Ultimate
One-Dish
Wonders

Ultimate One-Dish Wonders

More Than 200 Hearty, Foolproof Casseroles for Everyday Dinners, Potlucks, and Make-Ahead Meals

Crystal Cook & Sandy Pollock
The Casserole Queens

RODALE.

© 2011, 2013 by Sandy Pollock and Crystal Cook

Photographs © 2011 & 2013 by Ben Fink

Photograph on page viii © Michael Lovitt

Published by arrangement with Clarkson Potter / Publishers, an imprint of the Crown Publishing Group, a division of Penguin Random House LLC

Back cover recipe photos *(top to bottom)*: The Nelly Frittata, page 187; Sheperdless Pie, page 189; and S'more Pie, page 300

Book design by Amy Sly

Library of Congress Cataloging-in-Publication Data is on file with the publisher.

ISBN 978-1-62336-771-8   direct mail hardcover

2 4 6 8 10 9 7 5 3 1   direct mail hardcover

We inspire and enable people to improve their lives and the world around them.
rodalestore.com

This book was inspired by the stories, memories, and traditions of our childhoods. From the heartfelt to the humorous, they simply would not exist if it weren't for the loving homes we grew up in. We would like to dedicate this book to our parents—Joe Kent and Charlotte Cook, and Max and Margie Pollock—for always making mealtime more than just nourishment, but about family.

Contents

Introduction

Meet the Casserole Queens

Meet Crystal. Meet Sandy. Together, we're bringing back the classic American casserole, along with other familiar recipes from a bygone era, and updating them with a retro-chic, gourmet flair. It's the best of the 1950s with a modern, sophisticated twist. We call it *sophistakitsch*.

We know what you're thinking. It's not the 1950s, and the idea of whipping up a home-cooked meal with a freshly powdered face seems unreal. But wait! You *can* have that wholesome dinner ready for your family to devour! And guess what? You'll actually enjoy doing it. Don't think you have to throw on an apron and cook every night of the week (although we think it's fun!).

We have loads of nifty tips, creative shortcuts, and easy-to-cook meals that are designed to fit your hectic lifestyle. You may be on a budget, or have zero time to cook, but still yearn for a meal that's healthy and filling. Or, maybe you're feeling adventurous and want to step it up a notch. (If so, you're in luck—we've included some of our best, world-class recipes derived from Sandy's training at the French Culinary Institute. The Queens are crafty like that.)

Whether it's a dinner party with friends, an evening meal with the family, or an all-out extravaganza, we hope our unique and quirky perspective, along with our delectable recipes, will inspire you to enjoy an evening gathered around the dinner table. And, just maybe, you'll find out what little Johnny is learning in science class.

Our Story

Let's back up a bit to a warm, summer night in Austin, Texas. Lots of folks have asked us how we got our business started, and the truth is that the idea for the Casserole Queens was conceived one night while contemplating life over a salty margarita (or two). (See "Idea-Generating Margaritas" opposite.)

As we sipped, Sandy spoke of how she was charmed by a recent holiday visit with her family. Sandy had decided to make all the Pollocks' signature dishes with her mom and siblings. The food was heavenly, and the conversation centered on the good memories generated by these favorite recipes. She described the evening (while Crystal continued to sip), and proposed the idea of a business designed to help bring families back together around the dinner table with home-cooked goodness. Crystal, being from the South, couldn't agree more. Food and family go hand in hand where she grew up. In a world where people are always in a hurry and have little time for dinners together, the idea of convenient home-cooked meals is something that Sandy and Crystal both truly believed in. Hence, the Casserole Queens was born.

Now, we aren't saying that all great ideas start this way, but we have been delivering fresh-from-scratch meals to customers in Austin for over 4 years, all the while sporting heels, aprons, and the timeless tradition of mom's best recipes. Our business has been featured in numerous publications. Heck, we've even been on national television, appearing on the Food Network's *Throwdown! with Bobby Flay*.

Idea-Generating Margaritas

Careful! Drinking more than two of these can make your ideas seem better than they actually are.

Makes 2 servings

Lime wedge

Sea salt

3 ounces premium silver tequila

3 ounces fresh lime juice

3 ounces fresh orange juice

1 ounce Triple Sec

1. Run the lime wedge around the rim of 2 margarita glasses, and then roll the rims in the sea salt. Add fresh crushed ice to glasses and set aside.

2. Fill a cocktail shaker with crushed ice. Add tequila, lime juice, orange juice, and Triple Sec. Shake vigorously, then pour over ice in salt-rimmed glasses. Let the ideas roll!

The Kitschy Kitchen
Retro Tips and How-Tos

To us, casseroles represent more than just a delicious and nutritious meal for the family. They also represent a way of life—part of the retro-chic brand that defines the Casserole Queens as a business and the two of us as individuals. When we think of the quintessential 1950s homemaker, we have to chuckle. Hurry, ladies! Rush and fluff the pillows, prepare his favorite drink, straighten your hair, and quiet down the kids—your husband is coming home from a hard day at work! Oh, how times have changed. Homemakers may be men or women, and few of us would seek advice on creating a comfortable environment for our spouse. And yet the kitchen remains an important place in many of our lives, not because we are expected to be there but because it is where we can show our devotion to the ones we love most.

When you choose to express yourself through the dishes you cook, it's about more than the ingredients. It's about passion, presentation, creation, and pleasing the senses. (Mmmm, smell that? That's my cookin'!)

5

Having the right items on hand to prepare a quick, delicious meal is key. But also, taking steps to appropriately equip and use your kitchen makes the time you spend there more enjoyable and fulfilling. The kitchen has always been a creative, fun environment for us—cooking and dancing like no one is watching. This section was created with care to ensure you never get stuck in a cooking rut! Use our handy tips to minimize fuss, avoid cooking "emergencies," and create meals that fit your family's budget, tastes, preferences, and time constraints. We hope to ignite your inner artist, sparking a culinary creativity you never knew you had. Or at the very least, help you cook a solid, memorable meal.

Let's Dish

Casseroles may have become popular in the 1950s as a way to relieve women of kitchen drudgery, but they were also a response to a more active and social lifestyle. We, on the other hand, think they became popular because they were a way to "one-up" your friends and neighbors by appearing at the potluck dinner with the most colorful dish!

In our kitchen, we celebrate the casserole dish any which way we can. To be completely honest, we have a fairly loose interpretation of what the casserole dish actually is. If it all goes in one dish, then it is a casserole. From the old-school 9 x 13-inch glass Pyrex, to the highly decorated soufflé dish, Dutch oven, ramekin, or pie pan, it's all comfort—it's all a casserole.

In addition to brightening your own table, these dishes make wonderful host/hostess gifts. Ding! Now you know what to get that person who's impossible to shop for. There are so many super-cute and affordable vintage dishes available on the Internet, the next time you're invited to a potluck, bring your contribution in a dish that can be left with the host as a gift! And if swanky is the look you're going for, check out a new fad called the casserole tote. Made from amazing vintage fabrics, these totes make for easy transport and have real down-home appeal. They're chic and sassy, and easy to make.

Find One That Suits Your Style!

The beauty of the casserole dish is its variety. You can find them in every shape, size, color, or pattern. Go on, girl, get crazy—express yourself! You'll find that our recipes mostly call for a 9 x 13-inch dish, which is a nice, standard size. But with so many fun options, you can match your casserole to any mood or occasion.

GLASS. Keeping it real. We love this no-fuss, family favorite because glass dishes are inexpensive, and many come with plastic, airtight lids for easy transport and leftover storage. They are great for freezing and easy to clean up, and most are dishwasher safe.

PORCELAIN. The entertainer. Available in an array of colors and sizes, ovenproof, microwave proof, and dishwasher safe, these dishes can go from freezer to oven, then straight to the table. Soufflé dishes, shallow gratin dishes, and—our favorite—the ramekin all find places in our cupboards. Ah, ramekins—an oh-so-versatile dish that is a must in any kitchen. Perfect for individual-size meals and desserts, ramekins can also be used to serve condiments at the dinner table, like dipping sauces, toppings, or fresh sea salt or cracked black peppercorns. (Yes, we are in love.)

DUTCH OVEN. The old-fashioned gourmet sidekick. Aside from the ramekin, the Dutch oven is a heavy contender for our second favorite dish. This sturdy pot doesn't speak Dutch nor is it an oven, but it is a deep pot with a secure lid that can go from the stove top directly into the oven. Dutch ovens are well suited for long, slow cooking, such as for roasts, stews, and (yep, you guessed it!) casseroles. When we talk about Dutch ovens, we are referring to the modern enameled cast-iron version that does not need to be seasoned before use. These enameled Dutch ovens come in different shapes and sizes and can usually be cleaned like ordinary cookware. Some brands may even be placed in the dishwasher. Get ready for a tricep toner, because once you fill this dish with food, it can be quite heavy.

Dish-Towel Apron

Sandy's family does a lot of group cooking during the holidays. One year, Sandy's sister Yvette made aprons for all the girls in the Pollock family. The aprons were made from an assortment of Christmas-themed dish towels, with red and green ribbons for tying. We all loved them so much and still wear them to this day. Make them for someone you love!

Materials Needed

- 1 dish towel
- 2 big buttons
- 2 yard-long pieces of ribbon
  (to accommodate any size body)
- Scissors
- A needle
- Thread

Step 1: ATTACH BUTTONS

On the best side of the dish towel, sew a button to each top corner of one long side.

Step 2: TIE RIBBON

Tie a piece of ribbon around each button, leaving a little tail. This will make it easy to remove the ribbons before washing the apron, which will keep them from unraveling.

Step 3: WEAR IT

To wear the apron, wrap the ribbons around your waist as many times as necessary and tie a bow.

Step 4: ENJOY!

Dress the Part

Imagine cooking the perfect dinner, with perfectly coiffed hair, red lipstick, a full skirt, and high heels. Okay, now snap out of it! We all know that June Cleaver left the kitchen years ago, but there is something to be said about feeling "put together" and in charge of your environment. For the Queens, a fun, flirty apron can transport you to another age, relaxed and comforted. We love aprons. Not only are they practical, but even on a rushed day, you can throw on an apron and feel a little more in control. As with everything we recommend, get one to match your personality. Maybe an apron with pockets is perfect for you, especially if you use it to store fun-size chocolates. Or perhaps you want to spice things up a bit in pink chiffon. It's all you!

Get into the Groove!

Music is a must when we cook. Our portable iPod speakers have a permanent home in our kitchen. The kitchen is our kingdom—and in our land, we sing and dance just as well as Beyoncé. Music sets the mood for energy and can also inspire and spur ideas. It just makes cooking that much more fun! Apart from the cuisine, there are few components more important than the right music. Music helps your guests relax and puts you in the proper entertaining mood. Choose tunes that match the ethnicity or region of your dish.

Need a microphone quick? Grab a big serving spoon or spatula.

Be Prepared

A well-stocked kitchen can be a lifesaver when you need to whip up dinner at a moment's notice. Here are some things we suggest keeping on hand, especially when there's an impatient crew on deck.

THINGS IN CANS. Don't laugh, we are serious! Items such as tuna, sliced black olives, green chilies, tomatoes, canned beans, and tomato sauces can be integral to any casserole meal. Regardless of what you might have heard, don't forget the cream soups.

For some, cream soups conjure up bad casserole memories. We disagree. In fact, we appreciate their value and, when used with the right spices and fresh ingredients, you can make something quite good. We take pride in the need to keep things fresh and real, and there are times when we will encourage you to step it up a notch by inviting you to make your own soups and broths from our "From Scratch: Yes, You Can" section of this book on page 320. But when life comes at you fast, these canned soups can be your best friend. They are the type of friends who would drive 1,000 miles to bail you out of a Mexican prison. And the fact is, just as we have grown up over the years, so have they. Most brands nowadays are heart healthy, offering low-fat and less-sodium versions.

SPICES. We encourage you to have myriad spices on hand. Not only are they handy when creating meals from leftovers but they are the magic that turns the staple family recipe into something you can call your own when you add a special twist. After all, cooking with herbs is like icing on a cake: it makes the dish complete. Herbs add that extra something that elevates everyday food.

ONIONS AND GARLIC. Onions and garlic play a role in almost all of our recipes. Cry if you have to, but we suggest having them on hand at all times. We always have shallots in our pantry, as well. Shallots, in our opinion, are the perfect blend of garlic and onion. Voilà!

YOUR FAVORITE CONDIMENTS. Stock your refrigerator and pantry with an assortment of condiments that you enjoy: mayonnaise, salsa, Tabasco, Worcestershire sauce, ketchup, and a variety of mustards. They always come in handy for rounding out or adding flavor to a recipe. Do a routine check every 3 months or so to make sure they are fresh.

BULK PROTEINS. Buy proteins such as red meat and poultry in bulk to keep them affordable. Meat freezes really well and can easily be stored in individual portions. Just remember to allow enough time to thaw these items in your refrigerator for maximum safety.

FROZEN VEGETABLES. We personally prefer to use fresh vegetables, but frozen vegetables work fine, too. While some consider frozen vegetables inferior to their fresh counterparts, the opposite is actually true in many cases. Vegetables purchased in the produce section of supermarkets have spent multiple days in transit, and many of the nutrients may have leeched out. Frozen vegetables are frozen at their freshest, thereby capturing these nutrients. They are also a good solution when money or time is tight, and they are available when the fresh stuff is out of season.

GRAINS AND STARCHES. For casserole toppings and hearty fillings, keep a variety of grains and starches in stock, such as pastas, rice, crackers, bread crumbs, cereals, and potatoes.

OILS, VINEGARS, AND COOKING SPRAYS. A variety of oils is key for sautéing and adding flavor. Vinegar is perfect when a little acidity is needed. Nonstick sprays are handy for greasing dishes and cutting calories.

EGGS AND DAIRY. Most casseroles are held together by eggs and dairy, so you'll need to have fresh eggs, milk, butter, sour cream, and a selection of your favorite cheeses.

BAKING SUPPLIES. All-purpose flour, light and dark brown sugars, granulated sugar, baking powder, baking soda, and cornstarch should always be in your kitchen. Aside from baking batches of yummy treats, you'll find these ingredients in a number of casserole recipes to make and thicken sauces.

WINE. "A bottle of red, a bottle of white. It all depends upon your appetite." As Mr. Billy Joel suggests, keep a bottle of red and a bottle of dry white wine on hand, for both your cooking and your drinking pleasure. If you don't use a lot of wine, the small four-pack of airplane-size wine bottles works extremely well.

Go-Go Kitchen Gadget

Now, we would like to take a moment to offer some insight into other items that make life in the kitchen a bit easier—our beloved tools of the trade. We could go on and on about all the different tools that you should have in your kitchen, but we won't send you out on that special paella pan mission just yet. Here are our top "must-have" suggestions for making things simpler in the kitchen.

THE RIGHT KNIVES. A collection of appropriate and sharp knives is a must, but hold off on spending your entire paycheck on a packaged block set. We swear on Mamaw's fried apple pie that you don't need it. You can get just about any job in the kitchen done with only a few key knives. We recommend the all-purpose *chef knife*, the *paring knife,* and the *serrated knife* (aka bread knife). Along with your knives, keep a pair of *kitchen shears*. From snipping twine and cutting flower stems to trimming vegetables and meats, a sharp pair of shears is indispensable.

Other Noteworthy Reasons to Scale and Freeze

- Your husband likes tofu, and your kids dig meat.

- Tired of dishpan hands? Cleanup is a cinch. Making casseroles beforehand means no mess in the kitchen that night. (You made that mess weeks ago, hooray!)

- You can't be a "hostess with the mostest" when you're all stressed out. Give the cook of the house more time to do the things she wants, like enjoy a glass of wine and a good conversation with family, friends, or guests.

- It's friendly on the family budget. Little Billy needs new gym shorts. Susie is in dire need of a sticker book. Casseroles are affordable—because we wouldn't dare take stickers away from a child.

LATEX GLOVES. Smack! Gloves are handier than you will ever know. For example, since Crystal's knife skills are lackluster at best, it has become her duty in the kitchen to bone the chickens while Sandy perfectly chops, dices, and minces for prep. The boning chore has sparked a deep love in Crystal for her latex gloves. Plus, it makes cross-contamination a nonissue. Make sure you don't have a latex allergy!

SHARPIES. Sandy says that every good chef always has a Sharpie on hand. Not only are these markers good for keeping your refrigerator/freezer inventory clearly labeled and up to date, but they are also fun for drawing mustaches on your business partner while she is boning chickens and is defenseless.

FOOD WRAPPERS. No kitchen (especially a casserole kitchen) is complete unless you have lots of aluminum foil, freezer bags, plastic wrap, and oodles of parchment and wax papers.

DISH TOWELS. You can never have too many for cleaning up messes and drying dishes or hands. We also like making aprons out of our favorite patterns (see page 8). They make nice everyday aprons that you don't worry about getting a little messy or wiping your hands on.

STORAGE CONTAINERS. We just love the sizes and affordable shapes available. We recommend having at least three large (2-quart), three medium (1-quart), and six smaller (2-cup or less) plastic containers. A couple of glass ones are nice for onions and stinky cheeses, since plastic tends to hold on to odors. Another great tip: Tired of spaghetti sauce–stained plastic containers? Spray them with nonstick cooking spray first to prevent this food-stain faux pas.

CHEESE GRATER. Block cheeses are less expensive than the preshredded kinds. Grating your own cheese makes casserole cooking even more affordable.

ICE TRAYS. Ah, the forgotten ice tray! What a clever retro tool. Call up this old friend and use it for any leftover white wine (as if), chicken broth, or tomato sauce. Just fill ice cube trays and freeze them, then transfer the cubes to labeled freezer bags when done. Each cube is 2 tablespoons, so two cubes equals ¼ cup. Just place them in the pan while cooking to defrost them as needed.

WINE OPENER/BOTTLE OPENER. Do we need to say more?

How to Scale Appropriately

It's just as simple to make two casseroles as it is one (one for now, one for later), and they are easy to divide into individual, oven-safe containers. There are no hard-and-fast rules for scaling casseroles, but here are a few general guidelines. If you want to make:

INDIVIDUAL CASSEROLES: Prepare the ingredients according to the recipe, then distribute evenly into smaller oven-safe containers (ramekins work great and look adorable). Reduce cooking time by about 25 percent and watch closely.

LARGER CASSEROLES: Double a standard 9 x 13-inch casserole recipe and use a disposable 20 x 12-inch foil steam pan (commonly used by restaurants and cafeterias). In this case, the thickness of the casserole doesn't change much, so the cooking time should be about the same. Allow extra time for large casseroles to thaw completely before cooking. (Note that you might want to measure your oven first; many won't accommodate a pan of this size.)

ADDITIONAL CASSEROLES USING THE ORIGINAL RECIPE SIZE (ONE FOR NOW, ONE FOR THE FREEZER): Simply multiply the recipe by the total number of casseroles you're making. (Okay, so this one isn't rocket science.)

Note that these are only guidelines. All recipes and ovens are different. There is no substitute for keeping an eye on your casserole and watching for the telltale signs of doneness: the casserole should be bubbling around the edges, hot in the center, and brown on the top.

Hi-Dee-Ho, It's Off to the Freezer They Go!

We deliver dishes to our customers frozen, so we know the recipes that freeze well and the ones that don't. Throughout the book, we highlight the freezer-friendly casseroles that you can plan on making ahead of time.

Bye-bye, freezer burn. Here are some general tips for preparing, storing, and thawing frozen goods so that they will come out perfectly every time.

TO PREPARE

- We have found that the best way to freeze a casserole is at the stage right before baking, when all the ingredients have already been prepped and cooked and beautifully assembled in your favorite baking dish.

- We *do not* recommend freezing any seafood casseroles. It is best to enjoy seafood dishes fresh. Trust us on this one.

- Some casseroles call for crunchy toppings of crackers, cereals, french-fried onions, chips, and the like. Wait to add such toppings until right before baking, instead of putting them on before freezing. They tend to get soggy when frozen, and you miss out on the delightful crunch.

- Do not freeze previously baked pastry dough. Add fresh or frozen unbaked pastry during reheating. (Or freeze with unbaked dough in place.) Pastries are at their peak tastiness immediately after baking, and they just don't reheat well. Take this into consideration for leftovers, as well. If you aren't serving a crowd, make smaller portions in order to enjoy pastry at its best—fresh from the oven!

- If your casserole recipe calls for starchy ingredients such as pasta, rice, or beans, prepare them al dente, or slightly undercooked. Between freezing and the additional cook time in the oven, they can become "mushy" if not prepared correctly.

- Freeze casseroles either in quantities just right for your family or in individual servings. (See the portion control section on the opposite page for more ideas on how to do this.)

TO FREEZE

- Low on casserole dishes? Keep what you have available by lining pans with heavy aluminum foil before assembling your recipe. Once it is frozen, you can simply lift it out of the dish and tuck it back into the freezer. Your dish is now ready for other upcoming projects. Not only does your casserole stay neatly wrapped in foil, in the freezer, but it also creates a lot more space for storing.

More Freezer Tips

Wait, there's more! Here are some useful freezer tips for staple casserole ingredients:

- We've found that soft cheeses are easier to cut when slightly frozen. Simply place the cheese in the freezer 20 to 30 minutes prior to shredding or cutting. The cheese will be easier to handle.

- Casserole recipes often call for creamed soups and fresh broths. If you choose to make your own soups from scratch (see pages 335 to 339), chances are you will have extra on hand. For the most part, soups and broths freeze very well. Thaw the cream soups in a double boiler to prevent the cream from burning. Clear soups and broths can simply be thawed in a saucepan set over medium heat until heated thoroughly.

- Bread crumbs and croutons are always handy for adding texture to casseroles, but they can go stale quickly once opened. Keep them fresh longer by storing them in the freezer.

- Hey sugar, what's your story? Brown sugar is used often in our casseroles and can be kept fresh by storing in the freezer. Place in a freezer bag or other airtight container for maximum freshness. Don't worry if it hardens; it will soften up as it thaws.

- Make several batches of pie crusts at one time to save yourself some time later on. You can form dough into disks. Wrap them tightly in plastic wrap and freeze. When ready to use, remove from the freezer and allow to thaw before using. Another big time-saver is to roll the dough out between several sheets of plastic wrap. Using a small pizza box for the storage container, stack the disks, and then store the box in the freezer. Use as needed for your favorite recipe.

- Keep your nuts fresh longer by storing them in the freezer. Package both shelled and unshelled nuts in freezer bags and freeze up to 6 months. Other benefits for freezing nuts are that unshelled nuts will crack easier when frozen, and there is never a need to "thaw" nuts—they can go directly from the freezer into your dish.

- When cutting dried fruit, you will find that it sometimes sticks to the blade of your knife. Dried fruits stay fresh and moist when frozen and are easier to chop frozen. Another way to tackle this problem is to coat your knife with cooking spray.

- Always keep in mind that you should cool your casseroles completely before freezing. A quick way to do this is by setting the casserole in a pan of ice water to cool it to room temperature. Take the time for this extra step, because if you put a casserole in the freezer hot, the outside of the dish will freeze quickly while the inside may not cool in time to prevent spoilage. Plus, you don't want to raise the temperature of your freezer and harm your other frozen goodies. Nobody likes melted ice cream!

- Cover your casseroles with freezer-friendly products such as freezer paper, heavy foil, or a tight-fitting lid. We don't use plastic wrap, as it sometimes sticks.

- Always have a permanent marker on hand to label the casserole with the contents, number of servings, and date of freezing.

TO SERVE

- To ensure quality, do not store your casserole in the freezer for longer than 2 months. You made it with love and fresh ingredients, so you'll want it to taste that way.

- Don't be tempted to cook your casseroles in the microwave—the dreaded flavor zapper. For best results—and to ensure that it cooks through—always bake in an oven.

- Frozen casseroles cook best when they're completely thawed. The best way to thaw a casserole before reheating is by letting it stand overnight in the refrigerator. Then cook as directed by the recipe. If the casserole is for some reason not completely thawed, bake an additional 15 to 30 minutes or until the center is hot.

- We realize that people sometimes stop by unannounced (gasp! there you stand in your sweats and mustard-stained T-shirt) and you may not have the luxury of thawing your casserole. You most certainly can cook a casserole without thawing it first, but keep in mind that it will take approximately double the time to cook.

- Do not refreeze casseroles after they have been cooked. Refrigerate any leftovers.

Gluten-Free

To whip up gluten-free recipes, we got creative with ingredients like polenta, grits, rice, gluten-free pasta, and gluten-free bread. Some of our favorite gluten-free recipes in this book are:

- Deconstructed Cabbage Rolls (aka Pigs Out of the Blanket) (page 56)
- Baked Sausages with Fennel (page 60)
- Monterey Chicken and Rice (page 112)
- Mashed Potato Pizza (page 140)
- Rosemary Baked Ham (page 150)
- Erin's Special Gluten-Free Corn Dog Casserole (page 162)
- Rustic Polenta Casserole (page 182)
- Brussels Sprouts with Bacon, Garlic, and Shallots (page 198)
- Nene's Spanish Rice (page 226)
- Pint-Size Caprese Salad (page 266)
- Crystal's May-I-Have-More-Mayo Potato Salad (page 270)
- Tomato, Goat Cheese, and Quinoa Salad (page 277)
- Granny Pansy's Baked Apples (page 309)

Lighten Up: Quick Tips to Cut Calories

We understand that sometimes substitutions are necessary in life, and although we have recipes that cater specifically to a lighter lifestyle, here are some quick ways to kiss those calories good-bye. Nifty, I lost 50!

Of course, when you alter a recipe, there may be some trial and error. Please keep in mind that, when making substitutions, the consistency or flavor of the dish can change slightly. So it might take a few times of testing on little Billy before you hit it out of the park.

- If a recipe calls for a canned fruit in heavy syrup, forget the can and substitute the real thing. If the fruit happens not to be in season, opt for a canned version in its natural juices.

- Okay, we admit it—we really love salt. But if you need to reduce or omit the salt in your diet, start experimenting with fresh herbs and spices. We also suggest looking for alternatives in our recipes by substituting soups and sauces. Most condensed soups like chicken broths, tomato sauces, and soy sauces are now available in low-sodium varieties. Or, if you have the time, you can always make your own.

- So maybe your mom was right when she told you to eat more veggies. Simply decrease the meat and increase the vegetables called for in the recipe. Or, if you are feeling adventurous, there are a lot of healthful soy-based meat alternatives. Seriously, we've tried them and they do a fine job standing in for the real deal! We are big fans of MorningStar Farms and Boca brands.

Use egg whites or egg substitutes in place of whole eggs. (Two egg whites equal one egg, and ¼ cup of egg substitute equals one egg.)

- Foods that are white in color are usually hiding a dirty secret: empty carbs. Choose whole-grain versions of pasta and bread. Wheat flour over white flour. Substitute white rice with brown rice, wild rice, bulgur, or pearl barley.

- Many casseroles are topped with a layer of cheese. Experiment with reduced-fat cheeses by combining low-fat grated cheeses with whole-wheat bread crumbs. We recommend this method over using the fat-free kind. Fat-free cheese products tend not to melt and taste rubbery. Buy part-skim mozzarella and/or feta cheeses, which are naturally lower in fat. Or, if all else fails, you can simply use less cheese than the recipe calls for. Brilliant!

- In the grocery store, look for lean meats and skinless poultry. Reduced-fat or turkey sausage and bacon are also good options.

- When baking your favorite sweets, substitute applesauce or prune puree for half the butter, shortening, or oil called for in the recipe. It works really well. But as we mentioned, it might take a few tries to get it just right!

Diabetic-Friendly

The recipes with a diabetic-friendly icon were developed to drastically reduce or cut out grains and sugar (especially processed grains such as crackers, cereal, pasta, etc.). They also limit high-starch vegetables such as white potatoes, corn, and peas. Try these winning recipes:

- Chicken with 40 Cloves of Garlic (page 65)
- Yvonne's Unstuffed Poblano Casserole (page 108)
- Awesome Aussie Meat Pies (page 100)
- Shakshuka (page 144)
- The Nelly Frittata (page 187)
- Butternut Squash Gratin with Asiago Cheese and Toasted Pine Nuts (page 188)
- Farro, Wild Mushroom, and Walnut Casserole (page 190)
- Asparagus Bundles Wrapped in Prosciutto (page 203)
- Spinach and Spice and Everything Nice (page 218)
- Tomato and Avocado Salad (page 267)

Vegetarian-Friendly

For our vegetarian friends, we have developed lots of recipes that are free of red meat, poultry, fish, and seafood—yet are still comforting and satisfying. Some of our favorites include these:

- Summertime Tomato Basil Pie (page 177)
- Cheesy Grits-Stuffed Eggplant Rolls with Tomato Sauce (page 180)
- Spinach and Gruyère Soufflé (page 184)
- Butternut Squash Gratin with Asiago Cheese and Toasted Pine Nuts (page 188)
- Broccoli Rabe with Shallots (page 196)
- Carrot Soufflé (page 204)
- Braised Endive Gratin (page 211)
- Royal Ratatouille (page 216)
- Risotto with Asparagus and Lemon (page 225)

Now you can feel good about what you eat, and enjoy it just the same!

- If you haven't noticed, the Casserole Queens love cooking spray. When we cook at home, we always grease our pans with cooking spray rather than butter, oil, or shortening. Another good tip: when recipes call for sautéing vegetables with oil, substitute cooking spray to reduce the fat.

- Try substituting low-fat 1 or 2 percent milk when a recipe calls for milk. Skim milk will work, too, but it may not thicken as well when cooked. In cases where a recipe calls for cream, try replacing all or part of it with evaporated skim milk.

- Use a low-fat or nonfat mayonnaise, sour cream, cream cheese, yogurt, and cottage cheese in recipes calling for them.

The Conscientious Casserole: Food to Fit Your Lifestyle

First and foremost, we want to clearly state that the Queens are not doctors. Nor would anyone in their right mind ever want to cast us to play doctors on TV. So please note that this book is not intended to be a nutritional guide, and that you should have your doctor or nutritionist advise you as to what is best for you and your specific needs.

With that said, we've discovered that food allergies and intolerances are an ever-increasing concern in our Casserole Kingdom, so we wanted to address these challenges. Everyone is entitled to deliciousness! But first, we admittedly needed some education. We consulted with another fabulous Austin-area business woman, Carly Pollack, who owns a company called Nutritional Wisdom. There are a staggering number of issues that people can be faced with when choosing what to eat—so many, in fact, that it would be impossible to cover all of them. So we settled on the categories that we felt were most relevant to our fans: vegetarian, gluten-free, and diabetic-friendly.

Throughout the book, you'll find lots of recipes (all identified by helpful icons) that we developed with certain restrictions in mind, as well as tips for tweaking dishes to suit your needs with easy adaptations. Regardless of the restriction or substitution, we feel confident that these are dishes the entire family will enjoy.

Casserole Queens-Approved Gluten-Free Brands

With some simple substitutions, casseroles can easily be a part of a gluten-free diet. Hooray! Please remember: it is extremely important when cooking for people with gluten intolerances or wheat allergies that you either make your items from scratch or purchase products from a company that's committed to operating out of a gluten-free factory. Here are some of our top brand recommendations, backed by our favorite nutritionist, Carly:

- For a cracker topping, or if you simply want to add some character to your casserole, Mary's Gone Crackers brand makes a tasty cracker that packs a crunch. Also try good ol' Kellogg's Corn Flakes for a crunchtacular cereal topping.

- Pasta? Yes way! Choose from quite a few gluten-free options. We like Glutino, though we also like Ancient Harvest Quinoa Gluten-Free Pasta.

- Many commercial soup products contain gluten. For gluten-free, we reach for Pacific Natural, which offers cream of celery, cream of chicken, and cream of mushroom.

- There's even a simple swap for bread crumbs! Make your own using Rudi's Gluten-Free Bread or Udi's prebaked bread and our recipe for bread crumbs on page 330!

You can find the breads in your grocer's freezer section. If it is a stuffing mix you need, try Aleia's Gluten-Free Savory Stuffing Mix.

- We think that the best ready-made gluten-free baking mix options are Pamela's Gluten-Free Baking Mixes, which come in varieties like flour, cookie, pancake, and brownie. Of course, we also love the flour mix recipe provided by nutritionist Carly and found on page 322. Not only does it work beautifully, but it is also high in fiber!

- If there is a dessert recipe that calls for a cookie crumble, Arrowhead Mills has an excellent variety of gluten-free cookies and snacks.

- Lots of our recipes call for condiments, sauces, or dressings. We do offer lots of substitution recommendations and from-scratch options, but we've found that Sass brand condiments and salad dressings are very good!

Let the Good Times Casserole

There are two things the Queens truly adore: great food and great company. Sounds dreamy, right? We have some fun entertaining ideas that will inspire you to cook up nights you'll never forget. With delicious new recipes and a game or craft, you'll not only get people to the table, but you'll also get them off their smart phones and engaged. Hey, little Susie, we'll give you somethin' to text about!

When's the last time you hosted a potluck? One surefire way to get people together is to make dinner a group effort. Hello, potluck, where have you been? Invite your family, your friends, their kids, even their neighbors' kids. With these recipes, you'll have plenty of potluck power to get them in the door. Making casseroles is inexpensive, serves plenty, and is having a comeback. Why order a pizza and watch reruns on TV when you can have great food and great times with all of your friends? Here are a few of our favorite ways to have a fabulous potluck.

The Casserole Queens Swap! Scandalous!

Let's face it, casserole fans! The idea of freezing make-ahead meals for a busy week sounds pretty much like a second job. Why not turn this potential chore into a party extravaganza by inviting friends over to sample and swap casseroles? What wonders you'll take home to your freezer! Cooking and freezing dishes for a casserole swap gives everyone some much-needed excitement in the kitchen. And wouldn't it be nice to cross one more thing off of your "to-do" list?

Casserole swaps are also ideal for helping others who could use an extra hand. Let's say someone in your group of friends is expecting a new baby. A "swap" can turn into a fun way to stock her freezer for those nights when the new parents are too tired to know what day it is. Whether it's an excuse to hang out with your BFFs or to stock your own freezer or a friend's, Casserole Queen Swaps are a novel way to save time, save money, and add some spice to your dinner preparation.

THE PREP

To ensure that there are a wide range of dishes to choose from, assign each guest a different casserole to bring. Since you are potentially providing others with meals for the week, you can choose from a variety of flavors to keep things interesting! Need ideas? Well, hot dog! This book just happens to be full of them. Here is a sample menu idea, but we have lots of recipes that are highlighted with a "freezes well" icon throughout this book. Find the ones that speak to you and go!

Sample Menu

- Macaroni-and-Beef Casserole (page 44)

- Yvonne's Unstuffed Poblano Casserole (page 108)

- The "Sitch" Chicken Parmesan (page 114)

- Chicken Paprikash (page 122)

- Cheesy Grits-Stuffed Eggplant Rolls with Tomato Sauce (page 180)

Each family and/or couple will cook two batches of their assigned casserole: one to freeze and swap, and one to enjoy at the party. (We found that approximately five families and/or couples work best since most people don't have more than one oven to keep the tasting casseroles warm.) This way, everyone gets to try each casserole and pick one to take home. Or if the goal of your get-together is to have more than just one additional meal on hand, you can cook more than two batches—it's easier to cook more of the same thing rather than cooking a gazillion different recipes.

THE SETUP

When setting up the swap, here are some important things to keep in mind:

- Assign casseroles with similar serving portions. It would be such a sad sight if Sally picked up a casserole that feeds eight, and Flo took home a casserole that feeds only two. Boo-hoo!

- Remind your guests that the best way to freeze a casserole is at the stage right before baking, when all the ingredients have already been prepped, cooked, and beautifully assembled in the pan. That way you'll get a freshly baked taste!

- Use disposable containers, such as aluminum pans. Cleanup will be a snap, and you don't have to worry about losing a dish! Also, look for pans with cardboard or flat aluminum tops, which take up less room in the freezer and stack better.

- Ask your guests to bring a recipe card, complete with baking or reheating instructions. It can easily be taped to the top of the casserole or cataloged into a recipe book. Ding! Party favor alert! Give your guests an empty photo album with 4 x 6-inch cards for them to start storing their recipes in. Wanna go the extra mile? Take a picture of the casserole for the opposite sleeve!

- If you are creating an entrée that should be served over rice or pasta, bring those extra dry ingredients in a plastic zip-top bag. It's simply the polite thing to do!

With each guest bringing a frozen casserole, you might want to clear out some freezer space, or have everyone BYOC (Bring Your Own Cooler)!

THE DRINKS

Much like Crystal and Sandy, casseroles and cocktails are two great things that go together! What better way to make the whole event even more festive? Just take a quick inventory of the flavor of your dishes and get creative! Pitchers of margaritas or sangria are easy to mix up (see "Red, Red Wine Sangria" below) and work well with Mexican and Spanish dishes; a variety of wines pair nicely with Italian or French cuisine; and a dry martini can turn any swap into a formal affair. Now, cheers to you for pulling off a casserole swap without breaking a sweat!

Red, Red Wine Sangria

(Don't hate us for getting that song stuck in your head.)

Serves 6

- ½ cup sugar (for simple syrup)
- 1 bottle dry red wine (we prefer Spanish Rioja)
- ½ cup Spanish brandy
- ¼ cup fresh lemon juice
- ⅓ cup fresh orange juice
- ½ cup triple sec
- 1 lemon, sliced
- 1 orange, sliced
- 1 lime, sliced
- Splash of ginger ale

1. Make a simple syrup by combining the sugar and ½ cup water in a small saucepan set over medium-high heat. Bring to a boil, reduce the heat to low, and simmer for about 2 minutes or until the sugar has dissolved. Let cool. The simple syrup may be made ahead and stored in an airtight container in the refrigerator for up to a month.

2. In a large pitcher or bowl, combine ½ cup simple syrup (or more to taste) with the wine, brandy, lemon juice, orange juice, and triple sec. Add the lemon, orange, and lime slices and stir. You can serve this immediately, adding a splash of ginger ale to each glass, but it's best if you refrigerate it overnight to let the flavors blend.

Game Nights . . .
Bring on the Bunco!

For a great game night, anything goes, really— Pictionary, dominos, cards, charades. But for the purpose of this book, we are going to focus on a little game called Bunco! If it's good enough for the *Real Housewives of Orange County*, it's good enough for us! Seriously, though, to us, Bunco is not just a dice game, but a tradition. Sandy's mom has been a part of a Bunco group for more than forty years, and now her daughters are carrying on the custom. Young or old, Bunco rocks! If you are new to Bunco, here are a few tips:

- You will need at least four players. The more tables of four that you have, the more fun the game will be. Twelve players is ideal.

- Decide which set of Bunco rules you want to use for the group. You will find several different ideas for rules at www.buncogame.com/bunco-rules.

- Purchase the few items you need for the game—dice, a bell, score sheets, and enough pens to go around. Set up tables of four with pens and score sheets.

- Plan the menu. Keep it simple for your own sake. An example of an easy dinner would be a delicious baked dish from this book, and then everyone else could bring a side

(continued)

Just Like Our Casseroles Aren't Your Mama's Casseroles, Bunco Isn't Your Mama's Bridge Game.

We think Bunco has become popular in American culture because it's a good excuse for girl time. The rules are simple, the pace is high energy, and it's guaranteed fun. The best part is, the person with the most points at the end of the night usually takes home a prize. In some cases, like in Sandy's Hargill group, it's a booby! (Prize that is.)

Bunco started in England during the eighteenth century and made its way to the United States in 1855. Now more than 17.4 million American women play regularly, according to Procter & Gamble, who sponsored the first World Bunco Championship tournament in Las Vegas. With a $50,000 grand prize, this nationally televised event was a huge hit. But most women aren't playing for the competition or a hefty cash prize. They're playing to take a mental break from deadlines, dirty clothes, dogs, and dishes. They're playing to catch up with friends, family, and neighbors over good food and good laughs. It's easy to play at any age, and we haven't met a woman who didn't have a fun time.

If you throw a Bunco party, we'd love to see the pictures! Send them to us at info@casserolequeens.com and we'll post them on our blog.

Craft Night!
Introducing the Casserole Tote

So you're a casserole-baking pro . . . then you need the perfect tote in which to carry your casseroles. Lucky for you, we're about to get crafty. Ding! Party favor alert! Give your guests a savvy tote, made especially by you—it's a handmade gift that they'll actually use. (Pssst, we won't tell if you just want to keep the tote for yourself.)

Note that these instructions are for a tote that will comfortably fit a 9 x 13-inch casserole dish. Once you have the hang of making this tote, the size can always be modified to fit other casserole dishes. Although it's not necessary, we recommend using prequilted fabric, which helps to insulate and keep hot foods hot. Not sure what to do with your grandmother's unfinished quilt scraps? Sounds tote-worthy to us!

Materials Needed

1 yard prequilted, reversible print fabric (see Note below)
  Scissors

2 (12-inch) straight purse handles, dowels, or bamboo handles
  Straight pins

4 pieces sew-on Velcro (6 inches long and 1 inch wide)
  Matching or coordinating thread

Note: If you want to create your own quilted fabric, place 1 yard of fabric face down. Layer 1 yard of Insul-Bright on top of this, and lay another yard of fabric on top, facing up. Quilt as desired. If opting for this technique, have fun with the patterns and mix and match. One layer will be seen on the outside of the carrier and the other as you open it.

All edges can be finished with a serger or with a zigzag or overcast stitch for a more finished look.

Steps

1. You want to have one main piece and two side pieces for this project. Cut one main piece 36 x 16 inches. Cut two side pieces that are each 24 x 8 inches.

2. Take the two 24 x 8-inch side pieces, turn under and pin a ½-inch hem toward the center along both (long) sides, and stitch.

3. Take the 36 x 16-inch piece and, on the narrow ends, fold 2 inches from the end into the center and pin. You are going to cut out a semicircle for the handles. Using a bowl or plate that is 8 inches in diameter as a circular template, place your circle on the short side, so that it overlaps by about 4 inches deep and 8 inches across. Trace the curve of the bowl or plate where it meets the 2-inch fold. Cut out the semicircle formed by the curve of the template and the straight edge of the folded fabric. Once the fabric is unfolded, you will end up with a half-moon shape just below the 2-inch fold. Repeat on the other end.

4. Once you have cut out your handle cutouts, remove the pins. Finish the curved edges of the semicircle with a simple narrow stitch.

5. On the 36 x 16-inch piece, refold the edges down 2 inches, toward the center, and stitch along the sewn edge to create a 2-inch hem/space for the handles. Repeat on both ends of the fabric. (Note that the purse handles are not inserted until the project is completed.)

6. Fold the 36 x 16-inch piece in half lengthwise so that handle cutouts are aligned. Mark the center on both sides with chalk or quilting markers. Fold the 24 x 8-inch pieces in half lengthwise and mark the center of each short end.

7. Match the center of the side of the 24 x 8-inch piece to the center of the 36 x 16-inch main piece, with the right sides together. Stitch the 24-inch side of the 24 x 8-inch piece to the 36-inch side of the 36 x 16-inch piece. Sew one side at a time, stopping 2 inches from the edge of the short side. Repeat with the second 24 x 8-inch piece on the other side. The two 24 x 8-inch pieces will extend away from the 36 x 16-inch piece, creating a flap on each side.

8. Place a 9 x 13-inch casserole dish in the center of the fabric to aid as a template. Fold the unsewn 2-inch pieces of the 24 x 8-inch piece toward its partner on the opposite side (this will create the end walls of the area where the casserole will sit).

9. Separate the sew-on Velcro. You will be sewing one side to each of the exposed 2-inch pieces, close to the edge and centered. If both edges are folded to the center, one will be on top and the other will be on the bottom. Check to see that they are placed correctly to hold the side flaps together before stitching. Once you have verified placement, stitch one-half of the Velcro to each side flap.

10. Insert handles, bamboo, or dowels into the 2-inch hem. Enjoy!

Reading written sewing instructions can be tricky, so be sure to also check out our website, www.CasseroleQueens.com/pages/cookbooks, for a step-by-step video demonstrating how to put it together.

to complement it (well, heck—even those can come from this book)! Check out Sandy's favorite Bunco night side dish, Hargill's Bunco Club Seven-Layer Salad, on page 269.

- Determine prizes. As the hostess, you will need three prizes: for first, second, and last places (also known as the booby prize). With 12 participants, each member can host one time a year and spread the hosting duties equally.

- Most important: don't take the game too seriously. You could be shunned from the group if you are too much of a stickler for the rules. The game is far more social than actually competitive.

Tips from the Casserole Queens' Kitchen

Cooking is easy and fun when you're prepared for the job at hand. Here are some helpful tips that we've gathered when working in our own kitchen that we hope will be handy in yours.

Declutter Your Culinary Space. *Mise en place*, people! *Voulez-vous* say what? *Mise en place* is a French term that means "everything in place." For cooks, it's a technique of organizing yourself, and it's simply the best time-saver out there—hands down! What you do is read through your recipe, prepare and measure out all of your ingredients, and put everything in its own bowl. Then you line up all of the equipment you're going to use. Preparing the *mise en place* ahead of time allows you to cook without having to stop and find things. Once you're all set up, putting a dish together is a snap!

Contain Yourself! Invest in some ramekins, Tupperware containers, zip-top baggies, and stackable mixing bowls. (The ten-piece glass set from Williams-Sonoma is Crystal's favorite!) They're very useful for preparing your *mise en place* and for just generally being ready to go. If you're dreading the dish mess afterward, simply reuse some of your plastic take-out containers or prepared grocery item tubs. Recycling is as easy as rinsing and putting it in the right bin!

Throw in the Towel. Head to your local restaurant supply store and buy a pack of absorbent cloth towels (nothing fancy or decorative) to have handy to wipe down surfaces and clean up spills. They are far more important for achieving ultimate kitchen Zen than one might think. And they're much more economical and eco-friendly than endless rolls of paper towels.

To Save Time with Dishes, Think Like Grouper Fishes! Put like utensils in the same section of the silverware tray in the dishwasher—knives with knives, small forks with small forks, and so forth. That way, you can pull them out by groups and put them away just as fast. You can also do the same for similarly sized plates and bowls.

It's a Soaker! This is what we call those pesky pans with baked-on food because it takes a good soak before they can be cleaned. We have a handy tip for tackling such tricky messes faster than ever: set your dirty pots on the stove with some vinegar and water or dish soap and water, and then let them boil while you eat. By the time you finish dinner and get started on the dishes, the hot water solution will have loosened stuck-on food.

Do Your Knives Make the Cut? If you're serious about cooking, then picking a knife is sort of like picking a mate. You will want to love it for life. When choosing a knife, pick it up and see how it feels in your hand. The weight and shape of the handle are important. How is the grip? Is it comfortable? Is it substantial enough without being too heavy? In addition to buying a good knife, you must also keep the edge sharp. Get a honing steel while you're at it, and ask the folks in the store to teach you how to use it.

Garlic: Prepping the Clove Before It Hits the Stove. Many great recipes call for garlic, and if it's all the same to you, buying jars of preminced garlic might be a real time-saver. But for those who feel allegiance to tradition, here are a few tips for some garlic peeling, prepping, chopping, and mincing techniques:

- Peeling. If a recipe calls for multiple cloves at once, put them in a small resealable bag and hit the bag lightly with a jar or onto a hard surface. The peels will loosen right up. You can also microwave the cloves (not in a bag) for 10 to 15 seconds if the skins are especially tough to remove.

- Paste. If you don't have (or see the need for) a garlic press, use the bottom of an unglazed, flat-bottom dish to smear a clove into a fine paste.

- Chopping/Mincing. To keep young, ripe garlic from sticking to the sides of your knife, sprinkle a few drops of oil on the cloves before starting—it saves time, and keeps your fingers away from the blade.

If you're sensing a lot of garlic in your near future: instead of mincing garlic each time you need it, pulse a lot of whole cloves in a food processor, refrigerate in an airtight container, and use within one week.

Tomato Tips. One or two tomatoes aren't hard to handle, but working with a bunch can quickly become frustrating. If you need to remove seeds and have a salad spinner, roughly chop your tomatoes and give them a few spins. Voilà! Most of the seeds will have separated from the meat. Need to peel a bunch at one time? To peel a tomato, first use your paring knife to cut out the stem. Then score a shallow X in the bottom end. Drop the tomatoes into boiling water for 15 to 30 seconds, let cool, and then peel. The skins will come right off. If you have only a few, use tongs or a fork to hold each one over a burner of a gas or electric stove until the skin just blisters, and then you can peel away. Campfire songs are welcome.

When Your Tea Kettle's Wheezy, Blanching Is Easy! When a recipe calls for blanched vegetables, you end up waiting for an entire pot of water to boil just so you can dunk something in it for a few seconds (or maybe a few minutes). We all know that a watched pot never boils, so the next time a recipe calls for blanching spinach, beans, or a small amount of anything, try this quick technique. Fill a tea kettle halfway with water and set it over high heat. Put whatever needs blanching in a colander in the sink. When you hear the whistle, slowly pour the boiling water over your veggies to give them a quick cook.

How to Use This Cookbook

Basic Recipe Assumptions and Techniques

Wondering what we mean by this? Well, maybe this little story about Crystal's grandmother—or, as we say in the South, Mamaw—can help clarify. Mamaw Cook was an amazing cook (with an appropriate last name), and her claim to fame was delicious, melt-in-your-mouth fried apple pies. Everyone adored them, so it was only natural that the family asked Mamaw for the recipe. The funny thing was—there wasn't one. "A pinch of this," a "handful of that," and still to this day, no one can come close to making them taste as special as she did.

So how does this story relate to the Queens? Well, we kind of work the same way. Like most great chefs, Sandy likes to cook intuitively, and with the help of her trusty sidekick, Crystal, she experiments until the dish is mastered. We have taken great care to ensure the lists of ingredients and preparations for each recipe are correct. Chances are, you won't be in the kitchen with us, so even though we take the time to detail instructions in our recipes, here are some generalities and techniques that are always good to keep in mind—even when not making our recipes.

BLANCHING: To impart the most flavor into your vegetables, we recommend blanching them in salty water. Here's how to do it: Fill a large pot with water, heavily salt it (should taste like the sea), and bring to a boil over high heat. Add the vegetables and boil until they start to soften, usually about 3 minutes. Lightly poke at the vegetables with a knife; when you can break the skin without much resistance, you know they're done. Now pour them into a strainer, and plunge the strainer into a large bowl of ice water. The cold water will stop the cooking immediately and help the veggies retain texture and color. Drain the vegetables and pat dry.

PROTEINS: Proteins such as ground beef, chicken, and pork are always seasoned with salt and pepper.

SEAFOOD: When working with seafood, you'll notice that it tends to get a little watery when cooked. Prior to cooking, please rinse, thoroughly drain, and pat seafood dry with paper towels before preparing. This will help tremendously.

PASTA AND RICE: Boil these items in salted water to season them, unless it is a recipe in the light section.

BUTTER: We always use unsalted butter so that we are controlling the amount of salt in the recipe. We like to be in control.

OVEN TEMPS: Your oven varies from Mrs. Henderson's oven down the road, so think of our baking times as basic guidelines. Cooking times may vary ever so slightly, so please pay attention during cooking. Check the casseroles a few times near the end of baking to look for bubbling at the edges and a hot center.

DANCING: We find that dancing while cooking helps a great deal. We are personally big fans of the Robot, but we have found that the Cabbage Patch tends to work just as well. Trust us.

Friendly Faces

I spy a helpful icon. Just to make your life even easier, we've created some memorable, helpful icons scattered throughout this book. With a glance, you will quickly know more important information about the recipe you're planning to whip up. Here's the legend that tells you what the icons mean, so you know exactly what to look for!

 FREEZES WELL

 SPOT THIS CLOCK, and you will be wowed with time-saving shortcuts!

 INTERESTING TIDBITS, stories, and shortcuts from the Queens!

 SANDY favorite or personal story.

 CRYSTAL favorite or personal story.

Fun for the Whole Family.

Neat-O!

Remember the days when there was nothing better to do but prepare delicious, home-cooked meals for your family? Yeah, neither do we. Those days may be gone, but with our easy, classic recipes, cooking doesn't have to be a full-time job.

Bringing families together around the dinner table is what we do, and with these dishes, yours will come running. Who doesn't love a good, home-cooked meal? Remember Grandma's chicken pot pie? Your mom's tuna noodle surprise? Some of these recipes may be familiar to you. They may even take you back. The flavors, however, are current—bold, fresh, and updated to modern tastes. And with a few of our time-saving tweaks, you can enjoy these classic dishes without spending all afternoon in the kitchen. June Cleaver was fictional, anyway.

Meatball
Casserole

Makes 6 servings

Cooking spray

1 pound ground beef

1 cup saltine cracker crumbs

¼ cup chopped onion

¼ cup chopped green bell pepper

½ teaspoon salt

¼ teaspoon freshly ground black pepper

1 large egg, lightly beaten

1½ cups Cream of Mushroom Soup (page 339)

1 cup whole milk

1 tablespoon vegetable oil

⅓ cup all-purpose flour

½ cup chili sauce (such as Heinz)

It usually hits you from out of nowhere. You walk into a kitchen and bam!—there it is—a smell so welcoming and so familiar that you find yourself transported to another time and place. Smells are magical like that. Every time Sandy starts to make this dish, her mind becomes filled with fond memories from her childhood of meals shared with her trio of sisters, Yvonne, Yvette, and Kellye. This was her family's favorite meal growing up, and we hope that it will create as many sweet memories for you as it has for Sandy.

Don't confuse chili sauce with hot pepper sauce or canned chili (been there, done that!). Chili sauce is found in the grocery next to ketchup.

We suggest serving this casserole over rice. Try our recipe on page 329.

1. Preheat the oven to 350°F. Lightly coat a 9 x 13-inch casserole dish with cooking spray.

2. Combine the ground beef, cracker crumbs, onion, bell peppers, salt, pepper, and egg in a large mixing bowl. In a separate bowl, combine the soup and milk. Add half of the soup mixture to the meat mixture and mix well.

3. Heat the oil in a large sauté pan set over medium-high heat. Form the meat mixture into balls. Toss each meatball in the flour and shake off any excess. Working in batches, cook the meatballs in the hot oil, turning to brown all sides, about 10 minutes. Don't overcrowd the pan. Transfer the meatballs to the prepared casserole dish.

4. Combine the chili sauce and the remaining soup mixture; pour over the meatballs. Bake for 30 minutes or until the liquid is bubbling and light brown on top.

Tater Tot
Casserole

Makes 10 servings

Cooking spray

2 pounds lean ground beef

1½ teaspoons salt

1 teaspoon freshly ground black pepper

¼ cup (½ stick) unsalted butter

1 pound button mushrooms, sliced

1½ cups Cream of Mushroom Soup (page 339)

2 cups shredded Cheddar cheese (8 ounces)

1 (2-pound) package frozen tater tots

Um, what's not to love about this dish? Did you read the name? Tater tots and a casserole—that's the best thing we've ever heard of! Ground beef and a creamy mushroom mixture are topped off with Cheddar cheese and tater tots. Yep, you keep the tots for the top so that they can crisp up and make a crunchy layer above the cheesy center. We kept this dish simple, but it is one of those dishes that can be easily modified to include whatever else you may have on hand. For example, add onions and garlic when browning the beef for an extra layer of flavor, or spice it up with some taco seasoning and chopped bell peppers. Not a mushroom fan? No problem! Substitute some chopped celery and cream of celery soup. It's that easy! Anyone who has ever cooked a casserole has to have some improvising skills. You know, like nunchaku skills, bow hunting skills, computer hacking skills. (Come on, you really didn't think we could stop ourselves from making a *Napoleon Dynamite* reference in a tater tot casserole recipe, did ya?)

1. Preheat the oven to 350°F. Spray a 9 x 13-inch casserole dish with cooking spray.

2. In a large sauté pan set over medium-high heat, combine the ground beef, 1 teaspoon of the salt, and ½ teaspoon of the pepper. Cook, breaking up any lumps with the back of a spoon, until the beef is browned through, about 8 minutes. Drain off the grease and place the beef in the prepared casserole dish.

3. Wipe out the sauté pan and return it to the heat. Melt the butter, then add the mushrooms. Cook, stirring, until the mushrooms release their juices and start to brown, about 6 minutes. Season with the remaining $\frac{1}{2}$ teaspoon of salt and the remaining $\frac{1}{2}$ teaspoon of pepper. Spread the mushrooms over the beef, and then spread cream of mushroom soup on top of the mushrooms. Sprinkle the cheese over the casserole and top with the tater tots.

4. Cover the dish with foil and bake for 45 minutes. Uncover the dish and bake for 15 minutes more, or until golden brown on top.

FREEZES WELL For best results, prepare the casserole through step 3. Wrap in foil and freeze for up to 2 months. Thaw the casserole overnight in the refrigerator before baking as stated in the recipe. Note that casseroles that have not been completely thawed may take 15 to 30 minutes longer, so be sure to check for bubbling edges and a hot center.

CQ's Royal
Cottage Pie

Makes 8 to 10 servings

- 2 pounds russet potatoes (about 4 medium), peeled and cut into 1-inch pieces
- ½ cup (1 stick) unsalted butter, softened
- 1 cup heavy cream, warmed
- 4 ounces sharp Cheddar cheese, grated (1 cup)
- Salt and freshly ground black pepper
- 2 pounds ground beef
- 1 medium onion, finely chopped
- 1 medium carrot, peeled and diced
- ½ teaspoon salt
- 2 medium garlic cloves, minced
- ¼ cup all-purpose flour
- 1 tablespoon tomato paste
- 2 cups Beef Broth (page 336)
- 4 teaspoons Worcestershire sauce
- 1½ teaspoons finely chopped fresh thyme
- 1 (15-ounce) can whole kernel corn, drained
- 1 cup frozen peas

Ah, the never-ending debate of shepherd's pie versus cottage pie. So, what's the difference? It's all about the meat. A shepherd's pie traditionally calls for lamb, and a cottage pie calls for beef (or sometimes only vegetables). We wouldn't think of calling our meat pie a shepherd's pie, as we'd rather keep ourselves out of the line of fire. The beauty of this meal is that it's a great way to use leftovers. Include what you have on hand, whether beef or lamb, or even just a great mix of vegetables. Our favorite interpretation is below, so once you master the steps, try your hand at a variation.

1. Preheat the oven to 400°F.

2. For the topping, put the potatoes in a large saucepan, cover with water, and bring to a boil over high heat. Reduce the heat to low and simmer until the potatoes are tender and a fork inserted into the center meets little resistance, 15 to 20 minutes.

3. Drain the potatoes and return them to the saucepan set over low heat. Mash the potatoes thoroughly with a potato masher. Fold in the butter until melted, then stir in the warm cream and cheese. Season with salt and pepper to taste. Cover the pan and set aside.

4. For the filling, season the beef with salt and pepper. Cook the beef in a 10-inch ovenproof skillet set over medium heat, breaking up any lumps with the back of a spoon, until it is browned thoroughly, about 10 minutes. Drain the beef, discarding all but 1 tablespoon of the rendered fat, and set aside.

5. Heat the 1 tablespoon of reserved beef fat in the same skillet set over medium heat until shimmering. Add the onion, carrot, and salt, and cook until the vegetables are soft, 5 to 7 minutes. Stir in the garlic and cook until fragrant, about 30 seconds. Stir in the flour and tomato paste and cook, stirring constantly, until the flour is cooked, about 1 minute. Slowly stir in the broth, Worcestershire sauce, and thyme, scraping up the browned bits on the bottom of the pan. Bring the mixture to a simmer, reduce the heat to medium low, and cook until the sauce has thickened, 3 to 5 minutes.

6. Remove the pan from the heat, stir in the reserved cooked beef, the corn, and peas, and season to taste with salt and pepper. Pour the filling into a 9 x 13-inch casserole dish, smoothing it into an even layer. Dollop the potato topping evenly over the filling, then spread it into an even layer. Bake for 30 minutes or until warmed through.

Adding warmed cream, versus cold, to the potatoes will keep them from becoming gummy. Sandy learned this great tip while working at Jeffrey's, a restaurant in Austin, and ever since, she's had a much improved relationship with mashed potatoes.

This dish can be made GLUTEN-FREE by replacing the flour with a gluten-free mix, either store bought (see page 21 for recommendations of our favorite brands) or homemade (see page 322 for our recipe) and using a gluten-free brand of Worchestershire sauce.

Macaroni-and-Beef Casserole

Makes 8 servings

Cooking spray

1 pound elbow macaroni

2 tablespoons olive oil

2 tablespoons unsalted butter

1 onion, chopped

1 green bell pepper, chopped

2 pounds ground beef

2 teaspoons salt

1 teaspoon freshly ground black pepper

2 tablespoons all-purpose flour

1 (15-ounce) can crushed tomatoes

8 ounces sharp Cheddar cheese, shredded (2 cups)

1 cup whole milk

¼ cup chopped fresh parsley

⅓ cup cornflakes

If you're looking for something that's easy to make and tasty enough to fill those growling bellies, this is your recipe. Growing up, Crystal's family usually kept a close eye on the budget, so her mother learned how to get creative in the kitchen. One night, her mom pulled an assortment of ingredients from her pantry and fridge and created this dish from scratch. It was like magic! This casserole is, to this day, Crystal's father's favorite thing to eat. It's amazing how you can go from "nothing in the pantry" to an instant family classic. We've modified the recipe a bit, but we have a feeling it'll work wonders for your family, too.

1. Preheat the oven to 350°F. Spray a 9 x 13-inch casserole dish with cooking spray.

2. In a large pot of boiling salted water, cook the macaroni until al dente. Drain well and transfer the macaroni to a bowl. Toss the pasta with 1 tablespoon of the olive oil.

3. In a large skillet set over medium heat, heat the remaining 1 tablespoon of olive oil and the butter. Add the onion and bell pepper and cook until softened, about 5 minutes. Add the ground beef, 1 teaspoon salt, ½ teaspoon pepper, and continue cooking, stirring occasionally, until the meat is browned and any liquid has evaporated, about 8 minutes.

4. Add the flour and stir well. Add the tomatoes. Bring to a simmer and cook until the sauce thickens, about 15 minutes. Add the cooked macaroni, 1 cup of the cheese, the milk, parsley, remaining 1 teaspoon salt, and remaining 1/2 teaspoon pepper. Pour the mixture into the prepared casserole dish.

5. Combine the remaining 1 cup cheese with the cornflakes and sprinkle the mixture on top of the casserole. Bake for about 20 minutes, until the casserole is bubbling and the cheese is melted. Let stand for 5 minutes.

This dish can be made GLUTEN-FREE by using your favorite gluten-free macaroni and replacing the flour with a gluten-free mix, either store bought (see page 21 for recommendations of our favorite brands) or homemade (see page 322 for our recipe).

FREEZES WELL
For best results, prepare the casserole through step 4. Wrap it with foil and freeze for up to 2 months. Thaw the casserole overnight in the refrigerator. The next day, prepare the topping and bake as stated in the recipe. Note that casseroles that have not been completely thawed may take 15 to 30 minutes longer, so be sure to check for bubbling edges and a hot center.

Individual Bacon-Wrapped Meatloaves

Makes 8 servings

Cooking spray

12 slices bacon

1 cup ketchup

¾ cup balsamic vinegar

2 teaspoons red pepper flakes

½ cup homemade Spicy Bloody Mary mix (page 97), or your favorite store-bought mix

2 large eggs, beaten

1 garlic clove, minced

¾ cup Seasoned Bread Crumbs (page 330) or store bought

2 tablespoons chopped fresh parsley

½ teaspoon dried oregano

½ teaspoon salt

¼ teaspoon freshly ground black pepper

2 pounds ground beef

8 ounces mozzarella cheese, shredded (2 cups)

½ cup grated Parmesan cheese (2 ounces)

There are certain food pairings that never vary in the Pollock house. When meatloaf is on the table, it's a given that scalloped potatoes and green beans are faithfully by its side. The Pollocks' classic family meatloaf recipe has evolved a bit in our kitchen, as it now includes a spicy Bloody Mary mix. We also wrap each one in bacon for an elegant touch and great flavor. But we still eat it with scalloped potatoes and green beans! For a quick and easy twist on scalloped potatoes, try Mamaw's Potato Casserole (page 221).

1. Preheat the oven to 400°F. Spray a 9 x 13-inch casserole dish with cooking spray.

2. In a large sauté pan set over medium-high heat, cook the bacon just until lightly browned, but still soft, 6 to 8 minutes. Drain on paper towels.

3. In a large bowl, combine the ketchup, vinegar, and red pepper flakes.

4. In a separate bowl, combine the Bloody Mary mix, eggs, garlic, bread crumbs, parsley, oregano, salt, and pepper. Add the ground beef and mix well. Scoop the mixture onto a sheet of wax paper and shape it into a 9 x 13-inch rectangle. Sprinkle the mozzarella over the top. Starting from a short side, carefully roll the meat up like a jelly roll. Cut it into 1½-inch-thick slices. Wrap the edge of each slice with 2 strips of the cooked bacon, overlapping as needed and securing the ends with wooden picks.

5. Pour 1 cup of the ketchup mixture into the prepared casserole dish. Put each meatloaf slice flat into the sauce. Top the casserole with ¾ cup of the ketchup sauce. Sprinkle with the Parmesan cheese and bake for 1 hour, until the sauce has thickened and the meatloaf is cooked through.

FREEZES WELL
For best results, prepare the casserole until it's ready to put in the oven. Wrap in foil and freeze for up to 2 months. Thaw the casserole overnight in the refrigerator. Note that casseroles that have not been completely thawed may take 15 to 30 minutes longer, so be sure to check for bubbling edges and a hot center.

This dish can be made GLUTEN-FREE by eliminating the bread crumbs and substituting oats that have been processed in a wheat-free factory. You can also purchase gluten-free bread crumbs (see page 21 for recommendations of our favorite brands) or make your own.

To make this dish DIABETIC-FRIENDLY, substitute oats for the bread crumbs. Oats work well instead of bread crumbs to help bind a meatloaf, and they are high in fiber, which is important for diabetics.

Mamaw's
Stuffed Peppers

Makes 6 servings

6 green bell peppers

1 pound ground beef

1 large onion, finely chopped

2 garlic cloves, minced

1 teaspoon salt

¼ teaspoon freshly ground black pepper

2 (14¾-ounce) cans diced tomatoes

1 teaspoon Worcestershire sauce

½ teaspoon ground allspice

1 cup cooked long-grain white rice (see page 329)

Cooking spray

1 tablespoon unsalted butter

½ cup Seasoned Bread Crumbs (page 330)

Crystal's Mamaw Cook served these delicious stuffed peppers with a delectable buttered bread-crumb topping. These bad boys are sauce-free, and preferred that way so that the taste of the pepper comes through. But neither Crystal nor Mamaw Cook will take offense if you want to add a little sauce. (See the opposite page for a tomato sauce that's a great match for this dish.)

1. Preheat the oven to 350°F.

2. Cut off the top of each bell pepper and remove the seeds. Put the peppers in a large pot of boiling salted water and cook for 5 minutes. Drain well and set aside.

3. Set a skillet over medium heat. Add the beef, onion, and garlic, and season with salt and pepper. Cook, breaking up any lumps with the back of a spoon, until the beef is browned thoroughly, about 10 minutes. Add the tomatoes and simmer for 10 minutes. Add the Worcestershire sauce, allspice, and rice; stir well.

4. Coat a 9 x 13-inch casserole dish with cooking spray. Stuff the peppers with beef mixture and place them in the prepared casserole dish. In a small saucepan, melt the butter. Remove the pan from the heat and stir in the bread crumbs. Scatter the bread crumbs over the peppers and place the dish in the oven. Bake for 25 minutes or until the bread crumbs are golden brown and the meat is heated thoroughly.

FREEZES WELL Once the peppers are stuffed, they freeze well. Just make the bread crumbs and/or sauce fresh the day you want to serve the dish. Thaw the peppers, assemble, and bake!

Mary Ann's Favorite Tomato Sauce

Crystal's Aunt Mary Ann prefers to accompany her stuffed peppers with a rich tomato sauce.

Makes 4 cups

2	tablespoons unsalted butter		1	tablespoon minced fresh parsley
1	medium onion, diced		1	teaspoon granulated sugar
2	garlic cloves, minced		1½	teaspoons salt
3	cups diced canned tomatoes		½	teaspoon freshly ground black pepper
½	cup finely minced celery			
1½	tablespoons white wine vinegar			

In a saucepan set over low heat, melt the butter. Add the onion and garlic; sauté for about 8 minutes or until tender. Add the tomatoes, celery, vinegar, parsley, sugar, salt, and pepper and cook about 10 minutes. Pour the sauce over the peppers before baking.

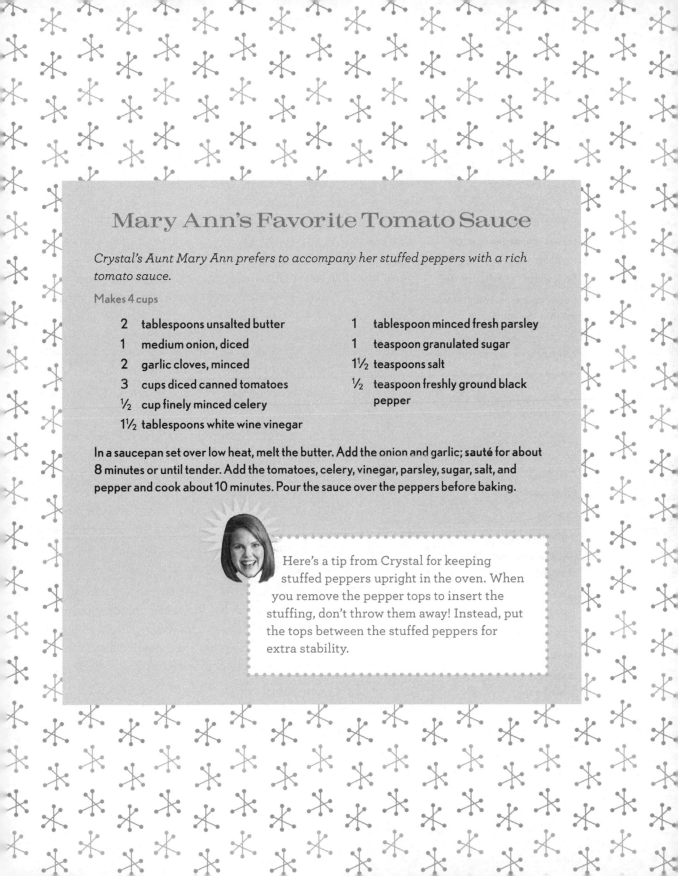

Here's a tip from Crystal for keeping stuffed peppers upright in the oven. When you remove the pepper tops to insert the stuffing, don't throw them away! Instead, put the tops between the stuffed peppers for extra stability.

Beef Stroganoff

Makes 8 to 10 servings

Cooking spray

1 (12-ounce) bag wide egg noodles

2 tablespoons unsalted butter

2 pounds boneless round steak, cut into ¾-inch cubes

Salt and freshly ground black pepper

¼ cup all-purpose flour

1 (10-ounce) container sliced button mushrooms

½ cup chopped onion

3 garlic cloves, minced

1 (10¾-ounce) can condensed tomato soup

1 cup sour cream

½ cup water

¾ cup coarsely grated Parmesan cheese (1½ ounces)

1 tablespoon Worcestershire sauce

10 drops Tabasco sauce

½ teaspoon salt

½ teaspoon freshly ground black pepper

From Russia with love! Our stroganoff has all the velvety richness of the original comfort-food favorite, with just a little kick (we can't help ourselves—we're from Texas, where Tabasco sauce is practically a food group). Our secret ingredient is tomato soup! We added the soup to brighten up the overall flavor of the dish. But don't worry, our variation of this classic is still enough to make you want to Cossack-dance your way back for seconds.

1. Preheat the oven to 350°F. Lightly coat a 9 x 13-inch casserole dish with cooking spray and set aside.

2. Cook the pasta according to package directions. Drain and set aside. Keep warm.

3. Melt 1 tablespoon of the butter in a large skillet set over medium-high heat. Season the beef with salt and pepper, then dredge in the flour, shaking off the excess. Place the steak cubes in the skillet and cook, turning, until browned on all sides, about 10 minutes. Transfer the meat to the prepared casserole dish. In the same skillet, add the mushrooms, onion, garlic, and remaining 1 tablespoon of butter. Cook, stirring, until the onion and garlic soften and the mushrooms start to get a little color, about 8 minutes.

4. In a medium bowl, combine the tomato soup, sour cream, water, ½ of the Parmesan cheese, the Worcestershire sauce, Tabasco sauce, salt, and pepper. Add the onion mixture, stir to combine, and pour over the meat in the casserole dish.

5. Bake for 45 minutes or until the meat is tender. Sprinkle with remaining cheese and bake an additional 15 minutes. Serve hot over egg noodles.

Reuben Sammy
Casserole

Makes 8 servings

Cooking spray

16 slices rye bread, cubed

¼ cup Thousand Island Dressing (page 261 or store bought)

8 ounces corned beef, thinly sliced and chopped

16 ounces sauerkraut, homemade (page 55) or store bought, well drained

4 kosher dill spears, chopped

1 teaspoon caraway seeds

2 cups shredded Swiss cheese (8 ounces)

3 cups whole milk

6 large eggs

¼ cup honey mustard

Sandy's dad loves a good Reuben sandwich smothered in his favorite Thousand Island dressing. Without fail, every Father's Day, his wife, Margie, would make this special Reuben casserole. But Marge refused to make it on any other day of the year—not even his birthday. Even though the whole family begged for it all the time, it was considered a very special treat. Only Marge knew the way to her man's heart—straight to the belly and covered in Swiss cheese! I guess it works, because they've been married over 55 years!

1. Preheat the oven to 350°F. Spray a 9 x 13-inch casserole dish with cooking spray.

2. Line the bottom of the casserole with half of the bread cubes, cutting to fit. Spread half of the dressing over the top. Cover with half of the corned beef, half of the drained sauerkraut, half of the pickles, and half of the caraway seeds. Sprinkle with half of the cheese. Repeat the layers.

3. In a bowl, combine the milk, eggs, and mustard. Beat well and pour the mixture over the layers. Let stand on the counter for 15 minutes to let the bread fully absorb the liquid.

4. Bake for 45 minutes, or until the casserole has set and the top is golden brown. Remove the dish from the oven and let stand 10 minutes before serving.

BBQ Pork Ribs

Makes 4 servings

Cooking spray

½ onion, chopped

1 celery stalk, chopped

2 tablespoons packed dark brown sugar

½ teaspoon salt

¼ teaspoon paprika

2 tablespoons unsalted butter, melted

½ cup ketchup

¼ cup Heinz chili sauce

2 tablespoons cider vinegar

1 tablespoon Worcestershire sauce

Juice of 1 lemon

5 drops Tabasco sauce

2 pounds pork ribs

The Queens have a little secret: we are slightly addicted to the thrill of competing in cook-offs. Well, at least Sandy is. Crystal just likes to dress up in costumes, decorate the camp, and mingle among the crowd all day! It's that combination of competitive spirit and social activity that makes cook-offs so unique and fun. Our particular favorite is the pride of Sandy's hometown, the Hargill Pan de Campo Cook-off. In recent years, we have taken home several trophies: second place in the Chili category, third place in Beans, and second place in Carne Guisada. But unfortunately we still haven't captured the top prize (insert *Throwdown! with Bobby Flay* flashbacks here) and, gosh darn it, we want those first-place braggin' rights! Our goal is to perfect our rib recipe this year and take the trophy home. But with Sandy living in a Washington, DC, apartment, it's hard for her to break out the smoker. Lucky for all of us, she's developed a pretty darn good recipe using just her oven. Serve with a side of Crystal's May-I-Have-More-Mayo Potato Salad (page 270), Spinach and Spice and Everything Nice (page 218), or Simple Herb-Roasted Vegetables (page 223), and you are set. Enjoy!

1. Preheat the oven to 350°F. Spray a 9 x 13-inch casserole dish with cooking spray.

2. In a large bowl, combine the onion, celery, brown sugar, salt, paprika, butter, ketchup, chili sauce, vinegar, Worcestershire sauce, lemon juice, Tabasco sauce, and $\frac{1}{2}$ cup water.

3. Put the ribs in the prepared casserole dish and pour in the sauce, making sure to thoroughly coat the ribs. Bake, uncovered and basting every 20 to 30 minutes, for 2 to $2\frac{1}{2}$ hours, until a meat thermometer registers 160°F.

This recipe is GLUTEN-FREE, as long as you make sure that the ingredients required (ketchup, Worcestershire, chili sauce) are all gluten-free brands. See page 21 for recommendations of our favorite brands.

Pork Chops with
Sauerkraut

Makes 6 servings

Cooking spray

2 (14-ounce) cans sauerkraut or homemade (opposite page)

6 (½-inch-thick) pork chops

Salt and freshly ground black pepper

4 russet potatoes, cut into ¼-inch-thick slices

2 medium onions, sliced

1 (14¾-ounce) can stewed tomatoes

Crystal's mother's maiden name is German. Well, actually it was Germaine, but the name was changed when her ancestors settled in South Carolina. The locals refused to call them "Germaine," and instead just said "that German family." To celebrate the German/Germaine family, we like to grab our favorite lager and whip out this traditional dish. The recipe calls for prepared sauerkraut, but if you like the idea of making your own, check out Crystal's family recipe (see opposite page).

1. Preheat the oven to 350°F. Coat a 9 x 13-inch casserole dish with cooking spray.

2. Scatter the sauerkraut on the bottom of the casserole dish. Season the pork chops with salt and pepper, then lay them on top. Layer the potato and onion slices over the pork, then scatter the tomatoes over the top. Cover with foil and bake for 1½ hours. Remove the foil and bake for 2 hours or until the potatoes are tender.

FUN FOR THE WHOLE FAMILY. NEAT-O!

That German Family Sauerkraut

Makes 4 to 6 quarts

- 1 head of green cabbage, chopped
- 4 to 6 quart canning jars with lids
- 4 to 6 teaspoons pickling salt (non-iodized)

Some simply don't have the patience to wait the weeks necessary for sauerkraut to ferment, but we prefer this old-school way of preparing it. The wait was actually a big part of the fun when Crystal was a kid (apparently there wasn't much to do in the North Georgia mountains).

Pack the cabbage into sterilized quart jars. Add 1 teaspoon of pickling salt to each jar and cover with water. Place the lid and bands on the jars and close as tightly as you can by hand. You might want to place your jars on a baking sheet or in a shallow dish, because during the fermenting process the lids will loosen and juice will run down the sides of the jars. This is why you don't seal them completely airtight as you do when you are canning. Store in a dry dark place to ferment for 3 weeks. Crystal's family stored theirs in their basement, which added to the fun (it was so scary down there!). If you do not have a basement, use a pantry or cover them with a towel.

Deconstructed
Cabbage Rolls

(aka Pigs Out of the Blanket)

Makes 8 servings

Cooking spray

1 tablespoon olive oil

2 pounds lean ground pork

1 small onion, chopped

½ green bell pepper, chopped

1 celery stalk, chopped

1 teaspoon salt

½ teaspoon freshly ground black pepper

1 (14.5-ounce) can condensed tomato soup

1 tablespoon cider vinegar

2 teaspoons minced garlic

¼ head cabbage, shredded

2 russet potatoes, peeled and thinly sliced

12 slices bacon

Even the Casserole Queens had to get their cooking career started somehow. Other than peanut butter and crackers, pigs-in-a-blanket was the first "gourmet" dish Sandy learned to prepare as a child, straight out of the 1957 edition of *Betty Crocker's Cook Book for Boys and Girls*. Those little pigs, all warm and cozy in their fancy blankets, became a weekly Saturday night staple. Then a friend of the family came to visit from up north (the big city!) and rocked Sandy's world by cooking a meal that put pigs-in-a-blanket smack on center stage as the main entrée. You can imagine Sandy's surprise when she realized that her friend's version called for ground pork to be rolled up in cabbage blankets and covered with a tomato sauce. Her friend said that this is how they are made in Poland, where her family came from. Sandy was hooked from the first delicious bite. In recent years, she's been deconstructing the recipe so that the dish is more layered, taking the pigs "out of the blanket" to become a true casserole!

1. Preheat the oven to 350°F. Spray a 9 x 13-inch casserole dish with cooking spray.

2. In a large sauté pan set over medium heat, heat the olive oil. Add the pork, onion, green pepper, celery, salt, and pepper. Cook for 15 minutes, until the pork is no longer pink and the veggies are soft.

3. Meanwhile, in a medium bowl, combine the tomato soup, vinegar, and garlic.

4. Layer half of the cabbage in the prepared casserole dish, followed by half of the pork mixture, half of the potatoes, and half of the tomato sauce. Repeat the layers with the remaining ingredients. Top with the bacon.

5. Cover the dish and bake for 1½ to 2 hours, or until the sauce is bubbling and the top is browned.

Deep-Dish Pizza,
Chicago Style

Makes 6 to 8 servings

Cooking spray

3 teaspoons olive oil

1 pound hot Italian pork sausage, casings removed

1 cup finely chopped onion

½ cup chopped green bell pepper

1 teaspoon red pepper flakes

1 (8-ounce) package sliced button mushrooms

3 garlic cloves, minced

1 tablespoon tomato paste

2 (8-ounce) cans tomato sauce

1 teaspoon dried oregano

½ teaspoon fennel seeds, crushed

1½ cups Homemade Pizza Dough (page 326)

8 ounces fresh mozzarella cheese, sliced (about 6 slices)

4 ounces mozzarella cheese, shredded (1 cup)

1 cup grated Parmesan cheese

Chicago's best-loved food is deep-dish pizza. Do it up right, just as they do in the Windy City, with heaping portions of spicy, hot Italian sausage, green peppers, fresh mushrooms, and onions. You can cheat a little and use refrigerated dough, but if you don't want to upset the mob, try making your own dough from scratch (see page 326).

Chicago-style pizza and our beloved home of Austin, Texas, have more of a connection than one might realize. Reportedly, the famous Chicago-style deep-dish pizza was invented by former University of Texas football star Ike Sewell. Go Horns!

1. Preheat the oven to 400°F. Lightly coat a 9 x 13-inch casserole dish with cooking spray.

2. Heat 2 teaspoons of the olive oil in a large nonstick skillet set over medium-high heat. Add the sausage, onion, bell pepper, and red pepper flakes to the pan and cook, breaking up any lumps with the back of a spoon, until the sausage is browned, about 8 minutes. Drain the sausage mixture, and set aside.

3. Return the pan to medium-high heat. Add the mushrooms and cook, stirring frequently, until the moisture evaporates, about 5 minutes. Transfer the mushrooms to a small bowl and set aside. Wipe the pan clean.

4. Return the pan to medium heat and add the remaining teaspoon of olive oil. Add the garlic and cook, stirring constantly until lightly browned. Add the tomato paste and cook, stirring frequently for 1 minute. Stir in the tomato sauce, oregano, and fennel. Reduce the heat to low and simmer for 5 minutes or until the sauce is slightly thickened.

5. Press the pizza crust dough into the bottom and halfway up the sides of the prepared casserole dish. Place a single layer of the mozzarella slices in the bottom of the pan to cover the dough (about 6 slices). Spoon the sausage mixture evenly over the cheese, then spoon the mushrooms over the sausage. Pour the sauce over the casserole and top with the shredded mozzarella and grated Parmesan cheeses.

6. Bake for 20 to 25 minutes or until the crust is browned and the cheeses bubble.

Baked Sausages
with Fennel

Makes 6 servings

Cooking spray

2 tablespoons olive oil

1 pound spicy Italian sausages

2 tablespoons unsalted butter

1 fennel bulb, cored and thinly sliced (see Note, opposite)

3 garlic cloves, minced

1 teaspoon fennel seeds

1 pound russet potatoes (about 2), peeled and chopped

½ teaspoon salt

⅓ cup dry white wine

1 (28-ounce) can diced tomatoes, drained

6 ounces Gruyère cheese, grated (about 1½ cups)

2 tablespoons chopped fresh parsley

Maybe you can relate to this, too: about three or four times a year, we get one of those stop-what-you're-doing immediate cravings for Italian sausage. Maybe it's TV commercials with tantalizing close-ups, or the smell of your neighbors barbecuing, or even a flashback to that memorable sausage pizza you had in Manhattan. Either way, if it's sausage you crave, then it's sausage you shall have! Instead of just eating it straight up, we've created a recipe that turns this delicious food into a complete meal. The potatoes and tomatoes help fill you up, while the fennel bulbs and seeds add a crunch and a slightly sweet taste. Trust us, this meal is bursting with flavor, and we guarantee it will satisfy that hankering for sausage! Try serving it with our Panzanella Salad (page 274) and some crusty bread.

1. Preheat the oven to 450°F. Spray a 9 x 13-inch casserole dish with cooking spray.

2. In a large sauté pan set over medium heat, heat 1 tablespoon of the olive oil. Add the sausages and cook, turning, until browned and cooked through, about 10 minutes. Transfer to a cutting board. When the sausages are cool enough to handle, cut them into ¼-inch slices.

3. Add the remaining 1 tablespoon of oil and the butter to the same pan and heat over medium heat. Add the fennel bulb, garlic, and fennel seeds, cover the pan, and cook for 5 minutes. Stir in the potatoes and salt, cover the pan again, and continue cooking until the vegetables start to soften, about 5 minutes. Stir in the wine and simmer until evaporated, about 10 minutes. Stir in the tomatoes. Increase the heat to medium-high and simmer until all of the liquid has evaporated, 2 to 3 minutes. Stir in the sausages and transfer the mixture to the prepared casserole dish.

4. Bake for 10 minutes. Remove the dish from the oven and sprinkle the Gruyère over the top. Return the dish to the oven and bake until the vegetables are tender and the cheese is melted, about 10 more minutes. Allow to sit for 5 minutes and then sprinkle the top with the parsley. Serve.

Fennel, the incredible edible plant! With a sweet, perfumey, anise-like flavor, virtually all of the fennel plant can be consumed in some manner. The roots and stalks can be cooked and eaten as a vegetable or used to add flavor to soups. The stems are a refreshing addition when chopped and added to salads, and the bulb is a welcome ingredient in baked fish or roasted vegetables. The seeds are great on pizza and are commonly used to flavor pickles, liqueurs, tomato sauces, and sausages. Even the fennel oil is used in candy and liqueurs!

"Like a Good Neighbor"
Ham and Gruyère Strata

Makes 10 servings

Cooking spray

2 tablespoons olive oil

4 shallots, finely chopped

1 tablespoon unsalted butter

2 pounds fresh baby spinach

1 teaspoon fresh lemon juice

2 teaspoons salt

1 teaspoon freshly ground black pepper

6 cups (about 14 ounces) sliced cremini mushrooms

1 cup shredded deli smoked ham

¼ cup chopped fresh parsley

8 cups cubed hearty white bread

1 cup shredded Gruyère cheese (4 ounces) (see Note, opposite)

3 cups whole milk

6 large eggs, lightly beaten

1 teaspoon dry mustard

We are just like everyone else. We stumble in high heels, burn the occasional meal, and even lock our keys in the car. Sandy wouldn't have discovered this recipe if she hadn't locked her keys in her car the week she started her first job after college. She was heading home from work and stopped at the grocery store to grab something really quick, so she left her car running (never a good idea, no matter how cold it is!). When she returned, her doors were locked! Luckily, her new neighbor, Mrs. Dominguez, happened to be walking out to her car at the same time. She not only came to the rescue by waiting with Sandy for Pop-a-Lock to arrive but invited her over that night to eat strata. Now that's being neighborly! But something special happened as Sandy enjoyed the conversation and the amazing mushroom flavor of the meal: she totally forgot about her troubles and got lost in the moment. So if you want to meet your neighbors, invite them over and serve this dish, which is perfect for making new friends. Throw in a side of Braised Endive Gratin (page 211), and you'll be friends for life!

1. Preheat the oven to 325°F. Spray a 9 x 13-inch casserole dish with cooking spray.

2. In a large sauté pan set over medium heat, heat 1 tablespoon of the olive oil. Add half of the shallots and sauté for 2 minutes. Add the butter and cook 1 more minute. Add the spinach, lemon juice, 1 teaspoon of the salt, and ½ teaspoon of the pepper, and cook for 3 minutes, until the spinach is wilted. Spoon the spinach mixture into a large bowl and set aside. Wipe out the sauté pan with a paper towel.

No Gruyère? That's okay. You can easily substitute Emmentaler, Swiss, or raclette cheese.

3. Heat the remaining 1 tablespoon of oil in the sauté pan set over medium heat. Add the remaining shallots and sauté for 2 minutes, or until translucent. Add the mushrooms and cook for 7 minutes, until they release moisture. Remove the pan from the heat and let cool slightly. Stir in the spinach mixture, the ham, and the parsley.

4. Put half of the bread cubes in the bottom of the prepared casserole dish. Top with half of the mushroom mixture and $\frac{1}{2}$ cup of the Gruyère. Repeat the layers with the remaining bread, mushroom mixture, and $\frac{1}{2}$ cup of cheese.

5. In a small bowl, combine the milk, eggs, dry mustard, the remaining 1 teaspoon of salt, and the remaining $\frac{1}{2}$ teaspoon of pepper. Pour this mixture over the layers. Cover with foil and bake for 30 minutes. Uncover and bake for 20 more minutes, until the strata is set in the middle and golden brown.

This dish can be made GLUTEN-FREE by using your favorite gluten-free brand of bread. See page 21 for recommendations of our favorite brands.

Traditional King Ranch
Casserole

Makes 8 servings

1½ cups Cream of Chicken Soup (page 338)

1½ cups Cream of Mushroom Soup (page 339)

1 cup Chicken Broth (page 335)

1 (10-ounce) can Rotel tomatoes or diced tomatoes with green chilies

1 teaspoon garlic salt

Cooking spray

12 (8-inch) corn tortillas, cut into quarters

1 (3-pound) roasted chicken, boned and shredded (page 340)

1 medium onion, diced

2 cups store-bought grated Mexican-blend cheese (8 ounces)

The King Ranch Casserole is as much a part of Texas history as the Alamo. So imagine when Crystal—originally from Georgia—marched into Sandy's kitchen with some ideas on how to improve the dish. Yep, you guessed it. Disaster. You just can't mess with Texas. Our recipe hasn't budged from the original, which has been in Sandy's family for as long as she can remember. Our fellow Austinites share the same love for this traditional recipe and have made the King Ranch one of our most popular menu items. Enjoy!

1. Preheat the oven to 350°F.

2. In a large saucepan set over medium-high heat, combine the cream of chicken soup, cream of mushroom soup, chicken broth, tomatoes, and garlic salt. Stir until warm, about 5 minutes. Remove from the heat and set aside.

3. Grease a 9 x 13-inch baking dish with cooking spray. Put half of the tortillas in the bottom of the pan. Layer in half each of the chicken meat and onion, then sprinkle with one-third of the cheese mix. Pour half of the soup mixture over the top, then repeat the layers. Top the casserole with the remaining third of the cheese.

4. Bake for 45 minutes or until the cheese has melted and browned slightly.

FREEZES WELL
See our freezer tips on page 16.

FUN FOR THE WHOLE FAMILY. NEAT-O!

Chicken with
40 Cloves of Garlic

Makes 8 servings

Cooking spray

2 medium onions, chopped

4 celery stalks, cut into ¼-inch slices

1 teaspoon dried tarragon

3 tablespoons chopped fresh parsley

8 chicken thighs, skinned (about 2¾ pounds)

8 chicken drumsticks, skinned (about 1¾ pounds)

3 tablespoons olive oil

1½ teaspoons salt

¼ teaspoon freshly ground black pepper

½ cup dry vermouth (you can use sherry or dry white wine in a pinch)

40 garlic cloves, separated but not peeled

It's a good thing this dish will ward off vampires, because nothing ruins a dinner party like unwanted guests. If you've never had the pleasure of eating Chicken with 40 Cloves of Garlic, please don't be alarmed. What, you'd rather have vampires knocking at your door? In all seriousness, the garlic mellows as it roasts, and it takes on a slightly mild nutty flavor. And to round out your meal, this recipe works extremely well with simple sides such as our Aunt Fannie's Cabin Squash Casserole (page 214); Brussels Sprouts with Bacon, Garlic, and Shallots (page 198); or our Wild Rice (page 228). Either way, it adds a surprisingly clever twist to the standard chicken dish that some people say is "to die for."

1. Preheat the oven to 325°F. Spray a 9 x 13-inch casserole dish with cooking spray.

2. Combine the onions, celery, tarragon, and parsley in the prepared casserole dish.

3. Rub the chicken pieces with the olive oil and season with the salt and pepper. Put the chicken on top of the onions and celery. Drizzle with the vermouth and tuck the garlic in and around the chicken.

4. Cover the casserole with foil. Bake for 1½ hours, or until internal temperature of the chicken is 160°F.

Chicken Casserole:
A Cook Family Favorite

Makes 8 servings

Cooking spray

2⅓ cups chicken broth from carton, or homemade (page 335)

4 boneless, skinless whole chicken breasts

½ cup (1 stick) unsalted butter

2 medium onions, chopped

1 (8-ounce) package herb-seasoned stuffing mix

1 tablespoon dried sage

1 teaspoon salt

½ teaspoon freshly ground black pepper

2½ cups Cream of Chicken Soup (page 338)

Many recipes are culinary heirlooms, passed down from generation to generation. This Cook family recipe is just such a thing. As far back as Crystal can trace, the source of this casserole is her great-aunt Eulene, and it was a dish beloved by both her aunt Mary Ann and her uncle Tommy. Today, Tommy and Mary Ann's children are preparing it for their kids, making it one of their favorites! We hope this can now become a favorite with your family, too! This casserole goes especially well with our Dill Bread (page 229).

1. Preheat the oven to 400°F. Spray a 9 x 13-inch casserole dish with cooking spray.

2. In a large saucepan set over low heat, bring the chicken broth to a simmer. Add the chicken breasts, cover with a lid, and poach them for 15 to 20 minutes, or until they are tender and the meat no longer shows sign of pink when sliced at the thickest part. Remove the pan from the heat and let the chicken cool in the poaching liquid. Reserve 2 cups of the cooking liquid. Cut the chicken into small cubes.

3. In a large skillet set over medium-high heat, melt the butter. Add the onions and cook, stirring, until translucent, about 5 minutes. Add 1 cup of the reserved poaching liquid, the stuffing mix, sage, salt, and pepper.

4. In a medium saucepan set over medium-low heat, combine the cream of chicken soup and the remaining 1 cup of poaching liquid. Heat for about 5 minutes.

5. Put the chicken in the bottom of the prepared casserole dish. Pour the soup mixture over the chicken and top with the stuffing mixture.

6. Bake for 30 minutes, or until the casserole is heated through and the edges are bubbling.

FREEZES WELL
For best results, prepare the casserole through step 5. Cover with foil and freeze for up to 2 months. Thaw the casserole overnight in the refrigerator before baking as stated in the recipe. Note that casseroles that have not been completely thawed may take 15 to 30 minutes longer, so be sure to check for bubbling edges and a hot center.

This recipe can be made GLUTEN-FREE by using a gluten-free stuffing mix and a gluten-free cream of chicken soup. See page 21 for recommendations of our favorite brands.

World's Greatest
Chicken Pot Pie

Makes 8 servings

- 2 tablespoons unsalted butter
- 1 (3-pound) roasted chicken, boned and shredded (see page 340)
- ¼ cup chopped red bell pepper
- 2 medium shallots, thinly sliced
- 3 tablespoons all-purpose flour
- 2 teaspoons salt
- 1 teaspoon dried tarragon, crushed
- 1 teaspoon freshly ground black pepper
- 2 cups whole milk
- 1 cup heavy cream
- ⅓ cup dry white wine
- 1½ cups fresh peas, blanched (see page 34)
- 1½ cups carrots, diced and blanched (see page 34)
- 2 russet potatoes, diced and blanched (see page 34)
- 1 sheet frozen puff pastry, thawed
- Egg wash (lightly whisk together 1 whole egg and 1 teaspoon water)

It's called a defining moment. For Madonna, it was "Everybody." For Brad Pitt, it was *Thelma and Louise*. For us, well, it was our chicken pot pie that started it all. Now, we aren't saying that we're the next Madonna or Brad Pitt. But, in all honesty, you wouldn't be reading this book if it weren't for this recipe. As seen on Food Network's *Throwdown! with Bobby Flay*, this signature dish is our claim to fame. It's not just any old pot pie—oh, no. We took great care to bring this everyday comfort food to new gourmet heights. White wine, tarragon, and shallots are just some of the surprise ingredients tucked under a perfectly golden brown puff pastry. It's the dish that made people sit up and take notice of us, and now it's your turn to take the spotlight.

1. Preheat the oven to 425°F.
2. In a large skillet set over medium-high heat, melt the butter. Add the chicken, bell pepper, and shallots, and cook, stirring constantly, for 5 minutes. Stir in the flour, salt, tarragon, and black pepper. Add the milk and cream, and cook, stirring frequently, until the mixture is thick and bubbly, about 10 minutes. Add the wine, peas, carrots, and potatoes and stir until heated thoroughly, about 5 minutes.

Take advantage of frozen vegetables if you are short on time. Replace the hand-cut and blanched veggies with a bag of frozen peas and carrots and ½ bag of frozen diced potatoes. Our lips are sealed! Just make note that by not blanching your veggies you'll miss some of the salt flavor. Taste the filling before you put it in the casserole dish and season with salt, if you like.

3. Transfer the hot chicken mixture to a 9 x 13-inch casserole dish. Place the puff pastry over the top of the casserole dish. Brush the edges of the puff pastry with the egg wash and press against the side of the casserole dish, then cut slits in the pastry to allow steam to escape. Brush the top of the puff pastry with egg wash—this will help the puff pastry brown evenly. Bake for about 35 minutes or until the top is golden brown. Serve immediately.

VARIATIONS

Here are two other great ways to make our chicken pot pie:

- Make individual pot pies! Portion out the filling into 6-ounce ramekins. Top each ramekin with some puff pastry and freeze. Cook at 425°F for 20 minutes or until puff pastry is golden brown. So cute!

- Use store-bought pie dough and make empanadas! Using a 3-inch circle pastry cutter, cut 12 circles out of the dough. Place a large spoonful of filling on one half of each circle. Brush the edge of the pastry with egg wash, then fold in half to make a half-moon shape. Press the edges together firmly and crimp with a fork. Put the empanada on a baking sheet and bake at 350°F for about 30 minutes or until golden brown.

FREEZES WELL
See our freezer tips on page 16.

Valley-Style
Arroz con Pollo

Makes 6 to 8 servings

- 1 (3-pound) chicken, cut into 8 pieces, skin removed
- 2 teaspoons salt, plus more for chicken
- 2 teaspoons freshly ground black pepper, plus more for chicken
- 3 tablespoons olive oil
- 1 cup long-grain white rice
- 1 (14½-ounce) can diced tomatoes
- 1 (8-ounce) can tomato sauce
- 1 cup finely chopped onion
- 1 cup finely chopped green bell pepper
- 1 cup frozen peas
- 2 tablespoons tomato paste
- 3 garlic cloves, minced
- 3 bay leaves
- 2 teaspoons ground cumin
- 1 (32-ounce) carton chicken broth, or homemade (page 335)

The Valley is what we, in Texas, call the Rio Grande Valley. It's located on the southernmost tip of the state, bordering Mexico, and it's where Sandy grew up. The Valley is a melting pot of American and Mexican cultures, and is known for its festivals, architecture, and cuisine. So when Sandy talks about comfort food, she thinks of dishes that are often heavily influenced by traditional Mexican flavors. Arroz con Pollo (rice with chicken) is one of her favorites. Many Spanish-speaking countries claim this dish, so there are many different ways to prepare it. This particular recipe is served up Valley style and is uniquely Texan.

1. Preheat the oven to 350°F.

2. Season the chicken with salt and pepper. Heat the olive oil in a large sauté pan set over high heat, and add 4 pieces of the chicken. Fry the chicken until browned, about 5 minutes on each side. Transfer the chicken to a paper towel–lined plate and set aside. In small batches, continue to fry the remaining pieces of chicken.

3. Add the rice to the oil remaining in the pan and fry over medium-high heat until it is golden brown, about 10 minutes. Add the tomatoes, tomato sauce, onion, bell pepper, peas, tomato paste, garlic, bay leaves, cumin, 2 teaspoons of salt, 2 teaspoons of black pepper, and $2\frac{1}{2}$ cups of the broth. Bring to a boil, then transfer to a 9 x 13-inch casserole dish.

4. Add the chicken to the casserole dish, nestling the white meat into the rice to prevent it from overcooking, and place the dark meat on top of the rice. Cover the dish with foil and bake until the rice is tender and the chicken is no longer pink, 40 to 50 minutes. If needed, add more chicken broth, 1 cup at a time, to the dish during baking to keep the chicken and rice moist.

Tuna Noodle
Casserole

Makes 8 servings

- 2 tablespoons unsalted butter
- 1 cup Seasoned Bread Crumbs (page 330)
- 1 (10-ounce) container sliced button mushrooms
- 1 medium onion, chopped
- 1½ teaspoons paprika
- ⅛ teaspoon cayenne
- ½ teaspoon salt, plus more for taste
- 3½ cups Chicken Broth (page 335)
- 1 cup heavy cream
- 1 (8-ounce) package wide egg noodles
- 2 (6-ounce) cans water-packed solid white tuna, drained well and flaked
- 1½ cups frozen peas
- 2 cups grated Parmesan cheese (8 ounces)
- 2 tablespoons finely chopped fresh parsley leaves
- Freshly ground black pepper

Love it or hate it, the tuna noodle casserole is an American classic. This dish and the renowned green bean casserole are the two most asked about casseroles that are not currently on our menu. Why, you ask? We deliver our products frozen, and neither of these dishes freezes well. They're best when enjoyed fresh from the oven. With that said—and after the umpteenth request for this old-school favorite—we pay our respects here.

1. Preheat the oven to 475°F.

2. Melt 1 tablespoon of the butter in a large nonstick skillet set over medium-high heat. Add the bread crumbs and toast until just golden brown, 3 to 5 minutes. Transfer the crumbs to a small bowl and set aside.

FUN FOR THE WHOLE FAMILY. NEAT-O!

3. Melt the remaining 1 tablespoon of butter in a medium sauté pan set over medium-high heat. Add the mushrooms, onion, paprika, cayenne, and $\frac{1}{2}$ teaspoon salt and cook, stirring often, until the mushrooms and onion are golden brown, about 8 minutes. Stir in the broth and cream, and then add the noodles. Increase the heat to high and cook at a vigorous simmer, stirring often, until the noodles are nearly tender and the sauce is slightly thickened, about 8 minutes.

4. Remove the pan from the heat and stir in the tuna, peas, Parmesan, and parsley, and season to taste with salt and pepper. Pour the mixture into a 9 x 13-inch casserole dish and sprinkle the bread crumbs over the top. Bake until the edges are bubbly, about 8 minutes.

Don't get foiled by oil! Choose a solid white chunk tuna packed in water. Crystal found that oil-packed tuna can cause the casserole to be greasy.

New England Pot Pie

Makes 10 servings

Olive oil, for dish

2 medium russet potatoes, peeled and diced

2 teaspoons salt

6 slices bacon, chopped

1 medium onion, chopped

⅓ cup all-purpose flour

2 (8-ounce) bottles clam juice

½ cup dry white wine

¼ cup heavy cream

2 garlic cloves, finely chopped

2 teaspoons freshly ground black pepper

1 cup frozen peas and carrots, thawed

1 cup frozen corn, thawed

1 tablespoon chopped fresh thyme

¼ cup chopped fresh flat-leaf parsley

1 cup fresh shrimp (31/35), peeled, deveined, and tails removed

1 pound skinless whitefish (such as cod, hake, pollock, or haddock), cut into 1-inch pieces

1 sheet puff pastry, thawed

Hearty, creamy, and with a flaky crust, this pot pie is straight-up comfort food. Growing up in the North Georgia mountains, Crystal mainly experienced seafood from a deep fryer. On rare occasions, her Uncle Bob would travel to a fish market and bring back huge bags of fresh shrimp, which quickly lent itself to a family shrimp-eating contest. (Boy, howdy! Could Uncle Bob, her brother, Kenny, and her daddy eat some shrimp!) But it wasn't until she went to Boston for college that she really started to appreciate and love all the flavors of the sea. It didn't take long before she started experimenting with the many varieties of fresh seafood and all the ways to prepare it. One of her favorite dishes is this amazing pot pie.

1. Preheat the oven to 400°F. Lightly oil a 9 x 13-inch casserole dish.

2. Fill a large saucepan with 1 quart of water and set it over high heat. Add the potatoes and 1 teaspoon of the salt and bring to a boil, about 5 minutes. Reduce the heat to medium, cover, and simmer for 5 to 7 minutes, or until the potatoes are tender. Drain the potatoes.

3. In a separate saucepan set over medium heat, cook the bacon until crispy, about 8 minutes. Transfer to a paper towel–lined plate to drain. When cool, crumble the bacon.

4. Increase the heat to medium-high. Add the onion to the bacon drippings and cook until golden brown, about 7 minutes. Using a wire whisk, stir in the flour and cook for 1 minute to cook out the raw flour taste. Slowly stir in the clam juice, white wine, cream, garlic, the remaining teaspoon of salt, and the pepper. Cook, stirring occasionally, until thick and bubbly, 5 minutes.

5. Add the cooked potatoes, bacon, peas and carrots, corn, thyme, and parsley and stir well. Cook 3 to 4 minutes, until the mixture is hot. Stir in the shrimp and fish. Spoon the mixture into the prepared casserole dish.

6. On lightly floured surface, unfold the pastry. Roll it into a 10 x 14-inch rectangle. Using a sharp knife, cut a few slits in the pastry to allow steam to escape. Put the pastry over the hot seafood mixture and press the pastry along the edges of the casserole dish to seal.

7. Bake for 30 to 40 minutes or until the crust is deep golden brown and puffed in the center. Let stand for 10 minutes before serving.

Tuna Tomato
Bake

Makes 6 servings

Cooking spray

2 (5-ounce) cans tuna, packed in water and drained

1½ cups mayonnaise

1 small onion, finely chopped

2 teaspoons smoked paprika

½ teaspoon salt

½ teaspoon freshly ground black pepper

1 (12-ounce) package wide egg noodles

8 to 10 plum tomatoes, sliced ¼ inch thick

1 cup shredded Cheddar cheese (4 ounces)

We don't care what people say . . . we love a good tuna noodle casserole! This dish is a little avant-garde. From the smokiness and color provided by the paprika, to the fresh flavors of the ripe tomatoes, this casserole leaves diners wowed and wondering what is next. How about dessert? We think that our Frozen Lemon Dessert (page 318) would be just the ticket!

1. Preheat the oven to 375°F. Spray a 9 x 13-inch casserole dish with cooking spray.

2. In a medium bowl, combine the tuna, mayonnaise, onion, paprika, salt, and pepper.

3. In a large pot, cook the noodles according to the package directions. Drain and return the noodles to the saucepan. Add the tuna mixture to the noodles and stir well.

4. Put half of the noodle mixture in the prepared casserole dish and top with half of the tomatoes and half of the cheese. Press down slightly. Repeat the layers.

5. Bake for 20 minutes, or until the cheese is melted and the casserole is heated through.

This recipe can be made GLUTEN-FREE by using gluten-free noodles. See page 21 for recommendations of our favorite brands.

Shrimply Delicious
Shrimp and Grits

Makes 8 servings

Chances are, if you grew up in the South, you have eaten your fair share of grits. You've probably eaten your share of shrimp, too. It's no wonder that these two Southern staples come together in one of the best dishes of all time. Crystal grew up eating grits almost every morning and had always considered them a breakfast dish—until the day she was served shrimp and grits for dinner. That was when her obsession began. Instead of seeking help, Crystal continued to make shrimp and grits on her stove top, working and reworking the dish to find the perfect recipe. Her work definitely paid off. Here is her winning combo of smoked Gouda cheese grits and Cajun spiced shrimp, topped off with an herbed tomato mixture. Perfection indeed.

GRITS

Cooking spray

2 teaspoons unsalted butter

4 cups chopped sweet onions, such as Vidalia (about 2 large)

2 garlic cloves, minced

3 cups Chicken Broth (page 335)

2 cups whole milk

½ teaspoon salt

1¼ cups quick-cooking grits

8 ounces smoked Gouda cheese, grated (2 cups)

2 large eggs, lightly beaten

¼ teaspoon freshly ground black pepper

TOMATO SAUCE

2 teaspoons olive oil

1 cup chopped sweet onion, such as a Vidalia

1½ cups chopped red bell peppers

1 tablespoon chopped fresh rosemary

2 (14½-ounce) cans Italian-flavored diced tomatoes

½ cup dry white wine

8 garlic cloves, minced

¼ teaspoon salt

SHRIMP

2 teaspoons olive oil

1 teaspoon freshly ground black pepper

1 teaspoon ground white pepper

¼ teaspoon cayenne

1 teaspoon paprika

1 teaspoon onion powder

1 teaspoon garlic powder

1 pound large shrimp, peeled and deveined

1. Preheat the oven to 375°F. Coat a 9 x 13-inch casserole dish with cooking spray.

2. For the grits, melt the butter in a large saucepan set over medium heat. Add the onions and garlic and cook for 8 minutes or until golden, stirring occasionally. Stir in the broth, milk, and salt and bring to a boil. Gradually add the grits, stirring constantly with a whisk. Reduce the heat to low, cover, and simmer for 5 minutes. Remove the pan from the heat; stir in the cheese, eggs, and pepper. Spoon the grits mixture into the prepared casserole dish. Bake for about 40 minutes or until firm.

3. For the tomato sauce, heat the oil in a large saucepan set over medium-high heat. Add the onion and sauté for 5 minutes. Add the bell pepper and rosemary and sauté for 1 minute. Stir in the tomatoes, wine, garlic, and salt. Bring the mixture to a boil, reduce the heat to low, and simmer for 30 minutes.

4. For the shrimp, heat the oil in a nonstick skillet set over medium-high heat. In a small bowl, stir together the black pepper, white pepper, cayenne, paprika, onion powder, and garlic powder. Toss the shrimp in the seasoning mix, and then put the shrimp in the pan. Cook and stir for 3 minutes or until the shrimp are opaque.

5. To assemble the casserole, spread the tomato sauce over the grits in an even layer. Top the sauce with the shrimp. Serve immediately.

Crystal grew up preparing shrimp for this dish. Here's how it's done: First, remove the shells and legs. Take a paring knife and make a shallow slit along the back of each shrimp. With the tip of the blade, lift up and remove the vein. The vein will tend to stick to your knife, so set a glass of water beside you while you work to dip your knife in and remove the vein before moving to the next shrimp.

Shrimp Gumbo
Casserole

Makes 8 servings

- 3 tablespoons olive oil
- 1 onion, chopped
- ½ green bell pepper, chopped
- 3 celery stalks with leaves, chopped
- 3 garlic cloves, minced
- 2 (28-ounce) cans diced tomatoes
- 1 (15-ounce) can tomato sauce
- 1 tablespoon plus ½ teaspoon salt
- 1¼ teaspoons freshly ground black pepper
- 1 teaspoon chili powder
- 1 teaspoon dried thyme
- 2 bay leaves
- 1 pound okra, sliced
- 1 pound fresh shrimp (31/35), peeled and deveined
- 2 teaspoons gumbo filé (see Note, opposite)
- 2 cups all-purpose flour
- 1 tablespoon baking powder
- ½ teaspoon cayenne
- 2 teaspoons granulated sugar
- ½ teaspoon baking soda
- 5½ tablespoons cold unsalted butter, cut into small pieces
- ¾ cup buttermilk

Sandy has been making this recipe for probably 20 years and has slowly perfected it over time. She knew she had finally mastered this dish when she took it to her friend's baby shower. She'd traveled up to Minneapolis, and it was freezing up there (something we Texas gals aren't used to). Sandy thought this would be the perfect thing to keep their bellies full and bodies warm. Well, she definitely picked the right recipe, because not 10 minutes into the baby shower, the electricity went out and didn't come back on for about 2 hours. All they had was a roaring fire in the fireplace and this casserole to comfort them! Luckily, the casserole hit the spot and kept them cozy with its Creole-spiced shrimp filling and satisfying biscuit topping.

1. Preheat the oven to 450°F.

2. In a large saucepan set over medium-high heat, heat the olive oil, then add the onion, green pepper, celery, and garlic. Cook, stirring, for 6 minutes, until soft. Add the tomatoes, tomato sauce, 1 tablespoon of the salt, pepper, chili powder, thyme, and bay leaves. Cover and cook slowly for 20 minutes. Add the okra, shrimp, and the gumbo filé, and cook for 3 to 5 minutes, until the shrimp turns pink. Remove the bay leaves.

3. In a medium bowl, combine the flour, baking powder, cayenne, sugar, baking soda, and the remaining $1/2$ teaspoon of salt. Using a fork, cut in the butter until the mixture resembles coarse cornmeal. Stir in the buttermilk until the mixure just comes together. Knead until a soft dough forms.

4. On a lightly floured surface, roll out the dough until it is $1/2$ inch thick. Using a $2^{1}/_{2}$-inch round cutter, stamp out 12 biscuits.

5. Pour the hot gumbo into a 9 x 13-inch casserole dish. Arrange the biscuits on top of the gumbo. Bake until the biscuits are golden brown, about 20 minutes.

Filé powder is a necessity for cooking authentic Creole or Cajun cuisine. In addition to contributing an unusual flavor, the powder also acts as a thickener when added to liquid. You can find it at most grocery stores or online at Amazon.com. We like the McCormick brand.

Super-Simple
Spinach-Stuffed Shells

Makes 8 servings

Cooking spray

3 cups shredded Italian cheese mixture (12 ounces)

2 (10-ounce) boxes chopped spinach, thawed and well drained

1 (15-ounce) container ricotta cheese

4 ounces cream cheese, softened

2 large eggs, beaten

½ teaspoon salt

½ teaspoon freshly ground black pepper

1 (24-ounce) jar marinara sauce or 3 cups Marinara Sauce (page 334; see Note, opposite)

1 (12-ounce) box jumbo pasta shells

We Queens are always on the lookout for easy go-to meal solutions. Our latest obsession happens to be these super-simple spinach-stuffed shells. They're meatless, easy, kid-friendly, and delicious! When you remove the foil for the last 10 minutes of baking, you can quickly throw together our Broccoli Rabe with Shallots (page 196) for a tasty sidekick. You're welcome!

1. Preheat the oven to 350°F. Spray a 9 x 13-inch casserole dish with cooking spray.

2. In a large bowl, combine 2 cups of the Italian cheese with the spinach, ricotta cheese, cream cheese, eggs, salt, and pepper.

3. Pour about 1½ cups of the marinara sauce into the prepared casserole dish, spreading the sauce around to cover the bottom of the dish.

4. In a large pot of boiling salted water, cook the pasta shells for 8 minutes, or until al dente. Rinse the shells under cool water to stop the cooking process. Stuff the shells immediately so they won't start sticking together. Stuff each shell with ½ cup of the cheese-and-spinach mixture. Put the filled shells into the casserole dish. Cover the pasta with the remaining 1½ cups of sauce. Sprinkle the remaining 1 cup of Italian cheese on top.

5. Cover the dish with foil and bake for 50 minutes. Remove the foil and bake for 10 minutes more. Remove the casserole from the oven and let it stand for 5 minutes before serving.

This recipe can be made GLUTEN-FREE by using a gluten-free pasta. See page 21 for recommendations of our favorite brands.

FREEZES WELL

For best results, prepare the casserole through step 4. Cover with foil and freeze for up to 2 months. Thaw the casserole overnight in the refrigerator before baking as stated in the recipe. Note that casseroles that have not been completely thawed may take 15 to 30 minutes longer, so be sure to check for bubbling edges and a hot center.

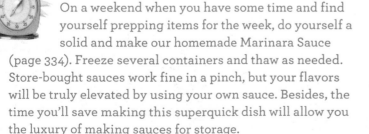

On a weekend when you have some time and find yourself prepping items for the week, do yourself a solid and make our homemade Marinara Sauce (page 334). Freeze several containers and thaw as needed. Store-bought sauces work fine in a pinch, but your flavors will be truly elevated by using your own sauce. Besides, the time you'll save making this superquick dish will allow you the luxury of making sauces for storage.

Four-Cheese Pasta

Makes 8 to 10 servings

Cooking spray

1 (16-ounce) box ziti or any other tube-shaped pasta

1 (14½-ounce) can diced tomatoes

3 tablespoons olive oil

1 cup chopped onion

12 garlic cloves, minced

⅔ cup dry white wine

2 cups heavy cream

1½ cups shredded Parmesan cheese (6 ounces)

1 cup crumbled Gorgonzola cheese (4 ounces)

2 cups mozzarella cheese, shredded (8 ounces)

1 cup shredded fontina cheese (4 ounces)

1 teaspoon salt

¾ teaspoon freshly ground black pepper

You haven't had a baked ziti like this before. Our version of this traditional favorite enhances the flavor with a creamy co-mingling of tangy Gorgonzola, nutty fontina, mozzarella, and sharp Parmesan cheese. Since this is such a rich and filling dish, it's great to serve when entertaining both vegetarians and meat lovers. Who doesn't love cheesy baked pasta?

If you can't find Gorgonzola or fontina at your local market, you can substitute! Use regular ol' blue cheese for the Gorgonzola and replace the fontina with shredded Italian cheese mix. These prepared cheese mixes usually include a variety of tasty Italian cheeses that complement this dish perfectly.

1. Preheat the oven to 425°F. Lightly coat a 9 x 13-inch casserole dish with cooking spray.

2. Cook the pasta according to the package directions. Drain the pasta and put it in the prepared casserole dish. Stir in the tomatoes and their juices. Set aside.

FREEZES WELL
See our freezer tips on page 16.

3. Heat the oil in a large saucepan set over medium-high heat. Add the onion and garlic and cook until just soft, about 8 minutes. Add the wine and cook for about 4 more minutes or until the liquid is reduced by half. Reduce the heat to medium and add the cream. Simmer gently, stirring frequently, for about 5 minutes or until the mixture starts to thicken slightly. Remove the pan from the heat. Stir in the Parmesan, Gorgonzola, mozzarella, and fontina cheeses, and season with salt and pepper.

4. Pour the cheese mixture over the pasta. Cover the pan with foil and bake for 30 to 35 minutes or until the sauce is bubbly. Remove from the oven and stir to make sure the cheese and pasta are thoroughly combined.

End up with extra Gorgonzola? Put it to good use! Sandy loves to stuff it into a fresh fig, then wrap the fig in a very thin slice of prosciutto. Voilà! A sophisticated garnish for a salad or an easy appetizer for your next cocktail party.

Easy Eggplant
Parmesan

Makes 6 servings

- 1 large eggplant, cut into 6 to 8 slices
- 1 teaspoon salt, plus more for the eggplant
- ⅓ cup plus 2 tablespoons olive oil
- 1 medium yellow onion, chopped
- 2 garlic cloves, minced
- 1 (14½-ounce) can diced tomatoes
- 1 (15-ounce) can tomato sauce
- 1 (6-ounce) can tomato paste
- 2 teaspoons dried oregano
- 1 teaspoon dried basil
- ¼ teaspoon dried rosemary, crushed
- 1 teaspoon granulated sugar
- ½ teaspoon freshly ground black pepper
- Pinch of ground cinnamon
- Cooking spray
- ⅓ cup grated Parmesan cheese (1½ ounces)
- 2 tablespoons all-purpose flour
- 2 tablespoons Seasoned Bread Crumbs (page 330)
- 1 large egg
- 8 ounces mozzarella cheese, shredded (2 cups)

Crystal's sister, Cindy, has always been a fantastic cook, but recently she has found a special connection in the kitchen. During a year-and-a-half-long treatment for breast cancer, she found that cooking is amazing therapy. Not only has Cindy been a great sounding board for our recipes, she concocted this easy, nutritious, and delicious dish that is so tasty that we just had to share it with the rest of the world. Go Cindy! Go Cindy!

1. Lay the eggplant slices on a wire rack that is nestled in a baking pan. Generously sprinkle the eggplant with salt and let them sit for up to 1 hour. Rinse the eggplant slices under cold water to remove the salt, then pat dry.

2. Heat 2 tablespoons of the olive oil in a large sauté pan or saucepan set over medium heat. Add the onion and garlic, and sauté until soft, about 8 minutes. Add the tomatoes, tomato sauce, and tomato paste, stirring until well blended. Add the oregano, basil, rosemary, sugar, 1 teaspoon salt, pepper, and cinnamon. Simmer for 20 to 30 minutes.

3. Meanwhile, preheat the oven to 350°F. Lightly coat a 9 x 13-inch casserole dish with cooking spray.

4. Combine the Parmesan, flour, and bread crumbs in a plate or other shallow dish. In a small bowl, beat the egg with 1 tablespoon of water.

5. Heat the remaining ⅓ cup olive oil in a large skillet set over medium heat. Dip each eggplant slice into the egg, shaking off the excess. Press the slices into the cheese mixture, coating both sides. Working in batches, put the slices in the hot oil and cook until crisp and golden brown, 2 to 3 minutes each side. Transfer the eggplant to a paper towel–lined plate and let drain. Repeat with the remaining eggplant slices.

6. Arrange the eggplant slices in the bottom of the prepared casserole dish. Sprinkle the eggplant slices with half of the mozzarella. Top with the tomato mixture, and sprinkle with the remaining mozzarella. (Top with an additional dusting of Parmesan cheese, if desired.) Bake for approximately 25 minutes, until the sauce is bubbling. Allow to stand for 5 minutes before serving.

This dish can be made GLUTEN-FREE by replacing the flour and bread crumbs with gluten-free store-bought alternatives (see page 21 for recommendations of our favorite brands) or make your own.

Jayne's
Baked Spaghetti

Makes 10 servings

- 1 (16-ounce) package angel hair pasta
- Cooking spray
- 2 tablespoons unsalted butter
- 1 cup chopped onion
- 1 cup chopped green bell pepper
- 1 (28-ounce) can diced tomatoes
- 1 (4-ounce) can sliced button mushrooms, drained
- 1 (2¼-ounce) can sliced black olives, drained
- 2 teaspoons dried oregano
- 8 ounces Cheddar cheese, shredded (2 cups)
- 1½ cups Cream of Mushroom Soup (page 339)
- ¼ cup whole milk
- ¼ ounce grated Parmesan cheese

Every family has a signature dish, and this one belongs to the Lovitt family. Sandy's other half, Michael, grew up on this dish, and to this day his mom makes it for him whenever he goes home to visit. In fact, Michael's mom, Jayne, has been making this dish ever since she was newly wed to her husband, Mike. The story goes that when Jayne and Mike were first married, they spent a lot of time with another couple in the neighborhood (we'll call them "Bob and Sally"). Jayne, Mike, Bob, and Sally would get together on a regular basis and play cards. Eventually, they decided that they would start making dinner for each other, too. This tradition didn't last long before Bob called and said they could no longer participate in the dinner parties. When Jayne asked if everything was okay, Bob said that Sally was very upset because there was no way she could ever compete with Jayne's baked spaghetti. They haven't spoken in 30 years!

1. Cook the pasta according to the package directions. Set aside.

2. Preheat the oven to 350°F. Lightly coat a 9 x 13-inch casserole dish with cooking spray.

3. In a large sauté pan set over medium heat, melt the butter. Add the onion and bell pepper and cook until tender, about 8 minutes. Add the tomatoes, mushrooms, olives, and oregano. Reduce the heat to low and cook for 10 minutes.

4. In the prepared casserole dish, layer half of the pasta, half of the sauce, and half of the Cheddar cheese. Repeat the layers with the remaining ingredients.

5. Combine the soup and milk, stirring until smooth, and pour over the top of the casserole. Sprinkle with the Parmesan cheese and bake for 30 to 40 minutes or until the pasta is bubbling around the edges.

VARIATION

- A simple way to enrich this dish is to add beef. Season 1 pound of ground beef with salt and freshly ground black pepper, and brown it in a large sauté pan set over medium-high heat. Add the meat to the sauce while it simmers so that the flavors have time to marry.

This dish can be made GLUTEN-FREE as long as you use a gluten-free brand of Worcestershire sauce.

Mexican *Spaghetti*

Makes 8 servings

Cooking spray

1 teaspoon olive oil

1 small onion, finely chopped

½ red bell pepper, chopped

1 (8-ounce) box *fideo*

¾ cup Chicken Broth (page 335) or store bought

¾ cup tomato sauce

2 garlic cloves, minced

½ teaspoon ground cumin

1 teaspoon salt

Another name for this great dish is *fideo,* which is also the Spanish word for vermicelli. Ask anyone from Sandy's neck of the woods in the Rio Grande Valley about it, and you'll likely get a chuckle and their family's favorite recipe. There is a version called *sopa de fideo,* which is typically a chicken soup prepared with some mixture of *fideo,* tomatoes, cilantro, jalapeños, and cumin. Our recipe uses *fideo* as a flavorful bed for any type of prepared chicken, beef, or pork dish. But don't fret if you don't eat meat. The *fideo* itself is filling enough for a main course. You will just need to replace the chicken broth with a vegetable broth to make it truly vegetarian. If you are unable to find *fideo,* you can use vermicelli or fine egg noodles.

1. Preheat the oven to 350°F. Spray a 9 x 13-inch casserole dish with cooking spray.

2. In a large saucepan set over medium heat, heat the olive oil. Add the onion and bell pepper and cook, stirring, until translucent, about 4 minutes. Add the fideo and cook until lightly toasted, about 5 minutes. Add the chicken broth, tomato sauce, garlic, cumin, and salt. Pour the mixture into the prepared casserole dish.

3. Bake for 30 minutes, or until most of the liquid has been cooked out.

This recipe can be made GLUTEN-FREE by using a gluten-free pasta. See page 21 for recommendations of our favorite brands.

This dish can be made VEGETARIAN-FRIENDLY by substituting vegetable broth for the chicken broth.

The Savory
Gourmet

Whether you're planning a weekend dinner party, a special occasion with your sweetheart, or a holiday gathering, there's a recipe in this chapter for you. These dishes may take a little more time and effort, or call for more than your everyday ingredients, but we'll guide you through them and you'll have fun at the same time.

As mentioned, we sought to use ingredients for these recipes not typically found in staple casseroles, such as buttery lobster, tender lamb, and fresh crab. Those with more sophisticated palates will be delighted that the humble casserole can meet their gourmet expectations. And the best part? These are still make-ahead dishes, which means more party time with your guests.

Osso Bucco
Fit for a Queen!

Makes 6 servings

- ¼ cup all-purpose flour
- Salt and freshly ground black pepper
- 6 (½-pound each) veal shanks or lamb shanks
- ½ cup vegetable oil
- ¼ cup (½ stick) unsalted butter
- 1 cup chopped carrots
- 1 cup chopped celery
- 1 cup chopped onion
- 4 garlic cloves, minced
- 3 fresh thyme sprigs
- 2 bay leaves
- 1 fresh rosemary sprig
- 1½ cups dry white wine
- 1 tablespoon tomato paste
- 3 cups veal stock or Chicken Broth (page 335), plus more as needed
- 1 (14½-ounce) can diced tomatoes
- 4 tablespoons chopped fresh flat-leaf parsley
- 1 tablespoon grated lemon zest

Put some lovin' in your oven! This fabulous dish gets its rich flavor from slowly brazing the veal until the meat is so tender, it literally falls off the bone with the touch of your fork. As it cooks, the aromas of the fresh herbs, earthy vegetables, and wine fill the kitchen. In fact, you may have to keep yourself busy by reading this cookbook until the timer goes off, lest you dig in before it's done. Seriously, if you have never tried osso bucco, this is your chance! It takes a little more time—and expense—to cook than other dishes, but it's completely worth it. Traditionally osso bucco is served over risotto, but we like it best over a bed of mashed potatoes or cooked white rice. So go ahead and treat yourself, you deserve it. If you're not keen on veal, you can use lamb instead.

1. Preheat the oven to 325°F.

2. Put the flour on a plate and season it with salt and pepper. Pat the shanks dry with paper towels. Dredge each shank in the seasoned flour, making sure to shake off any excess flour. Heat the vegetable oil in a heavy Dutch oven or large sauté pan set over high heat until just smoking. Working in batches so as not to crowd the pan, place shanks in the oil in a single layer. Cook the shanks until browned on each side, about 4 minutes per side. Remove the shanks from the pan and set aside.

3. Reduce the heat to medium high, then add the butter, carrots, celery, and onion to the pan and sauté for about 8 minutes or until the vegetables begin to soften. Add the garlic and sauté for 2 more minutes.

4. Meanwhile, make a bouquet garni: place the thyme, bay leaves, and rosemary on a square of cheesecloth, gather the corners at the top, and tie the cloth closed with some kitchen twine. Add the bouquet garni to the sautéed vegetables. Increase the heat to high and add the wine. Bring the mixture to a boil and cook, making sure to scrape up the browned bits at the bottom of the pan, until the liquid is reduced by about half, about 10 minutes. Add the tomato paste and stir to combine.

5. Return the shanks to the pan and add the stock and diced tomatoes. Cover the pan and place it in the oven. Now, go make yourself a cocktail and wait. This dish will need to braise for 1½ to 2 hours or until the meat is super-tender and falling off the bone. Check on it occasionally to make sure there's enough liquid in the pan. The shanks should be submerged in liquid by about three-fourths of the way up the shank. If the pan dries out some, just add more stock. Flip the shanks a couple of times during cooking so that both sides sit in the amazing juice for a while.

6. The meat is done when it is falling off the bone. Transfer the shanks to a serving platter. Remove the bouquet garni and discard. Spoon the liquid from the pan over the shanks and sprinkle with the parsley and lemon zest.

Sandy's first restaurant job out of culinary school was at a locally owned restaurant here in Austin called Jeffrey's. This restaurant has a fabulous reputation and Sandy was lucky enough to work with amazing chefs who inspired and challenged her in the kitchen and taught her many invaluable lessons. One of her most vivid memories of working there was the excitement around the addition of osso bucco to their menu each fall. Rich and decadent, it was only around for a limited time. Our osso bucco recipe is a nod to the talented crew at Jeffrey's.

Charlotte's
Prime Rib

Makes 6 to 8 servings

- 1 (5-pound) rib roast, bone-in
- 2 garlic cloves, quartered
- 2⅓ cups beef broth
- 2 tablespoons Lawry's seasoned salt
- Freshly ground black pepper
- 2 (14½-ounce) cans chopped tomatoes
- 2 medium onions, quartered
- 2 celery stalks, roughly chopped
- 2 bay leaves
- 2 tablespoons Worcestershire sauce

Crystal's mom, Charlotte, should have installed a revolving door in their home, as it was the place where everyone stopped by—conveniently right around dinnertime. Charlotte fed almost everyone in Blue Ridge—the small town located in the North Georgia Mountains where Crystal grew up—for years and finally decided to make a successful catering business of it. Her prime rib was by far one of the most requested items and has become a Cook family holiday favorite. Lucky for Charlotte, her recipe made it into this book, so now she can stop by someone else's house for dinner.

1. Preheat the oven to 375°F.

2. Make 8 slits in top of the roast and stuff each with a garlic piece. Place the roast in a roasting pan and cover with the broth, seasoned salt, pepper, tomatoes, onions, celery, and bay leaves. Cover with foil and bake for about 1 hour. Remove roast from pan, let rest 10 minutes, then wrap tightly with plastic wrap and place in refrigerator overnight. Place the pan juices in a covered container and refrigerate overnight.

3. The next day preheat the oven to 375°F. Remove the container of pan juice from the refrigerator, skim the grease from the top of the juice, strain out the vegetables, and add the Worcestershire sauce. Unwrap the meat and put the roast and juices into a 9 x 13-inch casserole dish and roast the meat again for 30 minutes or until the internal temperature reaches 130°F (medium-rare).

This dish is GLUTEN-FREE as long as you use a gluten-free brand of Worcestershire sauce.

Spicy Bloody Mary

Makes 6 servings

- 3 cups tomato juice
- ¼ cup plus 2 tablespoons fresh lime juice (from 6 limes)
- ¼ cup fresh lemon juice (from 4 lemons)
- 3 garlic cloves, minced
- 2 tablespoons Old Bay seasoning, plus more for garnish
- 1 tablespoon prepared horseradish
- 1 tablespoon Worcestershire sauce, or to taste
- Salt and freshly ground black pepper
- 1 lime, cut into wedges
- 1½ cups Pepper Vodka (see below) or unflavored vodka
- Pickled okra, for garnish
- 6 celery stalks, for garnish

In Crystal's house, along with the salt and pepper shakers sits a trusty can of Old Bay faithfully by their side. Her boyfriend, Tim, has quite the obsession with the spice mixture and requests it on pretty much everything: meats, roasted veggies, eggs, you name it. But mostly it is reserved for Sundays when they celebrate the taste of Maryland with steamed crabs and these incredibly spiced Bloody Marys! The Bloody mixture (sans the vodka) is also the secret ingredient to our Individual Bacon-Wrapped Meatloaves (page 47).

1. In a blender, combine the tomato juice, lime juice, lemon juice, garlic, Old Bay, and horseradish, and blend until smooth. Season the mixture to taste with the Worcestershire sauce, salt, and pepper. Refrigerate the mixture in a nonreactive container for at least 6 hours, and up to 3 days, before serving.

2. To serve, run a lime wedge around the rim of each of 6 (16-ounce) tumblers and dust with Old Bay. Fill the tumblers with ice, divide the tomato juice mix among the glasses, and top off each glass with the vodka. Garnish with the pickled okra and celery stalks and serve.

This drink can be made GLUTEN-FREE as long as you use a gluten-free brand of Worcestershire sauce.

This drink can be made VEGETARIAN-FRIENDLY as long as your Worcestershire sauce doesn't contain anchovies.

Pepper Vodka

Makes 1½ cups

- 1½ cups vodka
- 4 serrano chili peppers, sliced lengthwise

Combine the vodka and peppers in a glass jar with a lid and cover tightly. Let sit for 12 to 24 hours, strain and discard the peppers, and serve.

Beef
Burgundy

Makes 8 servings

- 8 slices bacon, chopped
- 3 pounds stew meat or boneless beef chuck, cut into ¾-inch cubes
- Salt
- ⅛ teaspoon freshly ground black pepper, plus more for beef
- ⅓ cup all-purpose flour
- 2 yellow onions, chopped
- 1 pound carrots, peeled and cut into 1-inch pieces
- 1 pound sliced button mushrooms
- 5 large garlic cloves, minced
- 3½ cups Beef Broth (page 336)
- 1 bottle dry red wine, preferably Burgundy
- ⅓ cup chopped fresh thyme leaves
- 1 tablespoon firmly packed light brown sugar
- 1 tablespoon tomato paste
- 1 bay leaf

This delicious, classic dish from the Burgundy region of France is designed to showcase the wines for which the area is famous. (We like anything that celebrates wine. Oui, oui!) Beef Burgundy can appear at first glance as a mere stew, but those of us who have had the pleasure of making this dish know that during the hours it slowly cooks in the oven something magical happens. The flavors of the broth are intensified by the wine, and it thickens into a velvety smooth sauce. Once finished, the cuts of beef are so tender they almost seem to melt. Traditionally, Beef Burgundy is made with wine from the French province of Burgundy. If you have trouble finding a true Burgundy (they can be pretty pricey!), the best substitutes are Pinot Noirs from California or Oregon. We suggest serving this over our Perfect Rice Every Time (page 329) and with our Rockin' Tomatoes Rockefeller (page 219).

1. Preheat the oven to 350°F.

2. Cook the bacon in a heavy ovenproof Dutch oven set over high heat until crisp, about 7 minutes. Transfer the bacon to a paper towel–lined plate. Set aside.

3. Season the beef generously with salt and pepper, and toss in the flour. Working in three batches so as not to crowd the pot, add the meat to the pot with the rendered bacon fat. Cook the beef, turning to brown all sides, about 5 minutes per batch. Transfer the meat to a large bowl.

4. Into the same pot, add the onions, carrots, mushrooms, and ⅛ teaspoon of the pepper and cook until the vegetables are light brown, about 8 minutes. Add the garlic and sauté for 1 minute. Transfer the vegetables to the bowl with the beef.

5. Add 1½ cups of the broth to the pot. Bring to a boil and cook, scraping up browned bits on the bottom of the pan, until reduced to a glaze, about 8 minutes.

6. Return the meat and vegetables and their juices to the pot. Add the wine, thyme, brown sugar, tomato paste, bay leaf, and the remaining 2 cups of broth. Bring to a boil, stirring occasionally. Cover the pot and place it in the oven. Braise until the beef is tender, about 2 hours. Remove the bay leaf before serving.

This dish can be made GLUTEN-FREE by replacing the flour with a gluten-free mix, either store bought (see page 21 for recommendations of our favorite brands) or make your own.

When it comes to cooking with wine, Sandy follows the sage advice of Julia Child, who said, "If you do not have a good wine to use, it is far better to omit it, for a poor one can spoil a simple dish and utterly debase a noble one."

Awesome Aussie
Meat Pies

Makes 6 servings

Cooking spray

3 tablespoons all-purpose flour

½ tablespoon ground cumin

1 teaspoon coriander

½ tablespoon salt

1 teaspoon freshly ground black pepper

2 pounds beef chuck roast, cut into ¼-inch cubes

½ tablespoon unsalted butter

1 tablespoon vegetable oil

1 onion, chopped

2 garlic cloves, minced

⅓ cup soy sauce

⅓ cup Worcestershire sauce

½ cup Shiner beer (we love a good Texas beer!), or any strong lager

2 cups Beef Broth (page 336) or store bought

1 sheet frozen puff pastry, thawed

Wouldn't you know it? The national dish of Australia is also a casserole! Rob Swander, a culinary grad and our dear friend's brother, perfected this traditional dish while traveling in the wilds of the outback. Well, not quite, but he did travel all over Australia, sampling countless variations of this dish (along with all of the local brews). He spent some time in our kitchen, as an honorary Casserole King, and passed along this little taste of "down under." So this is the real deal and the perfect dish for your mates. Get your veggies in by accompanying this dish with our Simple Herb-Roasted Vegetables (page 223).

1. Preheat the oven to 350°F. Spray six (6-ounce) ramekins with cooking spray.

2. In a large bowl, whisk together the flour, cumin, coriander, salt, and pepper. Add the beef and toss to coat well.

3. Heat a stockpot over medium heat. Add the butter and oil. Shake any excess flour from the beef and add the beef to the pot. Cook, turning to brown all sides, for 8 to 10 minutes. Transfer the beef to a paper towel–lined plate.

4. Add the onion to the pot and cook, stirring, until it has caramelized, 10 minutes. Add the garlic and cook for about 1 minute, then quickly add the beef back to the pot, followed by the soy sauce, Worcestershire sauce, and beer. Cook for about 3 minutes and add the beef stock. Reduce the heat to medium, so that you have a low simmer, and cover the pot. Cook until the sauce has become thick like gravy, about 45 minutes to 1 hour. Divide the beef mixture among the prepared ramekins.

5. Put the puff pastry on a floured work surface. Using a rolling pin, roll it out enough to get six 4-inch circles to cover the top of the ramekins. Dust with flour if the pastry is sticky. Lay the puff pastry over the meat filling in the ramekins. Press the pastry that hangs over the side onto the edges of the dish to seal, and cut a slit in each pie.

6. Bake for 45 minutes, or until the pies are golden and crispy looking on top.

FREEZES WELL For best results, prepare the meat pies through step 4. Wrap in foil and freeze for up to 2 months. Thaw the pies overnight in the refrigerator. The next day, top them with the pastry and bake as stated in the recipe. Note that casseroles that have not been completely thawed may take 15 to 30 minutes longer, so be sure to check for bubbling edges and a hot center.

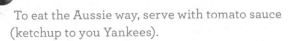

To eat the Aussie way, serve with tomato sauce (ketchup to you Yankees).

Greek
Pastitsio

Makes 8 to 10 servings

1 (16-ounce) package dried macaroni

1½ cups (3 sticks) unsalted butter, melted

2 cups whole milk

6 large eggs, beaten

8 ounces mizithra cheese, shredded, or romano cheese, grated (2 cups)

8 ounces feta cheese, crumbled (2 cups)

¾ cup grated Parmesan cheese (3 ounces)

¼ teaspoon grated nutmeg

1 teaspoon ground white pepper

1½ pounds ground beef

Salt and freshly ground black pepper

3 tablespoons olive oil

1 medium onion, chopped

1 garlic clove, minced

1 (6-ounce) can tomato paste

½ cup dry red wine

½ cup Beef Broth (page 336)

2 tablespoons chopped fresh parsley

½ teaspoon granulated sugar

10 sheets frozen phyllo pastry, thawed

This Greek casserole is traditionally pasta baked in a flavorful meat sauce and topped with another sauce, such as béchamel. But we decided to skip the extra layer of sauce and cover ours with layers of buttery, flaky phyllo dough instead. The phyllo adds a nice crunch to this delicious dish, making a truly scrumptious, savory pie. Don't pull out your best dinnerware for this one. It's so tasty, you'll want to throw your plate and yell "Opa"!

Note that the cheeses won't really melt. They will soften and become nice and creamy, but it won't be gooey like a Cheddar or American cheese.

1. Preheat the oven to 350°F.

2. Cook the macaroni according to the package directions and drain well. Return the cooked macaroni to the pot and add 1 cup of the melted butter, the milk, eggs, mizithra, feta, and Parmesan cheeses, nutmeg, and white pepper. Stir until well combined. Pour the macaroni mixture into a 9 x 13-inch casserole dish.

3. Heat a large skillet over medium-high heat. Add the ground beef, season with salt and pepper, and cook, stirring until browned thoroughly, about 10 minutes. Drain well and set meat aside. Return the skillet to medium-high heat and add the oil, onion, and garlic. Sauté until soft, about 8 minutes. Return the meat to the pan and add the tomato paste, red wine, beef broth, parsley, sugar, and salt and pepper to taste. Cover and simmer for 20 minutes. Remove the pan from the heat and let cool for 5 minutes. Pour over the macaroni mixture. Place one sheet of the phyllo on top of the macaroni. Using a pastry brush and the remaining ½ cup of melted butter, lightly coat the phyllo with butter. Working quickly, add another sheet of phyllo and brush it with butter. Repeat the

layers until you have used all 10 sheets of phyllo. (You may need to overlap the phyllo sheets to entirely cover the pasta.) Cut two or three vents in the top of the pastry.

4. Bake for 45 to 55 minutes, or until the pastry is golden brown and the eggs and cheese are set. Cool the casserole slightly before cutting into squares and serving.

Though working with phyllo dough takes a little extra work, Crystal is always thrilled with the results we get. So light and flaky, it makes a tasty topping for many casseroles and pastry dishes. We always work with frozen sheets of phyllo (it's inexpensive and awesome) and find that it is easiest to use when thawed in the refrigerator overnight.

Here are a few of Crystal's tips for working with this delicate dough. Have a few things on hand when you start to layer the sheets: a pastry brush, a small bowl of melted butter, damp paper towels, and parchment paper. To get started, remove the pastry sheets from the package and unfold them onto parchment paper. Cover the dough with damp paper towels to keep the pastry moist. (Phyllo dries out quickly, so it's important to keep the dough covered.) Work with one sheet at a time, keeping the rest covered.

You can store the sheets in the refrigerator for up to 3 days, wrapped well in foil, but do not try to refreeze any sheets that have been thawed. Unused packages can be stored in the freezer for up to a couple of months.

Moussaka

Makes 8 servings

Cooking spray

3 large eggplants

1 teaspoon salt

½ teaspoon freshly ground black pepper

4 tablespoons olive oil

1 medium onion, chopped

2 garlic cloves, minced

½ lemon, cut in thin slices

¼ cup chopped fresh oregano leaves

¼ cup chopped fresh flat-leaf parsley

2 pounds ground lamb

1 cinnamon stick

3 tablespoons tomato paste

1 (15.5-ounce) can crushed tomatoes

1 cup feta cheese, crumbled (8 ounces)

1 cup freshly grated Parmesan cheese (4 ounces)

3 cups Béchamel (page 106; optional)

1 cup bread crumbs (see page 330)

Moussaka always reminds Crystal and her niece Maggie of the movie *My Big Fat Greek Wedding*. If you've seen it, you may recall a scene where a grade-school-age Nia Vardalos brings moussaka to lunch, and the other girls at the table think it's called "moose caca." Well, they sure missed out, because this is a very special casserole that is perfect for Sunday dinners or potluck gatherings. And the beauty of it is that it freezes well, with no loss of flavor. We've opted to omit the traditional béchamel sauce to cut back on some of the calories, but we have included our favorite béchamel recipe if you would like to indulge. Just pour it over the top before adding the bread crumbs. What are you waiting for? Make this dish for your family, and they'll treat you like their own Greek goddess. This dish pairs nicely with our Tomato and Feta Salad (page 265).

1. Preheat the oven to 350°F. Spray a 9 x 13-inch glass or ceramic casserole dish with cooking spray.

2. Cut off the stems of the eggplants and, using a vegetable peeler, peel them. Cut them lengthwise into ½-inch-thick slices. Season both sides of the pieces with ½ teaspoon of the salt and ¼ teaspoon of the pepper.

3. In a large skillet set over medium heat, heat 3 tablespoons of the oil. Working in batches, fry the eggplant in a single layer, turning once, until brown on both sides, about 8 minutes per side. Transfer the eggplant to a paper towel–lined plate to drain.

4. Add the remaining 1 tablespoon of oil to the pan and add the onion, garlic, lemon slices, oregano, and parsley. Cook, stirring, until soft, about 3 minutes. Add the lamb, cinnamon stick, the remaining $\frac{1}{2}$ teaspoon of the salt, and the remaining $\frac{1}{4}$ teaspoon of the pepper, and cook until lamb is browned through. Stir in the tomato paste and crushed tomatoes. Simmer until the liquid has evaporated, stirring occasionally. Remove from the heat. Remove cinnamon stick and lemon slices.

5. Line the bottom of the prepared casserole dish with a third of the eggplant slices; they should completely cover the bottom. Spread half of the meat sauce over the eggplant, and sprinkle half of the feta and half of the Parmesan on top. Repeat the layers again, ending with a final layer of eggplant. If using the béchamel sauce, pour it over the top. Cover with a layer of bread crumbs.

6. Bake for 30 to 40 minutes, or until the top is golden. Let cool for 10 minutes before serving.

FREEZES WELL For best results, prepare the casserole (without the béchamel) through step 5. Wrap in foil and freeze for up to 2 months. Thaw the casserole overnight in the refrigerator before baking as stated in the recipe. Note that casseroles that have not been completely thawed may take 15 to 30 minutes longer, so be sure to check for bubbling edges and a hot center.

This dish can be made GLUTEN-FREE by using gluten-free bread crumbs, either store bought (see page 21 for recommendations of our favorite brands) or homemade. If you want to add the béchamel to the recipe, you can make it gluten-free by eliminating the flour and substituting a gluten-free all-purpose mix, which you may purchase at most local grocery chains, or you can make your own (see page 322).

(continues)

Béchamel

Makes about 6 cups

4 cups whole milk

½ cup (1 stick) unsalted butter

½ cup all-purpose flour

1 teaspoon salt

½ teaspoon ground nutmeg

4 large egg yolks

The moussaka recipe calls for only 3 cups of the béchamel, but you may want to serve extra on the side, too. This sauce is delicious on lots of things—especially salmon croquettes or vegetable lasagna.

1. In a medium saucepan set over medium heat, heat the milk for about 10 minutes or until milk registers 160°F on a thermometer.

2. In a separate medium saucepan set over low heat, melt the butter. Slowly whisk in the flour and continue to whisk for 2 minutes.

3. Little by little, and while whisking constantly, pour in the steaming milk. It will set up and thicken dramatically at first, but as you continue adding milk, the sauce will loosen. Increase the heat to medium. Add the salt and nutmeg and stir well.

4. Put the egg yolks in a bowl and whisk well. Slowly, and while whisking constantly, pour a couple of cups of the hot béchamel into the eggs. Slowly pour the egg mixture back into the saucepan and whisk well. Keep the sauce on very low heat until ready to use; do not let simmer or boil. Per the recipe, you will use only half for this recipe, but you may serve extra on the side.

Bobotie

Cooking spray

2 thick slices white bread, torn into small pieces

¾ cup milk

¼ cup (½ stick) unsalted butter

1 large onion, finely chopped

½ pound ground lamb or beef

½ pound ground pork

1 cup slivered almonds, toasted

1 Granny Smith apple, peeled, cored, and diced

⅓ cup golden raisins

1 cup chopped dried apricots

2 tablespoons apricot jam

Juice of 1 lemon

1 tablespoon curry powder

⅛ teaspoon dried oregano

1 teaspoon salt

½ teaspoon freshly ground black pepper

1 large egg

6 lemon leaves, for garnish (see Note)

Who would have thought that the national dish of South Africa is—you guessed it—a casserole! Similar to the shepherd's pie of Great Britain or Greece's moussaka, bobotie is an all-in-one meal consisting of meat with a rich egg topping. Plus it happens to be fun to say (pronounced "buh-boor-tea").

If you're a little sheepish about eating lamb, trust us, this is the way to go for your first try. You can make this dish with beef, too, but the bites of tender lamb mixed with the sweetness of apricots, apple, and raisins are really delicious.

1. Preheat the oven to 325°F. Spray a 9 x 13-inch casserole dish with cooking spray.

2. In a small bowl, combine the bread and ¼ cup of the milk, and let soak for 5 minutes.

3. In a large sauté pan set over medium-high heat, melt 2 tablespoons of the butter. Add the onion and cook until it starts to soften, about 3 minutes. Add the lamb and pork and cook for 3 more minutes. Add the soaked bread, almonds, apple, raisins, apricots, jam, lemon juice, curry powder, oregano, salt, and pepper. Cook for 5 minutes. Pour the mixture into the prepared casserole dish.

4. In a small bowl, whisk together the remaining ½ cup milk and the egg. Pour half of this mixture over the meat. Dot with the remaining 2 tablespoons butter. Bake for 30 minutes. Add the remaining milk mixture and bake 5 more minutes or until set. Garnish with lemon leaves before serving.

This South African specialty is often adorned with a lemon leaf garnish. Lemon leaves can often be found at a florist. You can substitute with orange or bay leaves. If you opt for bay leaves, grate a bit of the lemon zest into the dish before adding the lemon juice (at step 3).

Yvonne's Unstuffed Poblano Casserole

Makes 8 servings

Cooking spray

4 poblano chilies, cut in half crosswise and seeded

1 pound ground beef

½ onion, chopped

1 teaspoon ground cumin

1 teaspoon salt

½ teaspoon freshly ground black pepper

3 cups shredded Monterey Jack cheese (12 ounces)

¼ cup all-purpose flour

4 large eggs, beaten

1½ cups whole milk

¼ teaspoon Tabasco sauce

When you think about peppers, comfort food usually isn't the first thing that comes to mind. But to Crystal and Sandy, it means home to them, and for different reasons. Crystal's mamaw always made great stuffed peppers, so we put that recipe in this book. And when Sandy tastes a poblano pepper, she's instantly reminded of this recipe, since Sandy's oldest sister, Yvonne, makes these for her every time she comes home for a visit!

Poblano peppers are smaller and spicier than their bell pepper cousins, but they're not too hot. Fairly mild overall, they pack a ton of flavor. Best of all, they're perfect for stuffing with a variety of ingredients. We love to serve this with our Tomato and Avocado Salad (page 267).

1. Preheat the oven to Broil. Spray a 9 x 13-inch casserole dish with cooking spray.

2. Put the poblanos, skin sides up, on a foil-lined baking sheet and flatten them with your hand. Broil for 10 minutes, or until the poblanos are blackened. Put the poblanos in a plastic zip-top bag and seal. Let stand 10 minutes.

3. Decrease the oven temperature to 350°F.

4. In a large skillet set over medium-high heat, combine the beef and onion. Cook, breaking up any lumps with the back of a spoon, until the beef is browned through, about 10 minutes. Drain off the fat, and then sprinkle with the cumin, ½ teaspoon of the salt, and the pepper.

5. Put half of the poblanos in the prepared casserole dish. Sprinkle with the cheese and top with the meat mixture. Arrange remaining poblanos over the meat.

6. Mix the flour and the remaining ½ teaspoon of the salt in a bowl. In a separate bowl, combine the beaten eggs, milk, and Tabasco sauce. Gradually add the egg mixture to the flour and stir until smooth. Pour over the casserole.

7. Bake for 45 to 50 minutes, or until a knife inserted just off-center comes out clean. Let cool for 5 to 10 minutes before serving.

This dish can be made GLUTEN-FREE by replacing the flour with a gluten-free all-purpose mix, either store bought (see page 21 for recommendations of our favorite brands) or make your own.

FREEZES WELL For best results, prepare the casserole through step 6. Wrap in foil and freeze for up to 2 months. Thaw the casserole overnight in the refrigerator before baking as stated in the recipe. Note that casseroles that have not been completely thawed may take 15 to 30 minutes longer, so be sure to check for bubbling edges and a hot center.

Chicken
Enchiladas

Makes 6 servings

Cooking spray

1 cup plus 2 tablespoons canola oil

3 tablespoons chili powder

2 tablespoons all-purpose flour

½ teaspoon ground cumin

1 cup tomato sauce

2 cups Chicken Broth (page 335) or store bought

5 cups shredded Monterey Jack cheese (20 ounces)

1 medium onion, finely chopped

3 garlic cloves, minced

18 corn tortillas

1 (3-pound) roasted chicken, boned and shredded (see page 340)

Sandy grew up in the Valley and her favorite school lunch at Edinburg High School (go Bobcats!) was chicken enchilada day! And if anybody is going to make enchiladas the right way, they're probably going to do it in the Valley. If you aren't aware, the Valley is deep in the southern part of Texas near the Mexican border, and it's known for delicious Mexican-influenced dishes. As with most of our childhood favorites, we have altered the recipe ever so slightly to fit our current palates. In other words, we can handle the heat! Here is Sandy's latest and greatest. She likes to serve it up with Nene's Spanish Rice (page 226).

1. Preheat the oven to 350°F. Spray a 9 x 13-inch casserole dish with cooking spray.

2. In a medium saucepan set over medium heat, heat 2 tablespoons of the oil. When the oil is hot, stir in the chili powder, flour, and cumin, and cook for 1 minute. Add the tomato sauce and chicken broth, bring to a simmer, and cook for 15 to 20 minutes, or until the sauce starts to thicken. Pour 1 cup of the sauce into the bottom of the prepared casserole dish.

3. In a medium bowl, combine the cheese, onion, and garlic. Mix well and set aside.

4. In a medium sauté pan set over medium heat, heat the remaining 1 cup of oil until hot. Turn off the heat, then, using tongs, dip each corn tortilla in the hot oil for 5 to 10 seconds to warm the tortilla and make it pliable, not crispy. Lay each hot tortilla on a paper towel–lined baking sheet to drain while you heat the remaining tortillas.

5. Take each tortilla, dip it in the sauce in the saucepan, and put it on a cutting board. Spoon ¼ cup of the cheese mixture onto the center of the tortilla and top it with roasted chicken. Roll the tortilla into an enchilada and put it seam side down in the casserole dish. Repeat with the remaining tortillas, cheese mixture (reserve 1 cup for top), and chicken. Top with the remaining sauce and reserved cheese.

6. Bake for 20 to 30 minutes, or until the cheese is bubbling and slightly brown. Let cool for 10 minutes before serving.

This dish can be made GLUTEN-FREE by replacing the flour with a gluten-free all-purpose mix, either store bought (see page 21 for recommendations of our favorite brands) or make your own.

FREEZES WELL For best results, prepare the casserole through step 5. Wrap in foil and freeze for up to 2 months. Thaw the casserole overnight in the refrigerator before baking as stated in the recipe. Note that casseroles that have not been completely thawed may take 15 to 30 minutes longer, so be sure to check for bubbling edges and a hot center.

Monterey
Chicken and Rice

Makes 6 servings

Cooking spray

1 (8-ounce) package cream cheese, softened

1 (3-pound) roasted chicken, boned and shredded (see page 340)

3 cups cooked rice (see page 329)

1 cup shredded Monterey Jack cheese (4 ounces)

1 (4-ounce) can diced green chilies

1½ cups Cream of Chicken Soup (page 338)

1 teaspoon salt

½ teaspoon freshly ground black pepper

¾ cup corn chips, coarsely crushed

This casserole comes together in a snap, so do yourself a favor and go ahead and double up the recipe. Casseroles prepared ahead of time and stored in the freezer are an easy solution for providing a home-cooked meal on a busy day. And this dish is so flavorful, your family will be happy to see it in frequent rotation. One thing to note is that this recipe calls for a crispy corn chip topping. Wait to add it until right before baking, instead of putting it on before freezing. Corn chips tend to get soggy when frozen, and you'll miss out on the delightful crunch.

1. Preheat the oven to 350°F. Spray a 9 x 13-inch casserole dish with cooking spray.

2. In a large bowl, stir the cream cheese until smooth. Add the chicken, rice, cheese, chilies, soup, salt, and pepper. Mix well and pour into the prepared casserole dish.

3. Sprinkle the top of the casserole with the corn chips. Bake for 25 to 30 minutes, until golden brown and bubbling around the edges.

This dish is GLUTEN-FREE as long as the cream of chicken soup is gluten-free. See page 21 for recommendations of our favorite brands.

FREEZES WELL For best results, prepare the casserole through step 2. Wrap in foil and freeze for up to 2 months. Thaw the casserole overnight in the refrigerator. The next day, sprinkle the top of the casserole with the corn chips and bake as stated in the recipe. Note that casseroles that have not been completely thawed may take 15 to 30 minutes longer, so be sure to check for bubbling edges and a hot center.

Curry Cure-All
Chicken Casserole

Makes 6 servings

4 tablespoons olive oil

1 large onion, chopped

½ red bell pepper, chopped

4 garlic cloves, minced

5 teaspoons curry powder

1 teaspoon salt

6 boneless, skinless chicken breasts, cut into 1-inch pieces

5 medium russet potatoes, peeled and diced

3 cups Chicken Broth (page 335)

When sick, people typically head straight for chicken noodle soup or some other mild-flavored, broth-based soup to nurse them back to health. Not Crystal. Oddly enough, when Crystal is feeling a little under the weather, she craves spice to comfort her. We're talking hot-and-sour soup, pho with lots of sriracha sauce, and her ultimate cure-all favorite, curry! Extremely satisfying, this dish's fragrant spices alone will perk you right up. Serve over steamed jasmine rice or with traditional Indian bread called naan.

1. Preheat the oven to 350°F.

2. In a large saucepan set over medium heat, heat the oil. Add the onion, bell pepper, garlic, curry powder, and salt, and sauté for about 8 minutes. Watch this step closely since the garlic and curry powder can burn easily if left unattended. Using a slotted spoon, remove the vegetables from the pan and set them aside.

3. Add the chicken to the pan and sauté for 8 minutes or until almost cooked. If the pan gets dry, add a little more oil. Add the potatoes and onion mixture to the saucepan and stir well. Pour the curry into a 9 x 13-inch casserole dish. Pour the chicken broth into the dish until the curry is just covered.

4. Bake for about 45 minutes or until the sauce starts to thicken to a gravy-like consistency and the potatoes are tender.

The "Sitch"
Chicken Parmesan

Makes 10 servings

Cooking spray

½ cup vegetable oil

2 large eggs, lightly beaten

1 teaspoon salt

½ teaspoon freshly ground black pepper

1 cup Seasoned Bread Crumbs (page 330)

4 whole boneless, skinless, split chicken breasts

2 (15-ounce) cans tomato sauce

2 tablespoons chopped fresh parsley

¼ cup chopped fresh basil

½ teaspoon chopped fresh oregano

½ teaspoon garlic powder

2 tablespoons unsalted butter

1 cup grated Parmesan cheese (4 ounces)

8 ounces mozzarella cheese, shredded (2 cups)

Anyone who knows Crystal is well aware that she is a funny, funny girl. She finds herself in the craziest situations—like randomly standing beside "the Situation" on a little reality show called *Jersey Shore* that's based on a group of Italian-Americans. Her cameo lasted a split second, but, nonetheless, it's a crazy story and we have a freeze-framed video clip to prove it. So what in the world does this have to do with our recipe? One of the characters on the show makes chicken Parmesan for a Sunday night, family-style dinner.

But let's go beyond the shores of Jersey and over to Italy. This dish is actually claimed by both Campania and Sicily and is based on *melanzane alla parmigiana,* or eggplant parmigiana, a classic southern Italian recipe. The addition of fresh basil and parsley really heightens the flavors. Pair it with a simple green salad tossed in our Lemon Parmesan Dressing (page 257) and your favorite bread.

1. Preheat the oven to 350°F. Spray a 9 x 13-inch casserole dish with cooking spray.

2. Heat the oil in a large sauté pan set over medium-high heat.

3. In a shallow dish, combine the eggs, salt, and pepper. Put the bread crumbs in a second shallow dish. Dip the chicken breasts in the egg mixture, then in the bread crumbs. Put the breaded chicken in the hot oil and cook until golden brown on both sides, about 6 minutes per side. Transfer the chicken to the prepared casserole dish.

4. In a medium saucepan set over high heat, combine the tomato sauce, 1 tablespoon of the parsley, basil, oregano, and garlic powder. Bring the sauce to a boil, reduce the heat to medium, and simmer for 10 minutes. Add the butter and when the butter has melted, pour the sauce over the chicken in the casserole dish. Sprinkle with the Parmesan cheese.

5. Cover the dish and bake for 30 minutes. Uncover the dish, sprinkle the mozzarella cheese on top, and bake 10 more minutes. Remove the pan from the oven, sprinkle the remaining 1 tablespoon parsley over the top of the casserole, and serve.

This dish can be made GLUTEN-FREE by using gluten-free bread crumbs, either store bought (see page 21 for recommendations of our favorite brands) or make your own.

FREEZES WELL For best results, prepare the casserole through step 4. Wrap in foil and freeze for up to 2 months. Thaw the casserole overnight in the refrigerator before baking as stated in the recipe. Note that casseroles that have not been completely thawed may take 15 to 30 minutes longer, so be sure to check for bubbling edges and a hot center.

Chicken Penne Pasta
with Pink Sauce

Makes 6 to 8 servings

- 6 ounces dried penne pasta
- 3 boneless, skinless whole chicken breasts
- 2 tablespoons olive oil
- Salt and freshly ground black pepper
- Cooking spray
- 2 garlic cloves, minced
- 1 cup coarsely chopped prosciutto
- ½ medium green bell pepper, cut into 1 x ¼-inch strips
- ½ medium yellow bell pepper, cut into 1 x ¼-inch strips
- 3 tablespoons drained capers
- 1 teaspoon dried basil, crushed
- 1 (15-ounce) jar marinara sauce, or 2 cups Marinara Sauce (page 334)
- 1 (10-ounce) jar alfredo sauce
- ⅓ cup grated Parmesan cheese (1½ ounces)

Tomato or cream sauce? Who says you have to choose? This casserole combines marinara and alfredo sauces to create a lovely pink sauce. The cream balances the acidity of the tomatoes, while sophisticated ingredients such as prosciutto and capers add an inviting gourmet touch to the meal. This recipe is perfect for Valentine's Day, first dates, or anniversaries. Not only will there be a pleasing blush to your meal, but perhaps to your sweetie, too!

1. Cook the pasta according to the package directions and drain well. Return the pasta to the pot and set aside.

2. Preheat the oven to 350°F. Coat the chicken breasts with 1 tablespoon of the olive oil and season with salt and pepper. Place the chicken on a baking sheet lined with foil and bake for 15 to 20 minutes or until cooked through. Remove the pan from the oven and let the chicken cool. When it is cool enough to handle, dice the chicken and set it aside.

3. Coat a 9 x 13-inch casserole dish with cooking spray.

4. In a large skillet set over medium-high heat, heat the remaining 1 tablespoon of olive oil. Add the cooked chicken and the garlic, and cook, stirring, for 2 minutes. Add the prosciutto, green and yellow peppers, capers, and basil. Cook, stirring frequently, for 2 to 3 minutes or until the peppers just start to soften. Add the chicken mixture to the reserved penne and mix well. Spread half of the mixture in the casserole dish.

5. In a medium bowl, combine the marinara and alfredo sauces. Ta-da! Pink sauce! Top the penne with 1 cup of the pink sauce. Put the remaining penne mixture over the sauce, then add the remaining pink sauce. Sprinkle the top with Parmesan cheese. Bake for 25 to 30 minutes or until the cheese is melted and slightly browned and the casserole is heated through. Remove the pan from the oven and toss the pasta thoroughly.

Crystal found a clever way to make peeling garlic a snap. Zap the garlic cloves in the microwave for 15 seconds and the peels will slide right off.

Chicken Divan Crêpes
with Gruyère

Makes 10 servings

- 1 head of broccoli, cut into florets, or 1 (10-ounce) package frozen chopped broccoli, defrosted and drained well
- 1 (3-pound) roasted chicken, boned and shredded (see page 340)
- 1½ cups Cream of Mushroom Soup (page 339)
- 8 ounces Gruyère cheese, grated (2 cups)
- ½ cup mayonnaise
- ½ cup sour cream
- ¼ cup dry white wine
- 1½ teaspoons fresh lemon juice
- ½ teaspoon curry powder
- Salt and freshly ground black pepper
- 1 (4.5-ounce) package prepared crêpes (10 crêpes), or homemade (opposite page)
- Cooking spray
- 1 cup grated Parmesan cheese (4 ounces)
- ½ cup Seasoned Bread Crumbs (page 330)
- 2 tablespoons unsalted butter, melted

Aunt Joan, Crystal's aunt, oozed charm and elegance. She always wore just the right dress or scarf. She was rarely without beautiful makeup and glam sunglasses. Her table was always set perfectly, and it was filled with foods that, for her young nieces, seemed exotic but tasty and comforting at the same time. The young ladies in Crystal's family all grew up aspiring to be as lovely and sophisticated as Aunt Joan. We have modified Aunt Joan's recipe for chicken divan by using it as a filling for crêpes. This recipe honors the beautiful and loving woman who graced so many lives and created so many special meals. Enjoy!

1. Preheat the oven to 350°F.

2. If working with fresh broccoli, steam the florets for 3 to 5 minutes. Drain well and put broccoli into a large mixing bowl. Add the chicken to the bowl, stir well, and set aside.

3. In a large bowl, combine the soup, cheese, mayonnaise, sour cream, wine, lemon juice, curry powder, salt, and pepper. Add half the soup mixture to the broccoli and chicken and stir well.

4. Lay the crêpes on a cutting board. Divide the chicken filling among the 10 crêpes, then roll them up. Lightly coat two 9 x 13-inch casserole dishes with cooking spray. Divide the crêpes between the two casserole dishes, placing the crêpes seam side down. Spread the remaining soup mixture over the crêpes. Combine the Parmesan, bread crumbs, and butter in a small bowl, and sprinkle over the tops of the crêpes. Bake until bubbly, 25 to 30 minutes.

Homemade Crêpes

Makes 10 to 12 crêpes

- 1½ cups all-purpose flour
- 3 large eggs
- 1½ cups whole milk
- ½ teaspoon salt
- ⅛ teaspoon curry powder (optional)
- 4 tablespoons (½ stick) unsalted butter, melted
- Cooking spray

We save time in this recipe by using ready-made crêpes. But if you have the extra time to make your own, you will only enhance your results. If working with crêpes is something you've never done, double the batter and give yourself plenty of time for a practice run!

1. In a large bowl, whisk together the flour and the eggs. Add the milk and whisk together. Add the salt, curry powder, and butter; whisk until smooth.

2. Lightly grease a medium skillet with cooking spray and set over medium-high heat. Pour ¼ cup of the batter into the pan. Working quickly, tilt the pan in all directions to coat the entire bottom surface of the pan with the batter. Let the crêpe cook until lightly browned, about 2 minutes. Flip the crêpe and cook the second side until lightly browned, about 1 more minute. Repeat with the remaining batter.

Coq au Vin

Makes 6 servings

- 4 slices bacon, chopped
- ½ cup chopped onion
- 1 celery stalk, coarsely chopped
- 1 (3-pound) chicken, cut into 8 pieces
- 8 shallots, thinly sliced
- 1 carrot, coarsely chopped
- 2 garlic cloves, minced
- 3 tablespoons cognac
- 2 tablespoons unsalted butter
- 1 (10-ounce) container sliced button mushrooms
- 4 flat-leaf parsley sprigs
- 2 bay leaves
- 2 fresh thyme sprigs
- 2 cups dry red wine, such as Pinot Noir

The Queens go "coo-coo" for Coq au Vin, a classic French dish of chicken cooked in red wine. An elegant but simple recipe, it's a great entry point to the world of French cuisine, which is often less complicated than it seems. Since this chicken dish has a decadent sauce, we love serving it in a shallow soup bowl over buttered egg noodles that have been tossed with chopped fresh parsley. We also garnish the rest of the plate with parsley, as the bright green pops against the red wine sauce. So pretty and so tasty!

1. Preheat the oven to 350°F.

2. In large sauté pan set over medium heat, cook the bacon, onion, and celery until the bacon is crisp and the onion is translucent, about 8 minutes. Transfer the bacon, onion, and celery to a plate, leaving the rendered fat in the pan. Add the chicken to the pan and cook, turning, until browned on all sides, about 10 minutes. Remove the chicken from the pan and set aside. Add the shallots, carrot, garlic, and cognac to the pan and cook, stirring, for 3 minutes.

3. In a separate small sauté pan set over medium heat, melt the butter and sauté the mushrooms until slightly browned, about 5 minutes. Set aside.

4. Make a bouquet garni by wrapping the parsley, bay leaves, and thyme in cheesecloth and tying the cloth closed with kitchen twine. Place the bouquet garni in the bottom of a 9 x 13-inch casserole dish. Add the chicken, vegetables, and mushrooms to the casserole dish.

5. Pour the wine into the sauté pan used to cook the chicken, set over high heat, and bring to a boil, using a wooden spoon to scrape up the brown bits from the bottom of the pan. Pour the wine over the chicken in the casserole dish. Cover the dish with foil and bake for 2 hours or until the chicken juices run clear when the meat is pierced. Remove the bouquet garni and serve.

This dish makes for an elegant presentation and is perfect for dinner guests. Consider making it a day ahead, so that the flavors can further meld together—and give yourself some extra time to enjoy your company! Just prepare the recipe up to the point before baking, cover, and store in the fridge. Now all you have to do the day your guests come is preheat your oven and create a mouthwatering aroma for your guests to enjoy as the dish bakes. Yep, it is that easy.

Chicken
Paprikash

Makes 6 servings

- 4 cups dried egg noodles (⅔ of a 12-ounce bag)
- 6 slices bacon, chopped
- 1 large onion, chopped
- 2 large carrots, chopped
- 2 celery stalks, chopped
- ½ teaspoon julienned lemon zest
- 2 tablespoons sweet paprika
- 1½ teaspoons salt
- ½ teaspoon freshly ground black pepper
- 1 (8-ounce) container sour cream
- ⅓ cup all-purpose flour, sifted
- 1¾ cups whole milk
- 6 boneless, skinless chicken breast halves (2 to 2¼ pounds)

Hungary's cuisine is as colorful as its culture. Chicken Paprikash is a classic Hungarian comfort food that's heavily seasoned with paprika and served over egg noodles. While we Americans are familiar with paprika the spice—a bright red powder that is either hot or sweet—in Hungary, this word really means "pepper." But don't go thinking this dish is superspicy, because ours is made with sweet paprika and has a rich, deep flavor.

1. Preheat the oven to 375°F.

2. Cook the noodles according to the package directions. Drain and set aside.

3. In a large saucepan set over medium heat, cook the bacon until crisp, about 10 minutes, and set it on paper towels to drain. Into the same skillet, put the onion, carrots, and celery, and cook over medium heat for 5 minutes, or until veggies start to become brown. Stir in the lemon zest, 1 tablespoon of the paprika, 1 teaspoon of the salt, and ¼ teaspoon of the black pepper.

4. Meanwhile, in a medium bowl, whisk together the sour cream and flour. Gradually whisk in the milk. Pour the milk mixture into the saucepan with the veggies. Cook, stirring, until the mixture is bubbly, 6 to 8 minutes. Stir in the cooked noodles and bacon.

5. Spoon the mixture into a 9 x 13-inch casserole dish. Arrange the chicken on top and sprinkle the chicken with the remaining ½ teaspoon salt, ¼ teaspoon pepper, and 1 tablespoon paprika.

6. Bake for 35 to 40 minutes, or until the chicken is no longer pink inside.

This dish can be made GLUTEN-FREE by replacing the flour with a gluten-free all-purpose mix, either store-bought or homemade (see page 322 for our recipe). You will also want to use gluten-free noodles. See page 21 for recommendations of our favorite brands.

FREEZES WELL For best results, prepare the casserole through step 5. Wrap in foil and freeze for up to 2 months. Thaw the casserole overnight in the refrigerator before baking as stated in the recipe. Note that casseroles that have not been completely thawed may take an additional 15 to 30 minutes longer, so be sure to check for bubbling edges and a hot center.

Pimpin' *Paella*

Makes 8 servings

- 1 tablespoon olive oil
- 5 slices bacon, chopped
- 1 (3½-pound) chicken, cut into 8 pieces
- Salt and freshly ground black pepper
- 2 cups chopped onions (2 large)
- 4 garlic cloves, minced
- 2 cups long-grain white rice
- 1 (7-ounce) jar roasted sliced pimientos with juice
- ½ teaspoon crushed saffron threads
- 2 cups bottled clam juice
- 1½ cups Chicken Broth (page 335)
- 1 pound fresh large shrimp, peeled and deveined
- 1 pound cleaned fresh squid, cut into ½-inch rings
- 1 dozen clams, scrubbed
- 1 dozen mussels, scrubbed and debearded
- 1 cup frozen green peas, thawed
- Lemon wedges

No special equipment needed here. Leave the paella pan at the store and let your casserole dish do the work. Packed with fresh seafood and accentuated with the alluring flavor of saffron, your kids may call this pimpin' dish "The Bomb," which means it's good.

This dish lives or dies by the freshness of the fish. The beauty of paella is that it is a flexible dish, so talk to your local fishmonger to get recommendations on the best catch of the day. If you don't like seafood, the dish actually works really well without it, too.

1. Preheat the oven to 450°F.

2. Heat the olive oil in a heavy, ovenproof Dutch oven over medium heat. Add the bacon and cook until crisp and the fat is rendered, about 6 minutes. Using a slotted spoon, transfer the bacon to a paper towel–lined plate to drain. Set aside.

3. Sprinkle the chicken pieces with salt and pepper. Add the chicken to the bacon drippings in the Dutch oven and cook over medium heat until browned on all sides, about 7 minutes per piece. Remove the chicken from the pot and set aside.

4. Add the onions and garlic to the Dutch oven and sauté until they just begin to brown, scraping up any browned bits as you go, about 8 minutes. Stir in the rice, pimientos with their juice, and saffron. Add the clam juice and chicken broth, and bring mixture to a simmer. Remove the pot from the heat.

5. Nestle the chicken, shrimp, squid, clams, and mussels into the rice mixture. Sprinkle with the bacon and peas, and cover the pot.

6. Bake the paella until the chicken is cooked through, the clams and mussels open, and the rice is tender, 25 to 30 minutes (discard any clams and mussels that do not open). Uncover the Dutch oven and let the paella stand for 10 minutes. Serve with the lemon wedges on the side.

Crystal was fascinated to learn that it takes 225,000 handpicked saffron stigmas to make a single pound, which explains why it's the world's most expensive spice—around $2,700 per pound!

Boo-Yah
Bouillabaisse

Makes 8 servings

¼ cup (½ stick) unsalted butter

1 medium yellow onion, chopped

1 red bell pepper, chopped

6 garlic cloves, minced

1 (46-ounce) can tomato juice

1 large tomato, chopped

3 tablespoons all-purpose flour

1 tablespoon packed light brown sugar

1 tablespoon sriracha hot sauce

2 teaspoons grated orange zest

1 teaspoon curry powder

¾ teaspoon dried thyme

¼ teaspoon saffron threads

2 teaspoons salt

1 teaspoon freshly ground black pepper

½ cup dry white wine

3 tablespoons fresh lemon juice

¼ cup plus 2 tablespoons chopped fresh parsley

2 bay leaves

3 pounds seafood (such as 1 pound shrimp, peeled and deveined; ½ pound crab meat, flaked; ½ pound sea scallops, quartered; 1 pound flaky white fish, such as snapper or cod)

1 loaf French bread, sliced and toasted

French-food lovers, fear not the long list of steps and ingredients for this traditional dish. It's easier than you think. Many of the ingredients are probably already in your pantry, and the rest can easily be found in your local grocery store. The key to great bouillabaisse is fresh seafood. We're talking fresh-from-the-sea fresh, not Joe's week-old specials. Nothing spoils a fish-based stew like subpar fish. Get to know the person at the fish counter and find out what's fresh that day. In fact, ask to sniff the fish before they wrap it up for you—you want it to smell like the sea. Much like paella, this dish has very flexible ingredients. It's part of the fun. Plus, you'll be amazed at how quickly and easily it comes together. It's time to start a French revolution—in your kitchen!

1. Preheat the oven to 400°F.

2. In a heavy, ovenproof Dutch oven, melt the butter. Add the onion, bell pepper, and garlic, and sauté until they begin to soften, about 8 minutes. Add the tomato juice, tomato, flour, brown sugar, hot sauce, orange zest, curry powder, thyme, saffron, salt, and black pepper, and stir until well combined.

Get to know sriracha, one of Sandy's favorite sauces. Also known as "Rooster Sauce" for the rooster that emblazons the bottle's label, this Thai chili sauce is fantastically spicy. If you don't have any on hand, you can substitute Tabasco sauce. Careful, though—Tabasco sauce will have a more vinegary taste, so be sure to adjust the amount of lemon juice to about half.

Bring the mixture to a boil, stirring often. Reduce the heat to medium so the mixture is at a gentle simmer. Add the wine, lemon juice, ¼ cup parsley, and the bay leaves. Simmer, uncovered, for 10 to 15 minutes. Taste for seasoning. If you would like to brighten flavors, add a bit more lemon juice.

3. Add the seafood to the pan, stirring gently so as not to break up the fish. Place the pot in the oven and bake for about 20 minutes or until the fish pieces are cooked through and flaky.

4. To serve, place two pieces of toasted bread in the bottom of 8 large soup bowls. Ladle the bouillabaisse over the bread and garnish with the remaining 2 tablespoons parsley. Serve immediately.

This dish can be made GLUTEN-FREE by replacing the flour with a gluten-free mix (see page 21 for recommendations of our favorite brands). And, of course, skip the French bread.

When cooking for our business, Sandy is a stickler when it comes to proper *mise en place*. This is a French phrase meaning "everything in place," and it refers to having all your ingredients prepped, measured, and ready to go before you start cooking. With recipes that have many ingredients, such as this bouillabaisse, you will find that taking the time to do the prep first will actually save you time in the long run. When everything is laid out in front of you, you'll be more organized and efficient. (Plus, you will look like a real chef!)

Seafood Lasagna Rolls
with Panko Crumb Topping

**Makes 6 servings
(2 rolls per person)**

PANKO CRUMB TOPPING

- 1 cup panko bread crumbs
- ½ cup (1 stick) unsalted butter, melted
- ⅓ cup grated Parmesan cheese (1½ ounces)
- 2 tablespoons shallots, finely chopped
- 2 tablespoons chopped fresh flat-leaf parsley
- ½ teaspoon chopped fresh thyme leaves

Unlike layered lasagna, which can lose its shape and become messy when served, these individual rolls are an elegant alternative that look as lovely on the plate as they taste. Crisp white wine and the nutty flavors of sherry come together beautifully in a creamy white sauce, adding a delicate accent that's perfect for the shellfish. Easily portioned, this dish is excellent for entertaining. Remember to do your prep early, as this recipe does take some time to assemble.

1. To make the topping, put the bread crumbs, butter, Parmesan, shallots, parsley, and thyme in a medium bowl, and mix thoroughly. Set aside.

2. Preheat the oven to 375°F. Lightly coat a 9 x 13-inch casserole dish with cooking spray.

3. In a large pot of boiling salted water, cook the lasagna noodles according to the package instructions. Drain the noodles, rinse with cold water, and lay them flat on a baking sheet while you make the sauce.

4. In a medium saucepan set over medium-high heat, melt the butter. Add the shallots and bell pepper, and sauté for about 3 minutes or until tender. Reduce the heat to medium and whisk in the flour, 1½ teaspoons of the salt, and 1 teaspoon of the white pepper. Cook for 2 minutes, whisking constantly, until the flour is cooked through. Pour in the clam juice, wine, and sherry and cook, whisking constantly, until a light sauce forms, 2 to 3 minutes. Add the cream and cook, whisking frequently, until the sauce thickens, about 5 minutes. Add 1 cup of the cheese and the spinach, and cook until the spinach wilts. Set the sauce aside.

LASAGNA ROLLS

Cooking spray

12 dried lasagna noodles

2 tablespoons unsalted butter

2 medium shallots, thinly sliced

1 red bell pepper, chopped

3 tablespoons all-purpose flour

2½ teaspoons salt

2 teaspoons ground white pepper

1 cup bottled clam juice

½ cup dry white wine

2 tablespoons sherry

2 cups heavy cream

8 ounces Monterey Jack cheese, grated (2 cups)

6 ounces fresh spinach leaves

1 pound shrimp, peeled and deveined

1 pound bay scallops

¾ pound cod, haddock, or other white fish fillets, cut into 1-inch cubes

½ pound lump crab meat

1 tablespoon chopped fresh flat-leaf parsley

5. Rinse the seafood under cold running water. Drain thoroughly and pat dry with a paper towel to remove any excess liquid. In a large bowl, combine the shrimp, scallops, cod, and crab meat with the remaining 1 teaspoon salt and 1 teaspoon white pepper and the parsley. Add 1 cup of the sauce mixture and fold until well combined.

6. Spread a heaping ⅓ cup of the seafood mixture on each noodle, leaving a ½-inch border on the edges. Roll up each noodle.

7. Spread about ½ cup of the sauce on the bottom of the prepared casserole dish. Arrange the rolled lasagna noodles seam side down snugly in one layer over the sauce. Pour the remaining sauce over the rolls. Sprinkle the casserole with the remaining 1 cup cheese, and then top evenly with the crumb topping. Cover the dish with foil, and bake until the sauce is bubbling and the filling is just cooked through, about 30 minutes.

8. Preheat the broiler. Remove the foil from the dish, and broil casserole about 3 inches from the heat until the crumb topping is browned, 3 to 5 minutes. Let stand for 5 minutes before serving.

Halibut Enchiladas
with Salsa Verde

Makes 5 servings

2 pounds halibut fillets

1 cup plus 2 tablespoons vegetable oil

Salt and freshly ground black pepper

1 tablespoon unsalted butter

½ cup chopped onion

¾ cup mayonnaise

¾ cup sour cream

1 (4-ounce) can diced green chilies

2 cups store-bought shredded Mexican cheese mix (8 ounces)

4 cups store-bought salsa verde or Salsa Verde (page 333)

10 (8-inch) corn tortillas

Salsa verde is a versatile sauce that Sandy has in her refrigerator all the time. She likes to warm 1 cup of the sauce in the morning and pour it over eggs and toast for breakfast. It's a spicy way to start the day!

Upscale enchiladas? You betcha! Take your enchiladas to serious new heights by baking fresh halibut, instead of frying it, and cooking the enchiladas in a delicious tangy verde sauce. Serve with black beans sprinkled with Cotija cheese, and a simple side salad for a truly flavorful meal.

1. Preheat the oven to 350°F.

2. Lightly coat the halibut with 2 tablespoons of the vegetable oil and season it with salt and pepper. Put the halibut in a 9 x 13-inch casserole dish and bake for 25 minutes. Allow the halibut to cool, then flake it into a bowl. Keep the oven at 350°F.

3. Melt the butter in a sauté pan set over medium heat. Add the onion and cook until translucent, about 8 minutes. Transfer the onion to a medium bowl and add the mayonnaise, sour cream, chilies, and 1 cup of the cheese mix. Mix thoroughly.

4. Pour 2 cups of the verde sauce into the bottom of a 9 x 13-inch casserole dish. Set aside.

5. Heat the remaining 1 cup of vegetable oil in a sauté pan set over medium heat until just warm, then turn off the heat. Put one tortilla in the oil at a time and leave it in the oil for 5 seconds (you are looking to just make the tortilla pliable, not brown or crunchy). Transfer the tortilla to a cutting board. Put ¼ cup of the fish mixture on one end of the tortilla. Roll up the tortilla and put it on top of the sauce in the casserole dish, seam side down. Repeat until all 10 tortillas are filled, then pour the remaining 2 cups verde sauce over the top to coat the enchiladas entirely. Sprinkle the remaining 1 cup cheese mix over the top.

6. Bake for 25 minutes or until the sauce is bubbling slightly and the enchiladas are heated through.

Caribbean Shrimp
Casserole

Makes 6 servings

Cooking spray

2 tablespoons unsalted butter

1 large green bell pepper, chopped

2½ pounds fresh or frozen shrimp, peeled and deveined (thawed if frozen)

1 (28-ounce) can crushed tomatoes

2 teaspoons chili powder

½ teaspoon dried thyme

1 teaspoon salt

1½ teaspoons freshly ground black pepper

2 cups cooked rice (see page 329)

The Queens simply adore shrimp, and for two main reasons: they are very versatile and relatively easy to cook, and they absorb flavors quickly, so dinners can come together in a flash! From prep to table, this dish takes less than 40 minutes, while your family will think you've been slaving away in the kitchen all day. (So maybe use the extra time you're NOT cooking to get a manicure!) For a balanced meal, pair with our Corn Pudding (page 206).

1. Preheat the oven to 350°F. Spray a 9 x 13-inch casserole dish with cooking spray.

2. In a large skillet set over medium-high heat, melt the butter. Add the green bell pepper and cook, stirring, until soft, about 5 minutes. Reduce the heat to medium and add the shrimp. Cook for 3 minutes, or until the shrimp turns pink. Stir in the crushed tomatoes, chili powder, thyme, salt, and pepper. Increase the heat to high and bring to a boil, then reduce the heat to medium and cook for 10 minutes.

3. Spread the rice in the bottom of the prepared casserole dish and press down firmly. Pour the shrimp mixture over the rice.

4. Bake for 15 minutes, or until heated through.

Shrimp
with Seared Polenta

Makes 6 servings

SEARED POLENTA

- 1 tablespoon unsalted butter
- 4 cups water
- 2 teaspoons salt
- 2¼ cups yellow cornmeal
- ¼ cup heavy cream
- 1 teaspoon dried thyme

SHRIMP

- 2 tablespoons olive oil
- ¼ pound pancetta, chopped
- 3 garlic cloves, minced
- ½ teaspoon red pepper flakes
- 1 (14-ounce) can diced tomatoes
- 1 pound large shrimp, peeled and deveined
- ¾ teaspoon salt
- 1 tablespoon chopped fresh flat-leaf parsley
- Cooking spray

Firm polenta serves as the base for a delectable shrimp sauce made with tomatoes, garlic, red pepper flakes, and crisp pancetta crumbles. Once seared, the polenta is perfectly crisp on the outside and velvety on the inside. You'll need to make the polenta a couple of hours before serving, since it needs time to cool and set before you can sear it. Luckily, it can be made ahead of time.

1. For the seared polenta, lightly grease a 9 x 13-inch casserole dish with ½ tablespoon of the butter. Set aside.

2. Combine the water and salt in a medium saucepan and bring just to a boil. Whisk in the cornmeal and continue whisking until it starts to thicken, about 3 minutes. Stir in the cream and thyme. Reduce the heat to low and simmer, stirring constantly, until the polenta is very thick.

3. Pour the polenta into the prepared pan and brush the top with the remaining ½ tablespoon of the butter. Let it stand at room temperature until cool, then cover and refrigerate until chilled. (Polenta can be kept in the refrigerator for 3 days before using.)

4. When ready to use, turn the chilled polenta onto a cutting board, and cut into 12 triangles. Set aside.

5. For the shrimp, heat the olive oil in a sauté pan set over medium heat. Add the pancetta and cook until crisp, about 10 minutes. Remove the pancetta from the pan and set aside. Add the garlic and red pepper flakes to the pan and cook, stirring, until the garlic is pale golden, 2 to 3 minutes. Return the pancetta to the pan along with the tomatoes and their juice. Bring to a simmer and cook until the liquid is reduced to about ¼ cup, 6 to 8 minutes. Add the shrimp and cook, stirring occasionally, until the shrimp are just cooked through, about 3 minutes. Season with the salt and garnish with the parsley.

6. Lightly grease a sauté pan with cooking spray. Sear the polenta triangles until all sides have a light golden crust, about 2 minutes per side. Place two triangles of polenta on each of 6 plates and top each with 1 cup of shrimp sauce.

> Crystal loves the flavor of pancetta. If you are unable to find it at your local grocery, you can substitute with prosciutto or even bacon.

Savory Salmon
Turnovers

Makes 6 servings

½ cup long-grain white rice

2 tablespoons unsalted butter

1 leek, thinly sliced, white and pale green parts only

1 carrot, cut into thin strips

1 celery stalk, cut into thin strips

1½ tablespoons all-purpose flour

1 teaspoon dried tarragon, crushed

Salt and freshly ground black pepper

1 cup whole milk

¼ cup heavy cream

2 tablespoons dry white wine

Cooking spray

3 sheets frozen puff pastry, thawed

6 (6-ounce each) salmon fillets, about 2½ inches thick, skin removed

1 egg

We actually got this brilliant idea from our World's Greatest Chicken Pot Pie (page 68), borrowing some of its staple flavors to create an entirely new dish. The mild flavors of the tarragon and white wine sauce complement the leek mixture in this new creation. Baking the salmon *en croute* keeps the fish moist and seals in its natural flavors. When you find a flavor combination you love, experiment and find new ways to make it work for you!

1. Cook the rice according to the package directions. Set aside.

2. Melt the butter in a heavy, medium skillet set over medium-low heat. Add the leek, carrot, and celery, and sauté until beginning to soften, about 4 minutes. Add the flour, tarragon, 1 teaspoon of salt, and 1 teaspoon of pepper, and cook for 1 minute. Add the milk and cream, and cook, stirring, until thickened and bubbly, about 8 minutes. Stir in the wine and heat thoroughly for an additional 2 minutes, stirring often. Remove from the heat and stir in the cooked rice. Set aside.

3. Preheat the oven to 400°F. Coat two 9 x 13-inch casserole dishes with cooking spray.

4. On a flat, lightly floured surface, roll the puff pastry sheets into 12-inch squares. Cut 4 equal squares from each sheet so that you have 12 squares total. Divide the rice mixture among 6 of the pastry squares, mounding the mixture into an oval shape with the ends toward two corners of the pastry square. Set a salmon fillet on top of each rice oval and sprinkle with salt and pepper. Make an egg wash by lightly beating together the egg and 1 teaspoon water. Brush the edge of the puff pas-

try with the egg wash, then bring the pastry corners up around salmon (the pastry will not enclose the salmon completely). Brush the edges of a second pastry square with egg wash and lay it on top of the salmon fillet, tucking its corners under the bottom of the pastry to enclose the fillet completely. Pinch the edges together to seal and brush the entire turnover with egg wash. Repeat for remaining turnovers. Cut a vent in the top of each turnover to allow steam to escape.

5. Arrange the salmon packages in the prepared casserole dishes, allowing each puff pastry package enough room to puff without touching each other. Bake until the pastry is golden brown and a thermometer inserted into the fish registers 145°F, about 30 minutes.

You can prepare this dish several hours ahead of time. Once you've made the turnovers, cover and chill them in the refrigerator until your guests arrive. Then, simply pop them in the preheated oven, serve, and enjoy. Easy entertaining at its best.

Lobster Boy
Casserole

Makes 4 to 6 servings

7 tablespoons unsalted butter

1 medium shallot, thinly sliced

1 pound meat from cooked lobster tails (4 tails), cut into bite-size pieces (see Note)

3 tablespoons all-purpose flour

½ teaspoon dry mustard

   Salt and freshly ground black pepper

2 cups light cream

3 tablespoons sherry

3 slices white bread, crusts removed and slices torn into small pieces

½ cup Seasoned Bread Crumbs (page 330)

Crystal's brother-in-law Jim is a native of Maine, and he has a passion so strong for lobster that we have nicknamed him "Lobster Boy." We have joked that if he were rich, he would eat lobster in some form or fashion every day—lobster rolls, lobster omelets, and even lobster casseroles. This casserole salutes you, Lobster Boy! We recommend serving it over buttered egg noodles that have been tossed with poppy seeds for color and a bit of a crunch.

1. Preheat the oven to 350°F.

2. Melt 4 tablespoons of the butter in a sauté pan set over medium heat. Add the shallot and cook for 3 minutes or until translucent. Add the lobster meat and cook for 2 minutes or until the lobster is heated through. In a separate bowl, combine the flour and dry mustard, and season with salt and pepper. Sprinkle the mixture over the lobster and toss to coat well. Add the cream slowly, stirring constantly, and cook until it thickens, about 6 minutes. Add the sherry and bread, and stir well.

3. Grease a 9 x 13-inch casserole dish with 1 tablespoon of the butter and pour in the lobster mixture. Melt the remaining 2 tablespoons of butter and stir in the bread crumbs, then sprinkle on top of the casserole.

4. Bake for 30 minutes or until the casserole is bubbly and browned on top.

If you don't want to be the one to do the deed, most fish markets will cook the lobster to your liking. All you'll need to do is take it home, remove the shells, grease your casserole dish, and get cooking!

Sherry versus cooking sherry: When cooking with high-quality ingredients such as fresh seafood, we recommend that you opt for the real thing! Cooking sherry is high in salt, and the quality just isn't good enough to stand up to the lovely buttery lobster in this dish.

TATER TOT CASSEROLE ✳ page 40

MAMAW'S STUFFED PEPPERS ✳ page 48

CQ'S ROYAL
COTTAGE PIE
page 42

DEEP-DISH PIZZA,
CHICAGO STYLE
page 58

CHICKEN WITH 40 CLOVES OF GARLIC ✳ page 65
ASPARAGUS BUNDLES WRAPPED IN PROSCIUTTO ✳ page 203
CARROT SOUFFLÉ ✳ page 204

WORLD'S GREATEST CHICKEN POT PIE ✳ page 68

SHAKSHUKA ✳ page 144

ROSEMARY BAKED HAM ✳ page 150
BROCCOLI SALAD ✳ page 273
AUNT FANNIE'S CABIN SQUASH CASSEROLE ✳ page 214

DAMN SKINNY YANKEE POT ROAST ✳ page 151

BEEF AND RICE FIESTA BAKE ✳ page 157

CHICKEN TETRAZZINI
page 168

ZUCCHINI
LASAGNA
page 154

GREEN CHILI AND CHICKEN BAKE ✳ page 166

RED SNAPPER
VERACRUZ
page 173

THE NELLY FRITTATA
page 187

BLACK BEAN ENCHILADA CASSEROLE ✳ page 179

CHEESY GRITS-STUFFED EGGPLANT ROLLS WITH TOMATO SAUCE ✳ page 180
HARGILL'S BUNCO CLUB SEVEN-LAYER SALAD ✳ page 269
DILL BREAD ✳ page 229

SHEPHERDLESS PIE
page 189

LUNCH LADY DORIS'S
SPICY MAC & CHEESE
page 194

HERB-BAKED
CAPRESE TOMATO
STACKS
page 200

BAKED SAUSAGES
WITH FENNEL
page 60

BRUSSELS SPROUTS
WITH BACON, GARLIC,
AND SHALLOTS
page 198

CORNBREAD SALAD TWO WAYS ✳ page 276

POLLOCK'S PEACH
COBBLER
page 297

GRANNY HALEY'S
ANGEL FOOD CAKE
WITH VANILLA
STRAWBERRY SAUCE
page 288

KEY WEST CLAFOUTI
page 312

CRUNCHY PEANUT BUTTER
CHOCOLATE BARS
page 305

PEANUT BUTTER FREEZER PIE WITH CHOCOLATE AND BANANAS * page 302

S'MORE PIE ✳ page 300

Asparagus and Crab Casserole

Makes 8 servings

- 2 tablespoons unsalted butter
- 2 tablespoons all-purpose flour
- 1⅔ cups whole milk
- 1 ounce Cheddar cheese, grated (¼ cup)
- 1 ounce Swiss cheese, grated (¼ cup)
- 1 teaspoon salt
- ⅛ teaspoon freshly ground black pepper
- 24 fresh asparagus spears
- 1 pound lump crab meat
- 1 cup grated Parmesan cheese (4 ounces)

Crystal *loves* crab. So much, in fact, that she is willing to risk physical harm to get it. You see, Crystal has recently developed an allergic reaction to crab meat. She feels as though the universe is playing some cruel joke on her—and she's just not ready to accept it. Allergy or not, this is one of her favorite casseroles. There is just something so irresistible about the sweetness of the crab and how it interacts with the earthy taste of the asparagus. Serve this creamy casserole over toasted French bread (much like an open-faced sandwich) and pour yourself a glass of a crisp white wine—you'll be very thankful that you are not allergic.

1. Preheat the oven to 375°F.

2. Melt the butter in a saucepan set over medium heat. Stir in the flour and cook, stirring, for 3 minutes. Gradually add the milk and stir until thick and smooth, about 5 minutes. Add the Cheddar and Swiss cheeses, and stir until melted. Add the salt and pepper. Set aside.

3. Hold an asparagus spear with both hands, about 2 inches from the ends. Gently bend the asparagus until it snaps. It will break at the point where the stem gets too tough to be enjoyable; discard the stem. Repeat for all your asparagus. Cook the asparagus in boiling water until just tender, 2 to 3 minutes. Drain.

4. Place the asparagus in a 9 x 13-inch casserole dish. Scatter the crab meat over the asparagus, then pour in the cheese sauce. Sprinkle with the Parmesan, then bake for about 30 minutes or until top is golden brown and the sauce is bubbling.

Cioppino-Style
Roasted Crab

Makes 10 servings

Cooking spray

¼ cup extra-virgin olive oil

1 medium onion, finely chopped

6 large garlic cloves, minced

2 cups bottled clam juice

1 cup dry white wine

2 (15-ounce) cans diced tomatoes

½ cup flat-leaf parsley leaves

1 teaspoon salt

½ teaspoon freshly ground black pepper

1 teaspoon red pepper flakes

2 bay leaves

2 (2-pound) cooked Dungeness crabs or Alaska king crab legs, cleaned, quartered, and cracked

We're about to tell you a crabby tale—a colorful story of how this dish originated. It all started with an Italian-American fisherman who gathered the crew's leftover catch after a day at sea. At the end of the day, he'd throw his assortment of fish and seafood into a communal pot for supper. All the fishermen would shout in broken English, "Chip in!" to one person and "You, chip in!" to another. Over time, this is how the name cioppino came to be.

However it originated, most people won't deny themselves a crab-infused recipe, especially if it's baked in a warm, delicious casserole. This Italian twist is a hit for many reasons, but we think it has something to do with the dry white wine. Not only does it bring out the flavor of the crab, but we made sure the recipe calls for just enough wine for there to be a bit left over for the chef to enjoy. Plus, when it's time to clean up after dinner, you can try this "chip in!" tactic on your family.

1. Preheat the oven to 400°F. Spray a 9 x 13-inch casserole dish with cooking spray.

2. Heat the oil in a large sauté pan set over medium heat. Add the onion and garlic and sauté until soft, about 5 minutes. Add 1 cup of water, the clam juice, wine, tomatoes, parsley, salt, black pepper, red pepper flakes, and bay leaves. Increase the heat to high and bring to a boil, 5 minutes. Reduce the heat to medium and simmer for 10 minutes. Add the crabmeat and pour the mixture into the prepared casserole dish.

3. Bake for 15 to 20 minutes, until the crab pieces are heated through. Remove the bay leaves before serving.

Crawfish Casserole

Makes 6 servings

Cooking spray

½ cup (1 stick) unsalted butter

1 cup chopped onion

2 pounds meat from crawfish tails (about 14 pounds whole crawfish)

½ cup chopped green bell pepper

½ cup chopped green onions, green parts only

1 (10-ounce) container sliced white button mushrooms

¼ cup chopped fresh flat-leaf parsley

1 teaspoon garlic powder

½ teaspoon cayenne

½ teaspoon freshly ground black pepper

½ teaspoon salt

2½ cups Seasoned Bread Crumbs (page 330)

1 egg, beaten

There is an old Louisiana legend that says that when the original Acadians fled Nova Scotia to head to Louisiana, the local lobsters followed them. During the long swim the lobsters lost a lot of weight and most of their length. By the time they reached the bayou swamps to reunite with the early Cajuns, they had turned into crawfish!

Crawfish, mudbugs, or crawdads—whatever you decide to call them, they're delicious. With Texas being so close to bayou country, we can't help but love these cute crustaceans. Though resembling tiny lobsters, only the extremely tasty tail is edible. When they are cooked with spicy Cajun flavors, you have yourself a mighty fine treat. Just remember that Louisiana crawfish are seasonal. A consistent supply can't be counted on except between early March and mid-June, with the height of the season mid-March to mid-May. If crawfish are not available, peeled and deveined shrimp serve as a good substitute.

1. Preheat the oven to 300°F. Lightly coat a 9 x 13-inch casserole dish with cooking spray.

2. Melt the butter in a large sauté pan set over medium heat. Add the onion and cook for about 8 minutes. Add the crawfish, bell pepper, and green onions, and cook for 5 minutes. Add the mushrooms, parsley, garlic powder, cayenne, black pepper, and salt and cook for 5 minutes. Remove the pan from heat, add 2 cups of the bread crumbs and the egg, and stir well.

3. Pour the mixture into the casserole dish and top with the remaining ½ cup bread crumbs. Bake for 25 minutes or until the casserole is set and the bread crumbs are golden brown.

Mashed Potato
Pizza

Makes 8 to 10 servings

1 tablespoon olive oil

3 cups mashed potatoes, leftover or homemade (opposite page)

2½ cups fresh or frozen broccoli florets (thawed and drained if frozen)

2 Roma tomatoes, chopped

2 cups shredded sharp Cheddar cheese (8 ounces)

6 slices bacon, cooked and crumbled

3 green onions, green parts only, sliced, for garnish

Turn your leftover mashed potatoes into a delicious crust for a tasty casserole spin on a deep-dish pizza! Don't worry if your mashed potatoes were seasoned with herbs or Parmesan cheese—we think seasoning will only enhance the flavor of the "crust." You can always make a fresh batch of spuds for this recipe, so check out our recipe on the opposite page.

1. Preheat the oven to 350°F.

2. Brush a 9 x 13-inch casserole dish with ½ tablespoon of the olive oil and press the mashed potatoes along the bottom. Brush the top of the potatoes with the remaining ½ tablespoon olive oil. Bake for 30 minutes, or until lightly browned. Remove the crust from the oven, and keep the oven on.

3. Cover the potato crust evenly with the broccoli, tomatoes, cheese, and bacon. Bake the pizza for 15 to 20 more minutes, or until the cheese has melted. Garnish with the green onions, slice up, and serve.

It's easy to make this dish into a VEGETARIAN-FRIENDLY feast. Simply omit the bacon or substitute with crumbled soy "sausage."

Mashed Potatoes

Makes 4 cups

2 pounds russet potatoes,
  peeled and cut into chunks

Salt

3 tablespoons unsalted butter

¾ cup heavy cream, warmed

Freshly ground black pepper

1. Put the potatoes in a saucepan and cover them with cold, salted water.

2. Set the pan over high heat and bring to a boil.

3. Reduce the heat to low and simmer until the potatoes are tender, about 30 minutes.

4. Drain the potatoes and mash them with the butter and cream until smooth.

5. Season with salt and pepper to taste.

It's easy to add depth to a multitude of dishes by simply roasting garlic cloves. For example, you can mash them up in your potatoes, spread them onto your pizza, blend them into a compound butter, toss them with pasta, or just spread them over French bread. They're very mild and quite sweet! Here's how you do it:

Preheat the oven to 400°F. Cut the top ¼ inch off a head of garlic so that the tops of each individual clove are exposed. Put the head of garlic on a large piece of heavy aluminum foil. Drizzle the top of the garlic with about 2 teaspoons of extra-virgin olive oil. Tightly wrap the garlic in the foil and roast for about 30 minutes. The garlic should be soft, fragrant, and golden. It will keep in the refrigerator for up to 5 days.

Oven-Baked
Spanish Tortilla

Makes 10 servings

Cooking spray

1 pound Yukon gold potatoes, diced

¼ cup olive oil

2 garlic cloves, minced

½ tablespoon red pepper flakes

4 green onions, finely chopped

1 medium red bell pepper, seeded and diced

10 large eggs

1 cup sour cream

½ cup Parmesan cheese, grated (2 ounces)

1 teaspoon salt

½ teaspoon freshly ground black pepper

If you've ever had the chance to visit Spain, it probably left a special place in your heart. From the rustic Spanish architecture to the vibrant quality of life and the renowned cuisine, Spain truly has its own distinct flair. When Sandy and her husband, Michael, spent some time in this country, they quickly fell in love with the variety of traditional foods, eaten at all hours of the day. This classic Spanish dish goes by two names: *tortilla de patatas* or *tortilla española*. How's that for a bit of worldly knowledge? It's an excellent option for a satisfying breakfast treat, lunch, dinner, or a unique tapa at a dinner party. Serve with our Salsa Verde on page 333. Like most of our casserole recipes, it can be made ahead and lends itself to many creative variations. Our version is vegetarian, but you can always add protein, such as small bits of precooked chorizo, bacon, or sliced prosciutto.

1. Preheat the oven to 375°F. Spray a large cast-iron skillet or a 9 x 13-inch casserole dish with cooking spray.

2. Put the potatoes in a small saucepan and cover with cold water. Bring to a boil, reduce heat to low, and cook for 5 to 7 minutes, until the potatoes are tender. Drain and set aside to cool slightly.

3. In a large skillet set over medium heat, combine the olive oil, garlic, red pepper flakes, green onions, and bell pepper. Cook, stirring, for about 5 minutes, or until the onions are soft but not browned. Let cool slightly, then stir in the cooked potatoes.

4. In a large bowl, combine the eggs, sour cream, cheese, salt, and pepper. Stir in the vegetable-potato mixture. Pour the mixture into the prepared casserole and smooth the top.

5. Bake for 40 minutes, or until golden brown, puffed, and set in the center. Let cool for 10 minutes before serving.

Savory French Onion Tart

Makes 8 servings

- 2 tablespoons unsalted butter
- 4 onions, chopped
- 1 pound bacon, cooked and crumbled
- 5 large eggs
- 3½ cups whole milk
- 1 tablespoon fresh thyme, chopped
- 1 teaspoon salt
- ½ teaspoon freshly ground black pepper
- 2 pie crusts, homemade (page 323) or store bought
- 1 cup grated Gruyère cheese (4 ounces)

During Sandy's days in culinary school, she learned how just a few simple ingredients can transform themselves into an elegant masterpiece. This simple onion tart is a perfect example. It has a thin, flaky crust, a creamy caramelized onion filling, and a delicious topping of Gruyère cheese. With a "touch" of crumbled bacon, this meal is over the top! And even though tarts are great cut up into small pieces for use at parties, we prefer serving ourselves a larger slice along with a simple green salad dressed in our homemade Balsamic Vinaigrette (page 262). Tuesday night just became date night!

1. Preheat the oven to 400°F.

2. In a large sauté pan set over medium heat, melt butter, then add the onions and cook for 5 minutes, or until softened, but do not let them brown. Add the bacon and cook for about 5 minutes.

3. In a small bowl, whisk together the eggs, milk, thyme, salt, and pepper.

4. Line a 9 x 13-inch casserole dish with the pie crusts and prick the bottom with a fork. Spread the onions and bacon in the casserole dish and sprinkle with the cheese. Pour the egg mixture over the top.

5. Bake for 25 to 30 minutes, or until the top is golden.

This dish can be made GLUTEN-FREE by replacing the pie crust with a gluten-free pie crust, either store bought or homemade (see page 324 for our recipe).

Shakshuka

Makes 8 servings

Cooking spray

¼ cup olive oil

2 jalapeño peppers, stemmed, seeded, and finely chopped

3 shallots, chopped

5 garlic cloves, crushed and sliced

2 teaspoons smoked paprika

1 teaspoon ground cumin

1 teaspoon salt

½ teaspoon cayenne

1 (28-ounce) can crushed tomatoes

1 (8-ounce) can tomato sauce

½ cup Veggie Broth (page 337) or store bought

8 large eggs

½ cup crumbled feta cheese (4 ounces)

1 tablespoon chopped flat-leaf parsley

8 pita bread rounds, for serving

Just imagine how worldly you will appear the next time you have houseguests and you say you are going to have Bobotie (pronounced "buh-*boor*-tea") (page 107) for dinner and shakshuka the following day for brunch. Equally impressive and equally as fun to say! Bobotie, shakshuka . . .

Shakshuka is a wildly popular and easy-to-make Israeli dish made with eggs (see, feels like home already!) poached in a flavorful sauce usually consisting of tomatoes, chili peppers, and onions, often spiced with cumin. Aside from the great taste, there are many reasons to love this recipe. It is naturally vegetarian, gluten-free, and diabetic-friendly, and it's very easy to make and/or adapt! Shakshuka is like that flexible friend who can go with you anywhere and fit in perfectly, no matter the crowd. Since it's egg based, you can serve it for breakfast, lunch, or dinner, but the Israelis usually eat it for breakfast. We love to serve it with some whole-wheat pita bread (to soak up all the delicious sauce!) for a light evening meal.

1. Preheat the oven to 350°F. Spray a 9 x 13-inch casserole dish with cooking spray.

2. In a large sauté pan set over medium heat, heat the oil. Add the jalapeños and shallots and cook, stirring occasionally, until soft and golden brown, about 6 minutes. Add the garlic, paprika, cumin, salt, and cayenne. Cook, stirring frequently, until the garlic is soft, about 2 more minutes. Add the crushed tomatoes, tomato sauce, and vegetable broth. Stir well. Pour the sauce into the prepared casserole dish, cover it with foil, and put it in the oven. Bake for 20 minutes, stirring midway through.

3. Pull the casserole dish out of the oven and crack the eggs over the sauce so that the eggs are evenly distributed throughout the casserole dish. Cover the dish with foil and cook until the yolks are just set, about 10 minutes. Sprinkle with the feta and parsley and serve with the pita bread.

As we mentioned in the headnote, this dish can easily be adapted to use whatever ingredients you have on hand or for taste. Don't have shallots? Simply substitute an onion. Want to incorporate an Indian flair? Keep the cumin, replace the other spices with garam masala, and switch out the feta with goat cheese or paneer. Want to give the tomato sauce an Italian twist? Substitute roasted red bell peppers for the jalapeños and switch out the spices with oregano and basil. Yum!

Gnocchi Bake

Makes 8 servings

- 1 pound russet potatoes, peeled and chopped
- 1 large egg
- 1 large egg yolk
- ½ cup grated Parmesan cheese (2 ounces)
- 1 cup all-purpose flour, plus more for dusting
- 2 teaspoons salt
- ½ teaspoon freshly ground black pepper
- Cooking spray
- 1 tablespoon olive oil
- 1 medium onion, chopped
- 1 red bell pepper, seeded and finely chopped
- 2 garlic cloves, minced
- 1 (15-ounce) can diced tomatoes
- ½ cup fresh basil leaves, torn
- 1½ cups shredded mozzarella cheese (6 ounces)

Over in Italy, you'll find wonderfully light dumplings called gnocchi. Really easy to prepare, they're a simple combination of cooked potatoes and flour formed into little bite-size pieces. The Queens take this amazing dumpling and combine it with other traditional Italian ingredients in our trusty 9 x 13-inch dish to make a gnocchi bake—our own casserole twist on a classic favorite. Ciao! If you're intimidated by the idea of making home-made gnocchi, you can find them frozen or vacuum sealed at most grocery stores. Look for a 16-ounce package for an easy substitution. Pair this dish with our Pint-Size Caprese Salad (page 266) or our Spinach and Spice and Everything Nice (page 218), and you'll have quite an Italian feast!

1. Put the potatoes in a large pot and add enough water to cover them by an inch. Bring to a boil, reduce the heat to medium, and simmer until the potatoes are tender, 25 to 30 minutes. Drain and set the potatoes aside to cool slightly. When the potatoes are cool enough to handle, pass them through a ricer into a large bowl. If you don't have a ricer, you can grate the potatoes using a fine grater.

2. In a small bowl, whisk together the egg and egg yolk. Add the egg mixture, the Parmesan, flour, 1 teaspoon of the salt, and ¼ teaspoon of the pepper to the potatoes. Using your hands, gently mix the ingredients to form a soft but not sticky dough. Transfer the dough to a floured surface. Gather into a ball, and then divide it into 4 pieces.

3. Line a rimmed baking sheet with parchment paper and dust it with flour. Working with 1 piece of dough at a time (keep the other pieces covered with a damp kitchen towel), roll the dough into a 24-inch-long rope. Cut crosswise into 1-inch pieces. Working with 1 piece at a time, press lightly on the gnocchi with the back of the tines of a fork and gently roll the gnocchi to create ridges on one side (see Note). Put the gnocchi on the prepared baking sheet and dust lightly with flour. Repeat with the remaining dough.

4. Preheat the oven to 350°F. Spray a 9 x 13-inch casserole dish with cooking spray.

5. Heat the oil in a large skillet set over medium-high heat. Add the onion and red bell pepper and cook for 5 minutes, until soft. Stir in the garlic and fry for 1 minute. Add the tomatoes, gnocchi, the remaining 1 teaspoon of salt, and the remaining ¼ teaspoon of the pepper, and simmer for 10 to 15 minutes, stirring occasionally, until the gnocchi are soft and the sauce has thickened. Stir in the basil and pour the mixture into the prepared casserole dish. Sprinkle the casserole with the mozzarella cheese.

6. Bake for 15 to 20 minutes, until the cheese is bubbling and golden.

Did you know that the ridges on gnocchi aren't just for decoration? They actually make it easier for the sauce to cling to the dumplings. Those Italians think of everything!

Meet the Lighter Side *of the* Casserole Queens

Cutting calories doesn't mean you have to cut flavor. The Casserole Queens are all about comfort food and the satisfaction of a good meal. So, do you really think we'd include recipes that didn't please the palate? You can rest assured that even though we've altered these recipes, you won't leave the dinner table feeling unsatisfied. Our approach about healthy eating is about neither sacrifice nor denial; instead, it is about taste and enjoyment, moderation, variety, and balance. By using the right combinations of fresh ingredients, seasonings, and herbs, lower fat cheeses, and heart-healthy fats, we trimmed calories without sacrificing that fabulous flavor you expect from a comfort-food dish. Who says watching your diet has to be boring? Not the Queens!

Rosemary
Baked Ham

Makes 16 servings

- 2 cups sweet vermouth
- 2 tablespoons agave nectar
- 1 (6-pound) fully cooked ham half
- Cooking spray
- 3 tablespoons chopped fresh rosemary
- 1 teaspoon freshly ground black pepper
- 5 garlic cloves, minced

A pig walks into a bar and orders a martini . . . Okay, this isn't the beginning of a horrible joke—it's a recipe for a delicious gluten-free ham sweetened with agave, rosemary, and sweet vermouth. You may wonder why you would need a recipe for a gluten-free ham, but prepared hams are often covered in a sweet glaze that usually contains wheat. Instead of second-guessing whether the glaze contains secret foes, we suggest making your own ham at home! The vermouth and agave add the sweet flavor you want, with no worries of hidden gluten.

1. Preheat the oven to 350°F.

2. In a small heavy saucepan set over high heat, bring the vermouth and agave nectar to a boil. Boil for 15 minutes or until the mixture is reduced to about ¾ cup. Remove the pan from the heat.

3. Trim the fat and rind from the ham. Score the outside of the ham in a diamond pattern. Put the ham on a broiler pan that's been coated with cooking spray. Rub the ham all over with the rosemary, pepper, and garlic.

4. Bake for 1 hour and 30 minutes, and then brush the ham with ¼ cup of the vermouth mixture and loosely cover it with foil. Continuing to baste the ham with the vermouth mixture every 15 minutes, bake for 45 minutes more, or until a thermometer inserted in the center of the ham registers 135°F. Transfer the ham to a serving platter and let stand for 30 minutes before slicing.

Damn Skinny
Yankee Pot Roast

Makes 10 servings

- 2 teaspoons olive oil
- 1 (4-pound) boneless beef chuck roast, trimmed
- 1 tablespoon kosher salt
- 1 tablespoon freshly ground black pepper
- 4 garlic cloves, minced
- 3 cups low-sodium beef broth or homemade (page 336)
- 1 (6-ounce) can tomato paste
- 2 teaspoons granulated sugar
- 2 tablespoons Worcestershire sauce
- 1¼ pounds small red potatoes
- 1 pound carrots, peeled and cut into 1-inch pieces
- 6 celery stalks, cut into 3-inch pieces
- 2 medium onions, quartered
- 2 tablespoons fresh lemon juice
- 2 tablespoons chopped fresh flat-leaf parsley

We all have a friend who can literally eat whatever she wants and continue to stay in shape. One of Crystal's dear friends, Carolyn, is that type of person: a Yankee from New Jersey—and a skinny one at that. Lucky for her, she introduced Crystal to this pot roast, and their friendship took off. Crystal soon found out that Carolyn actually cooks everything with lighter ingredients. Now we're on to Carolyn's secret!

1. Preheat the oven to 300°F.

2. Heat the olive oil in a large Dutch oven set over medium-high heat. Season the roast with salt and pepper. Put the roast in the pan and brown it on all sides, about 4 minutes per side. Add the garlic to the pan, and sauté until lightly browned, about 1 minute. Remove the roast from the pan and set aside. In a separate bowl, combine the broth, tomato paste, sugar, and Worcestershire sauce and stir until the sugar dissolves. Pour over the roast and bring to a simmer.

3. Cover the Dutch oven, transfer to the oven, and roast for 2 hours. Add the potatoes, carrots, celery, and onions, in that order, to the pot. Cover and roast for 1 more hour, or until the vegetables are tender and the meat has an internal temperature of 140°F (medium rare). Remove the roast from the pan and set it on a cutting board to rest for 20 minutes. Strain the vegetables out of the liquid in the pan. Pour this liquid into a medium saucepan, set over medium-high heat, and reduce by half. Stir in the lemon juice.

4. Slice the roast. Place 2 slices of meat on each plate. Ladle sauce over the meat and garnish with the parsley.

Mamma Mia! Lasagna

Makes 10 servings

- 1 pound lean ground beef round
- Salt
- ½ teaspoon freshly ground black pepper, plus more to taste
- Cooking spray
- 1 cup chopped onion
- 5 garlic cloves, minced
- 1 (28-ounce) can diced tomatoes
- 1 (14½-ounce) can Italian-style stewed tomatoes
- 1 (8-ounce) can tomato sauce
- 1 (6-ounce) can tomato paste
- ¼ cup dried parsley
- 2 teaspoons dried oregano
- 1 teaspoon dried basil
- 2 cups fat-free cottage cheese
- ½ cup finely grated Parmesan cheese (2 ounces)
- 1 (15-ounce) container fat-free ricotta
- 1 egg white
- 12 no-boil lasagna noodles
- 8 ounces store-bought shredded Italian cheese mix (2 cups)

Just like Mamma used to make, only better for you! By using a mixture of fat-free ricotta and fat-free cottage cheese, we've slashed loads of unnecessary calories while maintaining a true traditional taste. People all over Austin have fallen in love with our layers of lasagna noodles combined with our homemade meat sauce and light cheeses. It tastes so much like the real deal that you won't believe it's light.

1. Season the meat with salt and pepper, and put it in a large saucepan set over medium heat. Cook the meat, breaking up any lumps with the back of a spoon, until browned throughout, about 10 minutes. Drain the fat from the meat and set the meat aside.

2. Wipe out the pan with a paper towel. Coat the pan with cooking spray and set it over medium heat. Add the onion and garlic, and sauté for 8 minutes. Return the meat to the pan. Add the diced tomatoes, stewed tomatoes, tomato sauce, tomato paste, 2 tablespoons of the parsley, the oregano, and basil. Stir well and bring the mixture to a boil. Cover the pan, reduce the heat to low, and simmer for 15 minutes. Uncover the pan and simmer for 20 more minutes. Remove the pan from heat.

3. Preheat the oven to 350°F. Coat a 9 x 13-inch casserole dish with cooking spray.

4. Combine the remaining 2 tablespoons of parsley, the cottage cheese, Parmesan cheese, ricotta, and egg white in a large bowl. Stir well, and set aside.

5. Spread $3/4$ cup of the tomato mixture in the bottom of the prepared casserole dish. Arrange four of the lasagna noodles over the tomato mixture; top with half of the cottage cheese mixture, $2^{1}/_{4}$ cups of the tomato mixture, and $2/_{3}$ cup of the Italian cheese mix. Repeat the layers once, then end with an additional layer of noodles. Spread the remaining tomato mixture over the top.

6. Cover with foil and bake for 1 hour. Uncover the dish, sprinkle the lasagna with the remaining $2/_{3}$ cup of cheese mix, and bake for 10 more minutes. Let the lasagna stand for 10 minutes before serving.

FREEZES WELL See our freezer tips on page 16.

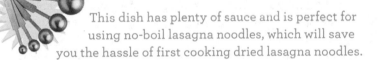

This dish has plenty of sauce and is perfect for using no-boil lasagna noodles, which will save you the hassle of first cooking dried lasagna noodles.

Zucchini
Lasagna

Makes 8 servings

- 2½ tablespoons extra-virgin olive oil
- 1 small onion, finely chopped
- ½ teaspoon red pepper flakes
- 1 pound ground turkey
- 1 (28-ounce) can diced tomatoes
- 3 tablespoons chopped fresh oregano
- 2 teaspoons salt
- 2 medium zucchini
- 1 cup part-skim ricotta cheese
- ¼ teaspoon freshly ground black pepper
- ½ cup freshly grated Parmesan cheese (2 ounces)

Citizens of Casseroleville, bow in the presence of the king of all baked dishes! This recipe gets two thumbs up not only for being gluten-free, but also for allowing you to keep your blood sugar in check. By replacing lasagna noodles with thin layers of sliced zucchini, the carbs stay low, but the flavor is still full and zesty. We suggest using a mandoline for even slices and quick prep. Just be careful—those things are sharp!

1. Preheat the oven to 375°F.

2. In a large straight-sided skillet set over medium heat, heat 2 tablespoons of the oil. Add the onion and red pepper flakes and cook, stirring occasionally, until the onion is tender, about 8 minutes. Add the turkey and cook, breaking up any large pieces with the back of a spoon, until brown throughout, 3 to 4 minutes. Add the tomatoes and bring the mixture to a boil. Reduce the heat to medium and simmer until it thickens, about 20 minutes. Stir in the oregano and salt. Let cool.

3. Slice the zucchini lengthwise into thin strips (about $\frac{1}{8}$ inch thick). Put 5 or 6 zucchini slices, overlapping slightly, in the bottom of an 8 x 8-inch baking dish. Top with 1 cup of the sauce. Dot with $\frac{1}{4}$ cup of the ricotta. Repeat the layers twice, alternating the direction of the zucchini. Top with the remaining zucchini and brush the top with the remaining $\frac{1}{2}$ tablespoon oil. Dot with the remaining $\frac{1}{4}$ cup ricotta and season with the black pepper. Top with the Parmesan cheese.

4. Bake for 50 to 60 minutes, until the lasagna is bubbling and the top is brown. Let stand for 10 minutes before serving.

Make this dish VEGETARIAN-FRIENDLY by simply omitting the turkey from the sauce or replacing it with ground meat substitute. We prefer MorningStar Farms Meal Starters Grillers Recipe Crumbles for use in sauces such as this.

FREEZES WELL For best results, prepare the casserole through step 3. Wrap in foil and freeze for up to 2 months. Thaw the casserole overnight in the refrigerator before baking as stated in the recipe. Note that casseroles that have not been completely thawed may take an additional 15 to 30 minutes longer, so be sure to check for bubbling edges and a hot center.

Ravioli
Lasagna

Makes 8 servings

Cooking spray

1 (24-ounce) jar marinara
sauce, or 3 cups homemade
(page 334)

1 pound fresh spinach, chopped

2 tablespoons dried parsley

2 teaspoons salt

1 teaspoon freshly ground
black pepper

1 (15-ounce) container
part-skim ricotta cheese

½ (16-ounce) container
2% low-fat cottage cheese

1 (25-ounce) package frozen
cheese-filled ravioli

3 cups shredded reduced-fat
Italian cheese mix (12 ounces)

If it looks like a duck, quacks like a duck, then it must be a duck—right? Same idea applies here . . . if it looks like lasagna, tastes like lasagna, then it must be lasagna! This ingenious casserole looks and tastes just like the real thing, but it requires only a fraction of the prep time. By using convenience items, you can make an impressive dish for your family and friends with little time and effort.

1. Preheat the oven to 350°F. Spray a 9 x 13-inch casserole dish with cooking spray.

2. In a large saucepan set over medium heat, heat the marinara sauce until heated through, about 10 minutes. Add the spinach, 1 tablespoon parsley, salt, and pepper, and cook for about 3 minutes, or until the spinach has wilted. Set aside.

3. In a medium-size bowl, combine the ricotta cheese, cottage cheese, and remaining 1 tablespoon parsley. Set aside.

4. Pour a third of the marinara mixture into the bottom of the prepared dish. Arrange half of the frozen ravioli in a single layer on top. Spread half of the ricotta mixture over the ravioli and sprinkle with 1 cup of the shredded cheese. Repeat the layers, ending with the remaining marinara mixture. Sprinkle the remaining 1 cup shredded cheese over the top.

5. Bake for 30 minutes, or until cheese starts to brown and the sauce is bubbling around the edges. If the cheese starts to get too brown, cover the dish with foil.

FREEZES WELL For best results, prepare the casserole through step 4. Wrap in foil and freeze for up to 2 months. Thaw the casserole overnight in the refrigerator before baking as stated in the recipe. Note that casseroles that have not been completely thawed may take 15 to 30 minutes longer, so be sure to check for bubbling edges and a hot center.

Beef and Rice
Fiesta Bake

Makes 6 to 8 servings

Cooking spray

½ pound lean ground beef

Salt and freshly ground black pepper

1 cup chopped onion

1 cup chopped green bell pepper

½ cup water

2 (14½-ounce) cans diced tomatoes

2 (4½-ounce) cans chopped green chilies

2 tablespoons chili powder

2 teaspoons ground cumin

1½ teaspoons granulated sugar

1 teaspoon dried oregano

4 cups cooked long-grain rice (see page 329)

1 cup fat-free sour cream

½ cup sliced green onions, green parts only

½ cup skim milk

3 ounces reduced-fat sharp Cheddar cheese, grated (¾ cup)

Say no to grapefruit diets, and yes to feeling satisfied. Similar to a burrito filling, this casserole boasts a creamy rice mixture made with low-fat sour cream and green onions, all covered in a spicy meat sauce and topped with reduced-fat Cheddar. Round out a healthy dinner by serving this dish with either a fruit or green salad and dinner rolls. It's also perfect to use as a filling for whole-wheat or corn tortillas.

1. Preheat the oven to 375°F. Coat a 9 x 13-inch casserole dish with cooking spray.

2. Season the beef with salt and pepper. Put the beef, onion, and bell pepper into a large skillet set over medium-high heat. Cook, breaking up any lumps with the back of a spoon, until the meat is browned, about 8 minutes. Add the water, diced tomatoes, green chilies, chili powder, cumin, sugar, and oregano. Stir and bring the mixture to a boil. Cover the skillet, reduce the heat to low, and simmer for 10 minutes. Uncover the skillet and simmer the mixture for 2 more minutes. Remove the skillet from the heat, and set aside.

3. Combine the rice, sour cream, green onions, and milk in a bowl. Spoon the rice mixture into the prepared casserole dish. Top with the beef mixture and sprinkle the top with the cheese. Bake for 30 minutes or until heated through and the cheese on top is bubbling.

FREEZES WELL
See our freezer tips on page 16.

Beef-Stuffed
Cabbage Rolls

Makes 8 to 10 servings

- 1 large head of green cabbage
- 1 pound lean ground beef chuck
- 1/3 cup cooked long-grain white rice (see page 329)
- 1 small onion, grated
- 2 large eggs
- 2 teaspoons salt
- 1/2 teaspoon freshly ground black pepper
- 1 large onion, sliced
- 3 (14 1/2-ounce) cans diced tomatoes
- 1 (15-ounce) can tomato sauce
- 4 teaspoons fresh lemon juice (from 1 large lemon)
- 1/4 cup packed light brown sugar

Or as we like to call them—Hungarian pigs in a blanket! (We're a bit silly, if you haven't noticed.) This dish traveled into our hearts long ago and has satisfied our families for generations. It was surprising to us that this comfort food that we grew up on wasn't that bad for you! Made with lean ground beef, rice, and veggies, and covered in a tomato sauce, these rolls will fill you up but not weigh you down.

1. Preheat the oven to 350°F.

2. Remove 15 large leaves from the cabbage and trim off the thickest part of each leaf. Pour boiling water over the cabbage and let the leaves soak until they are pliable, about 4 minutes. Remove from the water, pat dry, and set aside.

3. In a large bowl, combine the beef, rice, grated onion, eggs, 1 teaspoon of the salt, and 1/4 teaspoon of the black pepper. Place 1/4 cup of the meat mixture in the cupped part of each of the softened cabbage leaves. Fold over the sides of each leaf and roll them up. Recipe will make 8 to 10 rolls. Place the remaining 5 cabbage leaves in the bottom of a 9 x 13-inch casserole dish. Arrange layers of cabbage rolls seam side down, then add a layer of sliced onion over the cabbage rolls.

4. In a large bowl, combine the tomatoes, tomato sauce, lemon juice, remaining 1 teaspoon salt, and remaining 1/4 teaspoon pepper. Pour over the cabbage rolls. Bake until bubbling, about 30 minutes. Sprinkle the casserole with the brown sugar, cover the dish with foil, and continue baking for 1 hour. Remove and serve hot. Spoon pan juices over rolls.

"I'll Never Go Hungary Again" Goulash

Makes 8 to 10 servings

Cooking spray

2 cups thinly sliced onions

1 cup thinly sliced celery

2 garlic cloves, minced

1½ pounds lean ground beef

1 (6-ounce) can tomato paste

3 tablespoons all-purpose flour

1 tablespoon paprika

4 cups water

2 (14½-ounce) cans stewed tomatoes

1½ pounds Yukon Gold potatoes, peeled and cut into ½-inch cubes

1 tablespoon low-sodium beef bouillon granules

2 teaspoons salt

1 teaspoon ground marjoram

⅛ teaspoon freshly ground black pepper

1 bay leaf

Pinch of parsley flakes

This Hungarian-style dish reminds us of learning to cook on our own while in college. The term "goulash" is very loose in its definition as it was a dish invented for using leftovers—or in our case, whatever we could find in the kitchen!

Sandy, in particular, has fond memories of goulash. She was the last of the four Pollock sisters to leave home. Lucky for Sandy, her sister Yvette lived nearby. While Sandy was living with her parents and attending college, Yvette was a young schoolteacher, just getting started in her career. Yvette didn't have a lot of money, but she was always generous and creative. From time to time, she would invite Sandy and her parents over for goulash, asking, "Oh, would you mind bringing over a can of corn from the house? And could you grab some cheese? And some beef? Oh, and an onion?" It turned out that her goulash was composed of whatever the Pollocks had in their fridge or pantry at the time. But Yvette would always set the table for the family and turn the borrowed ingredients into the most delicious meal.

1. Preheat the oven to 325°F.

2. Coat a 4-quart oven-safe saucepan or Dutch oven with cooking spray and set over medium heat. Add the onions and celery, and sauté for 8 minutes. Add the garlic and sauté for 5 more minutes or until the onions are translucent. Add the beef, tomato paste, flour, and paprika; cook for 5 minutes, stirring constantly. Stir in the water, tomatoes, potatoes, bouillon, salt, marjoram, pepper, bay leaf, and parsley. Bring to a boil, then remove the pot from the heat and cover. Place the pan in the oven and cook for 1½ hours or until bubbling and potatoes can easily be pierced with a knife. Stir every ½ hour.

Mandarin
Meatloaf

Makes 6 servings

Cooking spray

1 pound ground turkey breast

½ pound lean ground pork

1 cup chopped green onions, green parts only

1 cup panko bread crumbs

½ cup chopped red bell pepper

½ cup chopped mandarin orange (drained, if using canned)

½ cup canned water chestnuts, chopped and drained

½ cup hoisin sauce

3 garlic cloves, minced

2 large egg whites

1 tablespoon low-sodium soy sauce

1 tablespoon grated fresh ginger

¼ teaspoon salt

Fruit in a meatloaf? What were we thinking? Trust us; we thought the exact same thing when Crystal's sister, Cindy, suggested it one night in our test kitchen. But since Cindy is usually right (don't even bother trying to play a game of Trivial Pursuit with her), we gave it a whirl and it worked! In fact, the sweetness from the mandarin orange brings an exciting new twist to this old-time dish. As soon as you try it, you'll understand. Substituting ground turkey keeps the calories and fat in check, and when served with a side of stir-fried veggies and brown rice, this healthy meal is sure to become a regular household favorite.

1. Preheat the oven to 350°F. Coat a 9 x 5-inch loaf pan with cooking spray.

2. Combine the turkey, pork, green onions, panko bread crumbs, bell pepper, orange, water chestnuts, ¼ cup of the hoisin sauce, the garlic, egg whites, soy sauce, ginger, and salt in a large bowl.

3. Put the mixture into the prepared loaf pan and spread the remaining ¼ cup hoisin sauce over the top of the meatloaf. Bake for 1 hour 15 minutes or until a meat thermometer registers 180°F. Let it stand for 5 minutes before serving.

Use a small funnel to quickly and easily separate an egg. The white will go through, while the yolk will stay in the top of the funnel.

Not Your Average Tamale Pie

Makes 6 to 8 servings

Cooking spray

1 pound lean ground turkey

1 medium onion, chopped

1 poblano pepper, roasted, seeded, and chopped

Salt and freshly ground black pepper

1 (15¼-ounce) can whole kernel corn, drained

1 (14-ounce) can diced tomatoes, drained

1½ tablespoons ground cumin

1 tablespoon chili powder

¼ teaspoon garlic powder

1 (8½-ounce) package cornbread mix

Tamales are a huge part of the Christmas celebration and tradition in the Rio Grande Valley, where Sandy was born and raised. As such, the holiday season simply wouldn't be complete without eating copious amounts of tamales.

Tamales are fun to make, but very time-consuming, so many people simply purchase them from a local restaurant. We go to Delia's in Edinburg, Texas. Around Christmastime, they make about 25,000 tamales and become so busy that the doors are closed to regular customers and the police are dispatched to direct traffic. If your order isn't in at least 2 weeks prior to Christmas, then you're out of luck! Our spin on the tamale is a casserole that saves you both calories and countless hours of preparation.

1. Preheat the oven to 400°F. Coat a 9 x 13-inch casserole dish with cooking spray.

2. Coat a large sauté pan with cooking spray and set it over medium-high heat. Add the turkey, onion, and poblano pepper and season with salt and pepper. Cook until the meat is browned throughout, about 7 minutes; drain well. Return the mixture to the pan and add the corn, tomatoes, cumin, chili powder, and garlic powder. Bring the mixture to a simmer and cook for 10 minutes. Pour the mixture into the prepared casserole dish.

3. Prepare the cornbread mix according to the package instructions. Pour the mixture over the top of the casserole. Bake for 20 to 25 minutes or until the topping is cooked and golden brown.

Erin's Special Gluten-Free
Corn Dog Casserole

Makes 8 servings

Cooking spray

2 tablespoons unsalted butter

2 celery stalks, minced

1 bunch green onions, green parts only, sliced

1½ pounds uncured hot dogs

1½ cups whole milk

2 large eggs

1 (20-ounce) bag Bob's Red Mill Gluten Free Cornbread Mix

2 teaspoons chopped fresh sage

¼ teaspoon salt

¼ teaspoon freshly ground black pepper

2 cups shredded sharp Cheddar cheese (8 ounces)

Our dear friend Erin loves our corn dog casserole, but she's discovered that her body can't handle gluten, and, sadly, the Jiffy mix we use contains it. We didn't want her to have to do without delicious corn dog goodness, so this is a special version that we created for her! We swapped out the Jiffy for Bob's Red Mill Gluten Free Cornbread Mix, and we also decided to use uncured hot dogs, which are both nitrate- and preservative-free. It sure turned into a mighty fine dish!

1. Preheat the oven to 400°F. Spray a 9 x 13-inch casserole dish with cooking spray.

2. In a large sauté pan set over medium-high heat, melt the butter. Add the celery and cook for 5 minutes. Add the onions and cook for 2 more minutes. Transfer the celery and onions to a large bowl and set aside.

3. Cut the hot dogs in half lengthwise, then cut into ½-inch pieces. Sauté the dogs in the same pan, turning to brown on all sides, about 6 minutes. Transfer the hot dogs to the bowl with the celery and onions.

4. In a medium bowl, lightly beat together the milk and eggs. Add the cornbread mix, sage, salt, and pepper, and stir well. Add the hot dogs, celery, and onions and $1\frac{1}{2}$ cups of the cheese and stir well. Pour the mixture into the prepared casserole dish. Sprinkle the remaining $\frac{1}{2}$ cup of cheese over the top.

5. Bake for 30 minutes, or until the casserole is golden brown and has risen slightly. You want a nice golden-brown crust on top.

This can easily be made VEGETARIAN-FRIENDLY by substituting your favorite vegetarian hot dog alternative for the regular hot dogs.

FREEZES WELL For best results, prepare the casserole through step 4. Wrap in foil and freeze for up to 2 months. Thaw the casserole overnight in the refrigerator before baking as stated in the recipe. Note that casseroles that have not been completely thawed may take 15 to 30 minutes longer, so be sure to check for bubbling edges and a hot center.

Queen Ranch Casserole

Makes 6 servings

- 3 large whole boneless, skinless chicken breasts
- 1 tablespoon olive oil
- Salt and freshly ground black pepper
- 1 tablespoon unsalted butter
- 1 medium onion, chopped
- 1 (14-ounce) can chicken broth, or 2 cups Chicken Broth (page 335)
- 4 teaspoons cornstarch
- 1 (10-ounce) can Rotel tomatoes or diced tomatoes with green chilies
- 1 (8-ounce) can diced green chilies
- 6 corn tortillas, cut into bite-size pieces
- 4 ounces low-fat Cheddar cheese, cut into ½-inch cubes (1 cup)
- Garlic salt

FREEZES WELL See our freezer tips on page 16.

All hail to the Queen! If you're a fan of our Traditional King Ranch Casserole (page 64), you will love this lighter version, which delivers on taste but not on fat. We cut out the creamy soups to home in on the flavors from the green chilies and Rotel tomatoes. That's not to say that this dish is super-spicy; it has a kick, but is overall very fresh.

The cornstarch and broth mixture is called a slurry, and is used to thicken soups, stews, and sauces. Here are a few tips for making a slurry: Never add cornstarch directly to a hot liquid or it will lump; slurries should be 1 part cornstarch to 2 parts liquid, and, when stirred, should have the consistency of heavy cream; if you don't have cornstarch, you can substitute flour—just use twice as much.

1. Preheat the oven to 350°F.

2. Coat the chicken breasts with the olive oil, then season with salt and pepper. Put the chicken on a baking sheet. Bake for 15 to 20 minutes or until no longer pink. Remove the pan from the oven and let the chicken cool. When it is cool enough to handle, dice it and set aside.

3. Melt the butter in a medium saucepan set over medium heat. Add the onion and cook until translucent, about 8 minutes. Add the cooked chicken. In a small bowl, whisk together the broth and cornstarch until smooth. Add the cornstarch mixture to the chicken mixture and cook for 5 minutes. Add the tomatoes and chilies and cook until thickened, about 6 minutes.

4. In the bottom of a 9 x 13-inch casserole dish, layer the tortilla pieces, cheese cubes, and chicken mixture, sprinkling each layer with garlic salt to taste. Bake for 30 minutes or until the cheese is melted and bubbling around the edges.

Summer Halibut
with Dill

Makes 4 to 6 servings

1 tablespoon extra-virgin olive oil, plus more to drizzle

4 (6-ounce each) halibut fillets

Salt and freshly ground black pepper

3 tablespoons chopped fresh dill

2 ripe but firm medium tomatoes, seeded and sliced

½ cup red onion, thinly sliced

½ cup Seasoned Bread Crumbs (page 330)

½ cup grated Parmesan cheese (2 ounces)

Dill is one of our favorite summertime herbs. Its fresh, clean flavor is perfect for a flaky white fish like halibut. It's lovely served with wild brown rice and crisp green beans. You can also make this with haddock or red snapper.

1. Preheat the oven to 450°F.

2. Lightly coat a 9 x 13-inch casserole dish with olive oil. Place the fish fillets in the dish, overlapping them slightly if necessary, and season with salt and pepper. Sprinkle half of the dill over the fish and cover with the sliced tomatoes. Scatter the onion slices over the top and sprinkle with the remaining dill. Drizzle with the olive oil and season lightly with salt and pepper. Sprinkle the seasoned bread crumbs and Parmesan cheese over the top.

3. Bake for 25 to 30 minutes or until bubbling on the sides and the fish is cooked through. Serve hot.

Green Chili
and Chicken Bake

Makes 6 servings

This Tex-Mex favorite combines the full flavor of Manchego and the creamy, mild flavor of Monterey Jack to create a sophisticated twist on a traditional chicken-and-rice dish. We also go the extra mile by toasting the rice, both to impart a nutty flavor and to reduce the total cooking time. Dotting the rice with butter adds flavor and helps provide a nice golden color when broiling.

Cooking spray

2 tablespoons olive oil

3 boneless, skinless whole chicken breasts, cut into cubes

1 teaspoon salt, plus more for the chicken

½ teaspoon freshly ground black pepper, plus more for the chicken

3 (4-ounce) cans diced green chilies

1 (14.5-ounce) can stewed tomatoes (Mexican style, if available)

1 (8-ounce) can tomato sauce

1½ teaspoons chopped fresh oregano

1½ cups chopped onion (about 2 small onions)

2 garlic cloves, minced

1 jalapeño pepper, seeds removed, and chopped

1 teaspoon ground cumin

1 tablespoon chili powder

1½ cups long-grain rice

3 cups Chicken Broth, homemade (page 335) or store bought

¼ cup (½ stick) butter, cut into small pieces

1 cup shredded Monterey Jack cheese (4 ounces)

1 cup shredded Manchego cheese (4 ounces)

2 tablespoons chopped fresh cilantro

½ cup crushed corn tortilla chips

1. Preheat the oven to 375°F. Spray a 9 x 13-inch casserole dish with cooking spray.

2. In a large sauté pan set over medium-high heat, heat 1 tablespoon of the olive oil. Season the chicken with salt and pepper and put it in the pan. Cook, stirring, until it's no longer pink, about 8 minutes. Add the green chilies, stewed tomatoes, and tomato sauce. Season with the 1 teaspoon of salt, the $\frac{1}{2}$ teaspoon of black pepper, and the oregano. Pour the mixture into the prepared casserole dish.

3. Bake the casserole for 20 minutes. Remove the dish from the oven and set the oven to Broil.

4. Meanwhile, in the same pot set over medium-high heat, heat the remaining 1 tablespoon of olive oil. Add the onions, garlic, jalapeño, cumin, and chili powder. Sauté until the onions are golden, 5 minutes. Stir in the rice and continue to cook until it is lightly toasted, about 5 minutes. Add enough chicken broth to cover the mixture, scraping up the brown bits on the bottom of the pan. Cover pan with a lid and cook until the rice is done, about 45 minutes.

5. Spread the cooked rice over the chicken in the casserole dish and dot with butter.

6. Preheat the oven to broil. Cook until the top of the rice is golden and crispy, about 6 minutes. Remove the dish from the oven and sprinkle the top with the Monterey Jack and Manchego cheeses. Return the dish to the oven and broil again until the cheese is melted, about 2 minutes.

7. Sprinkle with the cilantro and the crushed chips and serve.

FREEZES WELL For best results, prepare the casserole through step 5. Cover with foil and freeze for up to 2 months. Thaw the casserole overnight in the refrigerator. Note that casseroles that have not been completely thawed may take 15 to 30 minutes longer, so be sure to check for bubbling edges and a hot center.

Chicken
Tetrazzini

Makes 6 to 8 servings

Cooking spray

½ (16-ounce) box spaghetti

3 whole boneless, skinless chicken breasts

1 tablespoon olive oil

Salt and freshly ground black pepper

1 tablespoon unsalted butter

1 cup finely chopped onion

1 cup finely chopped celery

1 (8-ounce) container sliced button mushrooms

¾ teaspoon salt

½ cup dry sherry

½ cup all-purpose flour

1⅓ cups Chicken Broth (page 335)

1 (4-ounce) package low-fat cream cheese

1⅓ cups grated Parmesan cheese (5½ ounces)

½ cup panko bread crumbs

Contrary to popular belief, chicken tetrazzini was served at many upscale restaurants throughout the United States in the early 1900s. The dish was inspired and named after the great Italian opera star Luisa Tetrazzini, and it was widely popular. In fact, it was so popular that home cooks everywhere began trying to re-create the famous dish in their homes, and it lost its appeal as a gourmet delicacy in fine dining establishments. Lucky for us at home, we can still enjoy this amazingly good comfort dish with our family and friends, unfettered by any unnecessary pretenses.

Typically it is made with heavy creams and lots of butter, but we have found some healthier substitutions, such as low-fat cream cheese, which still provides the decadence and creaminess of the original. The opera isn't over until the fat lady sings, but this much lighter version of a comfort food favorite will leave you enjoying the music!

1. Preheat the oven to 350°F. Lightly coat a 9 x 13-inch casserole dish with cooking spray.

2. Bring a large pot of heavily salted water to a boil. Break the noodles in half and cook according to package instructions. Drain the pasta and set aside.

3. Coat the chicken pieces with olive oil and season with salt and pepper. Place the chicken on a baking sheet and bake for 15 to 20 minutes or until no longer pink. Remove the baking sheet from the oven and let the chicken cool. When cool enough to handle, dice it and set aside.

4. In same pot as you cooked the noodles, melt the butter over medium heat. Add the onion, celery, and mushrooms, and cook, stirring, until soft, about 8 minutes. Season with the salt, add the sherry, and cook for about 1 minute. Gradually add the flour to the pot while stirring to coat the vegetables. Cook, stirring constantly, until the mixture is thick, about 5 minutes. Begin gradually adding the chicken broth while stirring constantly. Bring the mixture to a boil, then reduce the heat to low. Simmer for about 5 minutes or until thickened. Add the cream cheese and stir until melted. Add 1 cup of the Parmesan cheese to the pasta and cooked chicken and stir until combined. Pour the mixture into the prepared casserole dish.

5. Mix the bread crumbs with the remaining $1/3$ cup of Parmesan cheese in a small mixing bowl. Sprinkle the topping evenly over the casserole. Bake for 30 minutes or until bubbly and browned on top. Let the casserole rest for 10 minutes before serving.

Tuscan
Ziti Bake

Makes 6 servings

Cooking spray

½ (16-ounce) box dried ziti

8 ounces hot Italian turkey sausage, casings removed

1½ teaspoons olive oil

5 cups thinly sliced zucchini (about 1½ pounds)

2 cups sliced onions (2 large onions)

3 garlic cloves, minced

½ teaspoon salt

¼ teaspoon freshly ground black pepper

¼ teaspoon red pepper flakes

½ cup fat-free, low-sodium chicken broth (page 335)

¼ cup dry white wine

1 tablespoon all-purpose flour

2 ounces feta cheese, crumbled (½ cup)

2 ounces part-skim mozzarella cheese, shredded (½ cup)

As well as being inexpensive and easy to make, pasta is actually low in fat. It typically tends to be what we combine it with (and how much we consume) that gets us into trouble! But if you are still worried about carbohydrates, you can always opt for low-carb or whole-wheat pasta. Instead of substituting the pasta, we avoided calorie pitfalls by adding lots of zucchini and using naturally lower fat cheeses, such as feta. The addition of hot Italian turkey sausage and red pepper flakes adds just the right amount of heat to keep your taste buds happy. Pair this dish with your favorite salad to make a quick and satisfying meal any night of the week.

1. Preheat the oven to 350°F. Coat a 9 x 13-inch baking dish with cooking spray.

2. Cook the pasta in boiling salted water for 6 minutes. Drain well and set aside.

3. Coat a large skillet with cooking spray and set it over medium-high heat. Add the sausage to the pan and cook, breaking up any lumps with the back of a spoon, until thoroughly browned, about 8 minutes. Transfer the sausage to a plate and set aside.

4. Wipe out the pan with a paper towel, set over medium-high heat, and add the olive oil. Add the zucchini, onions, garlic, salt, pepper, and red pepper flakes. Cook, stirring occasionally, for 10 minutes or until the vegetables are tender and the zucchini begins to brown.

5. In a small bowl, whisk together the broth, wine, and flour. Add the broth mixture to the pan with the vegetables and cook for 2 minutes. Combine the vegetable mixture, pasta, sausage, and feta cheese in a large bowl; toss well. Spoon the pasta mixture into the prepared baking dish. Sprinkle the mozzarella cheese evenly over the top. Bake for 20 minutes or until bubbly and lightly browned.

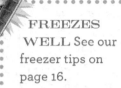

FREEZES WELL See our freezer tips on page 16.

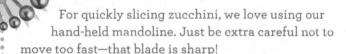

For quickly slicing zucchini, we love using our hand-held mandoline. Just be extra careful not to move too fast—that blade is sharp!

Mediterranean
Medley

Makes 4 servings

Cooking spray

1½ pounds large shrimp, peeled and deveined

1 tablespoon fresh lemon juice

½ cup chopped onion

2 garlic cloves, minced

3 plum tomatoes, diced

3 tablespoons bottled clam juice

3 tablespoons dry white wine

2 teaspoons chopped fresh oregano

1 tablespoon chopped fresh basil

2 tablespoons chopped fresh flat-leaf parsley

¼ teaspoon freshly ground black pepper

3 ounces feta cheese, crumbled (¾ cup)

1 (16-ounce) box linguine, cooked

4 lemon wedges, for garnish

Light on calories. More than delicious. We took the best of Mediterranean flavors and brought them together harmoniously in this fresh and delightful dish. Scrumptious shrimp and feta are baked with fresh herbs and tomatoes in a light sauce of wine and clam juice that is perfect for serving over a bed of linguine.

1. Preheat the oven to 450°F. Coat a 9 x 13-inch casserole dish with cooking spray.

2. Rinse the shrimp and pat dry with paper towels. Combine the shrimp and lemon juice in a large bowl and toss well. Set aside.

3. Coat a large skillet with cooking spray and set over medium-high heat. Put the onion in the pan and cook for 8 minutes or until translucent. Add the garlic and cook for 1 minute. Add the tomatoes, clam juice, wine, oregano, basil, 1 tablespoon parsley, and pepper. Bring the mixture to a boil, reduce the heat, and simmer for 5 minutes. Remove the pan from heat. Stir in the reserved shrimp.

4. Put the shrimp mixture in the prepared casserole dish. Sprinkle the feta cheese evenly over the top. Bake for 12 minutes or until the shrimp are opaque and the cheese is melted. Remove the dish from the oven and sprinkle the remaining 1 tablespoon parsley over the top. Serve immediately over the linguine, with lemon wedges on the side.

This dish can be made GLUTEN-FREE by using gluten-free pasta instead of linguine made with wheat (see page 21 for recommendations of our favorite brands).

Red Snapper Veracruz

Makes 8 servings

- 4 tablespoons (½ stick) unsalted butter
- 1 medium onion, chopped
- 1 (8-ounce) container sliced button mushrooms
- ½ green bell pepper, chopped
- 1 fresh jalapeño pepper, chopped (half the seeds removed for less heat)
- 1 (14¾-ounce) can tomato puree
- 1 (14¾-ounce) can diced tomatoes, drained
- ½ cup dry white wine
- 4 tablespoons chili sauce (such as Heinz)
- 3 tablespoons fresh lemon juice
- 3 tablespoons capers, drained
- 1 tablespoon chopped fresh flat-leaf parsley
- 2 garlic cloves, minced
- ½ tablespoon dried thyme
- ¼ teaspoon salt, plus more to taste
- 2 pounds fresh red snapper fillets
- ½ pound shrimp, peeled and deveined
- Freshly ground black pepper

Sometimes we forget that there is more to Mexican food than our favorite enchiladas and puffy tacos. In fact, there are many specialty seafood dishes throughout the country, varying in style and preparation, yet equally delicious. Veracruz is a central Mexican city on the Gulf of Mexico, and it's where many Spanish conquistadors landed when first coming to the Americas. Here, culinary traditions began to meld—not only Spanish but also Mediterranean, French, and Caribbean. The result is Veracruz style. We love serving this dish over a bed of quinoa, which is excellent at soaking up the delicious juices.

1. Preheat the oven to 425°F.

2. In a large sauté pan set over medium-high heat, melt the butter. Add the onion, mushrooms, bell pepper, and jalapeño, and cook until softened, about 8 minutes. Add the tomato puree, diced tomatoes, wine, chili sauce, lemon juice, capers, parsley, garlic, thyme, and salt, and cook for 5 minutes.

3. Pour half of the sauce into the bottom of a 9 x 13-inch casserole dish. Season the snapper fillets and the shrimp with salt and pepper, and lay them on top of the sauce. Pour the remaining sauce over the seafood. Bake for 15 to 18 minutes or until the fish is flaky.

Never heard of quinoa? Crystal invites you to get to know one of her favorite ingredients. Although quinoa (pronounced keen-wah) has been around for centuries, it isn't a mainstream pantry item in American kitchens. It has a similar texture to that of couscous or rice, with a slight crunch and a somewhat nutty flavor when cooked. Look for quinoa at your local grocery. Your body will thank you for it.

Baked Fish and Vegetables
with Tangy Caper Sauce

Makes 6 servings

- 2 pounds red potatoes, peeled and cut into $\frac{1}{8}$-inch slices (about 6 cups)
- 4 cups thinly sliced fennel (about 2 small bulbs)
- 1 tablespoon olive oil
- $\frac{3}{4}$ teaspoon salt
- $\frac{1}{2}$ teaspoon freshly ground black pepper
- 1 teaspoon fennel seeds
- 3 garlic cloves, minced
- 1 (28-ounce) can whole tomatoes, drained and chopped
- $\frac{3}{4}$ cup dry white wine
- 6 tablespoons chopped fresh flat-leaf parsley
- 2 tablespoons grated lemon zest
- 3 teaspoons chopped fresh oregano
- 6 (6-ounce each) sea bass fillets, or other firm white fish fillets
- Tangy Caper Sauce (opposite page)

"Good for you" doesn't have to mean "bland." Crystal is a sucker for lots of flavor, and this dish is an extravaganza for her palate! It's light, fresh, and oh-so-flavorful. While the fish and roasted vegetables have a wonderful taste all on their own, Crystal adores the tangy caper sauce that makes this dish sing! Capers—small green pockets of salty goodness—are actually the unopened flower buds of a Mediterranean bush, *Capparis spinosa*. Once harvested, they are dried in the sun and then pickled in either a vinegar brine or packed in salt. There is a rather large variety of capers, varying in size and origin. Feel free to experiment to find the ones you like best, but we typically prefer the smaller nonpareille size that hails from southern France. If you are trying to watch the amount of salt in your diet, rinse the capers and pat dry with a towel before adding them to the sauce.

1. Preheat the oven to 450°F.

2. Combine the potatoes, fennel, 2 teaspoons of the oil, $\frac{1}{4}$ teaspoon of the salt, and $\frac{1}{4}$ teaspoon of the pepper in a 9 x 13-inch casserole dish; toss gently to coat. Bake the vegetables for 30 minutes or until they can easily be pierced with a fork.

3. Heat the remaining 1 teaspoon of oil in a medium skillet. Add the fennel seeds and garlic, and sauté for 1 minute. Add $\frac{1}{4}$ teaspoon of the salt, $\frac{1}{8}$ teaspoon of the pepper, the tomatoes, wine, 4 tablespoons of the parsley, 1 tablespoon of the lemon zest, and the oregano to the pan. Bring the mixture to a boil, reduce the heat to low, and simmer for 8 minutes.

4. Sprinkle the fish fillets with the remaining $\frac{1}{4}$ teaspoon salt and the remaining $\frac{1}{8}$ teaspoon pepper. Arrange the fillets over the potato mixture in the casserole dish. Sprinkle with the remaining tablespoon of lemon zest and spread the tomato mixture over the fish. Bake at 450°F for 20 minutes or until the fish flakes easily with a fork. Sprinkle with the remaining 2 tablespoons parsley. Spoon the caper sauce over the fish before serving.

Tangy Caper Sauce

Makes $\frac{1}{4}$ cup

2 tablespoons fresh lemon juice

2 tablespoons extra-virgin olive oil

1½ teaspoons chopped fresh oregano

1 teaspoon salt

1 teaspoon grated lemon zest

2 garlic cloves, minced

3 tablespoons capers, drained

Dash of freshly ground black pepper

Put the lemon juice, olive oil, oregano, salt, lemon zest, garlic, capers, and pepper in a small bowl. Whisk to combine.

Orzo with Zucchini,
Tomatoes, and Goat Cheese

Makes 6 servings

- 1 (16-ounce) package orzo
- 1 tablespoon olive oil
- 2 medium zucchini, quartered lengthwise and thinly sliced
- 1 garlic clove, minced
- 1 (14.5-ounce) can diced tomatoes with garlic and oregano, drained
- 1 (7-ounce) jar roasted red bell peppers, drained and chopped
- ¼ cup chopped fresh parsley
- 1 teaspoon chopped fresh oregano
- ½ teaspoon salt
- ¼ teaspoon freshly ground black pepper
- ½ cup freshly grated Parmesan cheese (2 ounces)
- ½ cup crumbled goat cheese (2 ounces)

Summers may be hot in Texas, but that doesn't make our parties any less sizzling! We just lighten up the dishes and keep the cold drinks a-flowin'. This light yet mighty and flavorful dish is perfect for those summer backyard barbecues. It's wonderful at room temperature or served cold, so it's easy to make it the day before and spend time having summer fun with your guests instead of in the kitchen.

1. Prepare the orzo according to the package directions, omitting any salt and fat. Drain, and toss with 2 teaspoons of the olive oil.

2. Heat the remaining 1 teaspoon of oil in a large sauté pan set over medium heat. Add the zucchini and cook, stirring, for 7 minutes. Add the garlic and cook, stirring, for 3 minutes. Add the tomatoes, roasted red peppers, parsley, oregano, salt, and pepper. Cook for 5 minutes or until thoroughly heated. Remove the pan from the heat and stir in the orzo. If you plan to serve the dish hot, stir in the Parmesan and the goat cheese now. If serving it chilled, refrigerate the dish for at least 2 hours and toss with the cheese before serving.

This dish can be made GLUTEN-FREE by substituting quinoa for the orzo.

Summertime Tomato Basil Pie

Makes 6 servings

- 1 pie crust, homemade (page 323) or store bought
- 4 large beefsteak tomatoes, peeled and thickly sliced
- 1½ teaspoons salt
- ¼ cup fresh basil leaves, chopped, plus more for garnish
- 3 green onions, green parts, chopped
- ¼ teaspoon freshly ground black pepper
- ½ cup Greek yogurt
- ¼ cup crumbled goat cheese (1 ounce)

Celebrate the bounty of summer by combining two of life's most simple but divine pleasures: fresh tomatoes and basil. There is little out there in food that excites Crystal more than these ingredients, and one of her favorite things is to put them in a savory pie. For this recipe we recommend beefsteak tomatoes, as they are widely available, but if you are able to find a glorious selection of heirloom tomatoes at your local farmers' market, go ahead and substitute!

1. Preheat the oven to 350°F.

2. Line a 9 x 13-inch casserole dish up to the rim with the pie dough (if homemade, use 1 recipe; if store bought, use both pie crusts and overlap to ensure total coverage). Bake for 15 minutes, or until golden brown. Set aside to cool.

3. Put the tomato slices in a colander in the sink in one layer. Sprinkle them with 1 teaspoon of the salt and let drain for 10 minutes. Next, press the tomatoes between layers of paper towels to squeeze out more juice, and then cut them into large pieces and put them in a large bowl. Add the basil and onions and mix well. Season with the remaining ½ teaspoon of salt and the pepper.

4. In a separate bowl, combine the yogurt and goat cheese.

5. Put the tomato mixture into the cooled pie shell and spread the yogurt mixture on top. Bake for 30 minutes, or until lightly browned. Let cool for at least 15 minutes.

6. Cut the pie into slices and serve warm with a sprinkling of basil.

This recipe can be made GLUTEN-FREE by using a purchased gluten-free pie crust or by making your own (see page 324 for our recipe).

Merry Mushroom
Bread Pudding

Makes 6 servings

Cooking spray

3 cups low-fat milk

8 cups rustic bread, cut into 2-inch cubes

2 (4-ounce) portobello mushrooms

2 teaspoons vegetable oil

6 cups quartered button mushrooms (about 12 ounces)

2 garlic cloves, minced

½ cup chopped fresh parsley

2 teaspoons chopped fresh rosemary

¼ teaspoon salt

¼ teaspoon freshly ground black pepper

3 large eggs

1 large egg white

1 cup shredded Gruyère cheese (4 ounces)

The Queens have an impressive selection of vintage casserole dishes—from Pyrex to Fire King, and a whole lot of everything in between. One of our favorites happens to be a Corning Ware dish with the "Merry Mushroom" pattern on it. The orange, yellow, and brown color palette screams 1970s, and we love it! We're constantly creating new mushroom recipes and proudly serving them up in this dish. Trust us, nothing perks up a buffet table like a "Merry Mushroom" painted casserole dish! This particular bread pudding is one of our finest mushroom masterpieces. The combination of portobello and button mushrooms makes it especially earthy and supercomforting.

1. Preheat the oven to 375°F. Spray a 9 x 13-inch casserole dish with cooking spray.

2. In a medium bowl, combine 2 cups of the milk and the bread. Cover and chill for 30 minutes, stirring occasionally.

3. Meanwhile, using a spoon, remove the brown gills from the undersides of the portobellos and remove the stems; discard the gills and stems; slice mushrooms. Heat the oil in a large nonstick skillet set over medium-high heat. Add the portobello and button mushrooms and sauté for 4 minutes, until the mushrooms start to release their juices. Stir in the garlic, parsley, rosemary, salt, and pepper, and cook for 1 minute.

4. In a medium bowl, whisk together the remaining 1 cup of milk, the eggs, and the egg white. Spoon 2 cups of the bread mixture into the prepared casserole dish. Top with the mushroom mixture and sprinkle with ⅓ cup of the cheese. Top with the remaining bread mixture and the remaining ⅔ cup cheese. Pour the egg mixture over the top. Bake for 45 minutes, or until set. Let cool 5 minutes before serving.

Black Bean Enchilada
Casserole

Makes 6 to 8 servings

Cooking spray

10 (6-inch) corn tortillas

2 (14½-ounce) cans diced tomatoes

1½ cups chopped green onions, green parts only

1 cup chopped onion

1 cup store-bought salsa or Salsa Rio Grande (page 332)

1 teaspoon ground cumin

2 (11-ounce) cans black bean soup

1 (15-ounce) can black beans, rinsed and drained

10 ounces reduced-fat Cheddar cheese, shredded (2½ cups)

If you find yourself short on time, feel free to buy baked tortilla shells from the grocery store instead of toasting them yourself.

Enjoy this flavorful Mexican dish with a casserole twist that's not only easy to put together but adds pure spice to the dinner routine. Since this recipe calls for you to layer ingredients as a stack, versus individually hand-rolling the enchiladas, we recommend that you bake the corn tortillas separately in the oven until crisp. With traditional enchiladas, the corn tortillas become mushy, but by toasting them in the oven, they help this casserole keep its shape. Serve with light sour cream, fresh salsa, and guacamole for a real fiesta. *Olé!*

1. Preheat the oven to 350°F. Coat a 9 x 13-inch casserole dish with cooking spray.

2. Bake the tortillas in a single layer on baking sheets for about 10 minutes or until crisp. Set aside to cool.

3. In a large skillet set over medium-high heat, combine the tomatoes and their juice, green onions, onion, salsa, and cumin. Bring to a boil, reduce the heat to low, and simmer, uncovered, for 8 minutes.

4. Stir in the soup and black beans, and cook 5 minutes or until heated through.

5. Spread one-third of the bean mixture over the bottom of the prepared casserole dish. Top with half of the tortillas, overlapping as necessary, and sprinkle over 1 cup of the cheese. Add another third of the bean mixture, top with the remaining tortillas, and sprinkle on 1 cup of the cheese. Finish the layers with the last third of the bean mixture and remaining ½ cup cheese.

6. Bake the casserole for 25 to 30 minutes or until heated through, and serve hot.

Cheesy Grits-Stuffed Eggplant Rolls
with Tomato Sauce

Makes 8 to 10 servings

- 2 (28-ounce) cans diced tomatoes
- 2 medium yellow onions, halved
- ½ cup (1 stick) unsalted butter
- 1½ teaspoons salt
- 2 eggplants, cut lengthwise into ⅛-inch slices
- 2 tablespoons olive oil
  Cooking spray
- 1 cup quick-cooking grits
- 1½ cups Veggie Broth (page 337)
- 1 cup heavy cream
- 1½ teaspoons Creole Seasoning (page 331)
- 1 (5-ounce) package fresh baby spinach, chopped
- 1 cup shredded Parmesan cheese (4 ounces)
- 1 cup shredded mozzarella cheese (4 ounces)

After the fun time we had on *Throwdown! with Bobby Flay,* we were asked to shoot a pilot for a Casserole Queens TV show. The setup was that we had to make a casserole for a Harlem church choir's potluck fundraiser. We immediately got excited thinking about all the eclectic flavors and different cuisines that Harlem had to offer, but the twist was that our church members had several dietary restrictions: no shellfish, no pork, no red meat. What a challenge! We decided on serving these remarkable eggplant rolls. Not only are they extremely delectable, they're also elegant and filling. Though the show didn't take off, we think we made out like bandits with this fabulous recipe!

1. In a heavy medium saucepan set over medium heat, combine the tomatoes, onion, and butter. Bring to a simmer and keep the sauce at a slow, steady simmer for about 45 minutes, or until it has thickened. Remove the pan from heat, discard the onion, and add 1 teaspoon of the salt.

2. Meanwhile, preheat the oven to 425°F.

3. Arrange the eggplant slices in a single layer on a nonstick baking sheet. Using a pastry brush, lightly brush both sides of each slice with the olive oil. Bake for 10 minutes, flip, and cook the second side for another 10 minutes.

4. Reduce the oven temperature to 350°F. Spray a 9 x 13-inch casserole dish with cooking spray.

5. In a medium saucepan set over medium-high heat, combine the grits, vegetable broth, heavy cream, the remaining $1/2$ teaspoon of salt, and the Creole Seasoning, and bring the mixture to a boil. Reduce the heat to low and simmer, stirring occasionally, for 5 minutes, or until thickened. Remove the pan from the heat and stir in the spinach, $1/2$ cup of the Parmesan cheese, and $1/2$ cup of the mozzarella cheese. Stir well.

6. Put 1 slice of eggplant on a work surface. Put 2 tablespoons of the grits mixture on the large end of the eggplant slice. Roll the eggplant from the large end toward the small end to enclose the grits. Put the eggplant roll seam side down in the prepared casserole dish. Repeat with the remaining eggplant slices and grits mixture. Pour the tomato sauce over the rolls and sprinkle the top with the remaining $1/2$ cup of Parmesan cheese and the remaining $1/2$ cup of mozzarella cheese.

7. Bake for 25 minutes or until heated through. Remove from the oven and let rest for 5 minutes before serving.

FREEZES WELL For best results, prepare the casserole through step 6. Wrap in foil and freeze for up to 2 months. Thaw the casserole overnight in the refrigerator before baking as stated in the recipe. Note that casseroles that have not been completely thawed may take 15 to 30 minutes longer, so be sure to check for bubbling edges and a hot center.

Rustic Polenta
Casserole

Makes 6 servings

Cooking spray

1 teaspoon olive oil

2 cups chopped onion (about 2 onions)

3 cups (12 ounces) coarsely chopped shiitake mushrooms

2 garlic cloves, minced

1½ teaspoons salt

⅓ cup red wine

1 tablespoon tomato paste

1 tablespoon chopped fresh thyme

1 (15-ounce) can diced tomatoes

1 cup polenta

½ cup shredded Asiago cheese (2 ounces)

¼ teaspoon freshly ground black pepper

½ cup fresh goat cheese

1½ teaspoons unsalted butter, cut into small pieces

This dish comes together fast for a simple weeknight meal, and it's also elegant enough to serve to any important guest. So the next time you get the unexpected call from your spouse saying that the boss is coming over for dinner, you will know what to serve! Pair it with our Panzanella Salad (page 274) for a delightful and filling vegetarian meal.

1. Preheat the oven to 400°F. Spray a 9 x 13-inch casserole dish with cooking spray.

2. Heat the oil in a medium sauté pan set over medium-high heat. Add the onions and cook for 8 minutes, until they start to brown. Add the mushrooms, garlic, and ½ teaspoon of the salt, and cook, stirring, for 4 minutes. Add the wine, tomato paste, and thyme and cook for 3 minutes. Stir in the tomatoes, reduce heat to medium, and cook for 10 minutes, or until thick.

3. Bring 4 cups of water to a boil in a medium saucepan. Stir in the polenta and the remaining 1 teaspoon of the salt. Reduce the heat to low and cook, stirring, for 20 to 30 minutes, or until thick.

4. Spread a third of the polenta into the prepared casserole dish. Spread half of the tomato sauce over the polenta and sprinkle with 2 tablespoons of the Asiago cheese and $\frac{1}{8}$ teaspoon of the pepper. Crumble and sprinkle half of the goat cheese across the casserole. Repeat the layers, ending with the last third of the polenta. Top with the remaining $\frac{1}{4}$ cup of the Asiago cheese and top with the butter.

5. Bake for 25 minutes, or until bubbly.

FREEZES WELL For best results, prepare the casserole through step 4. Wrap in foil and freeze for up to 2 months. Thaw the casserole overnight in the refrigerator before baking as stated in the recipe. Note that casseroles that have not been completely thawed may take 15 to 30 minutes longer, so be sure to check for bubbling edges and a hot center.

Spinach and Gruyère Soufflé

Makes 8 servings

- 2 tablespoons unsalted butter, plus more for the dish
- 2 tablespoons all-purpose flour, plus more for the dish
- 1 cup whole milk
- ¼ teaspoon cayenne
- ¼ teaspoon ground nutmeg
- ½ teaspoon salt, plus a pinch more for the egg whites
- ½ teaspoon freshly ground black pepper
- 6 large egg yolks (see Note, opposite)
- 8 ounces fresh spinach
- 1½ cups Gruyère cheese (6 ounces)
- 6 large egg whites, at room temperature

Canapés. En croûte. Flambé. Soufflé. Why do all those words with the little accent marks seem so intimidating? Technically, canapés are just tiny appetizers. En croûte ("in a crust") is basically just wrapping puff pastry around something. To flambé is to set fire to something. And the secret to a successful soufflé is to beat the heck out of some egg whites. Seriously, folks, if you've never made a soufflé before, don't be afraid. They are actually quite easy to make, and our recipe contains simple shortcuts to make the process easier on you. Traditionally, savory soufflés rely on a béchamel sauce (again another scary word with an accent mark), but we skip the sauce and just use eggs and cheese for the custard. What cheese you ask? Why Gruyère (with the accent mark) of course!

1. Preheat the oven to 375°F. Butter a 9 x 13-inch casserole dish and dust with flour.

2. In a medium saucepan set over medium heat, melt the butter. Add the flour and cook for 2 minutes, stirring constantly. Remove the pan from the heat and add the milk, cayenne, nutmeg, the ½ teaspoon of salt, and the pepper. Whisk well, making sure to get all the flour off the bottom of the pan. Return the pan to the heat and cook, whisking constantly, until the mixture is thick and smooth, 3 to 5 minutes. Remove the pan from the heat and add the egg yolks, spinach, and cheese. Stir well.

3. In a large bowl, whisk the egg whites with a pinch of salt until stiff peaks form.

4. Whisk a quarter of the egg whites into the cheese mixture to lighten it, then gently fold in the rest of the egg whites. Pour the mixture into the prepared casserole dish. Bake for about 35 minutes, until the soufflé has risen and is firm to the touch. The key to serving a soufflé is to get it to the table before it falls. Have a serving tray right near the oven, or a trivet placed on the dinner table. That way, when the soufflé comes out, it can be served immediately with a large spoon.

This dish can be made GLUTEN-FREE by replacing the flour with a gluten-free all-purpose mix, either store bought (see page 21 for recommendations of our favorite brands) or homemade (see page 322 for our recipe).

Eggs separate more easily when cold, but the whites whip up better at room temperature.

The Great Pumpkin Pasta

Makes 6 servings

Cooking spray

1 pound uncooked penne pasta

2 teaspoons olive oil

1 medium onion, finely chopped

2 garlic cloves, minced

2 small zucchini, halved lengthwise and sliced

1 bunch kale, thick stems removed and leaves coarsely chopped

1 teaspoon dried sage

½ teaspoon dried thyme

2 teaspoons salt

½ teaspoon ground cinnamon

1 (15-ounce) can pumpkin puree (not pumpkin pie filling)

1 cup part-skim ricotta cheese

½ cup Veggie Broth (page 337)

1 cup shredded Parmesan cheese (4 ounces)

¼ cup pumpkin seeds, toasted

There is something magical that happens in late September: pumpkin-flavored foods are suddenly everywhere you turn. There are pumpkin-spiced lattes, pumpkin breads, pumpkin beer, and hold on . . . there are even pumpkin-flavored Pop-Tarts! To all of those things, we say, yes, please! And we continue to say yes until the end of November, when flavors turn to peppermint and gingerbread. We love the fall for this pumpkin explosion, and we decided that there's no need to wait until then to satisfy our craving. This amazing pasta delivers that pumpkin fix whenever we need it.

1. Preheat the oven to 400°F. Spray a 9 x 13-inch casserole dish with cooking spray.

2. In a large pot, cook the pasta according to the package directions. Drain and set aside.

3. In a large sauté pan set over medium-high heat, heat the olive oil. Add the onion and garlic and cook for about 5 minutes, until softened. Add the zucchini, kale, sage, thyme, salt, and cinnamon and sauté for about 5 minutes, or until the kale wilts. Stir in the pumpkin and ricotta cheese. Add the pasta and the vegetable broth to the pan and mix well. Spoon the mixture into the prepared casserole dish and sprinkle the top with the Parmesan cheese and pumpkin seeds.

4. Bake for 10 to 15 minutes, until heated through.

This dish can be made GLUTEN-FREE by using a gluten-free brand of pasta, such as Gilda's Gluten Free House La Rosa Penne. See page 21 for recommendations of our other favorite brands.

The Nelly Frittata

Makes 6 to 8 servings

- 1 tablespoon unsalted butter
- 1 tablespoon vegetable oil
- 1 bunch asparagus, trimmed and chopped
- 1 medium onion, cut in half and sliced
- 1/2 cup grated Parmesan cheese (2 ounces)
- 8 large eggs
- 1/4 cup whole milk
- 1 teaspoon salt
- 1/2 teaspoon freshly ground black pepper
- 1 tablespoon chopped fresh thyme

Get it? Nelly Frittata . . . Nelly Furtado . . . funny, right? All kidding aside, this is one serious frittata. Packed with asparagus, thyme, onions, and Parmesan cheese, this frittata is bursting with flavor and is naturally gluten-free, vegetarian, and diabetic-friendly! Fabulous, healthy, and all around awesome, just like Nelly herself! Serve with your favorite salad greens and our Lemon Parmesan Dressing (page 257) or our A Few of Sandy's Favorite Things Orzo Pasta Salad (page 275) for a light dinner or special brunch.

1. Preheat the oven to 350°F.

2. In a 12-inch ovenproof skillet set over medium-high heat, heat the butter and oil. Add the asparagus and onion and sauté for 12 to 14 minutes, or until the onion is tender. Remove the pan from the heat, and stir in 1/4 cup of the cheese.

3. In a medium bowl, whisk together the eggs, milk, salt, and pepper until well blended. Pour over the vegetable mixture.

4. Bake for 13 to 15 minutes, or until set. Increase the oven temperature to Broil, and broil for 1 to 2 minutes, or until the edges are lightly browned. Remove the pan from the oven and sprinkle with the remaining 1/4 cup of cheese and the thyme. Serve hot.

Butternut Squash Gratin
with Asiago Cheese
and Toasted Pine Nuts

Makes 8 to 10 servings

- ¼ cup (½ stick) unsalted butter
- 2 medium butternut squash, peeled, seeded, and cut into ¾-inch cubes
- 2 tablespoons olive oil
- 1 teaspoon salt, plus more to taste
- ½ teaspoon freshly ground black pepper, plus more to taste
- 2 leeks, white and pale green parts, cleaned and thinly sliced (3 cups)
- 1½ teaspoons chopped fresh sage
- 1½ cups Asiago cheese, shredded (8 ounces)
- 1 cup heavy cream
- ½ cup pine nuts, toasted

When Sandy and Crystal really like something they see on a menu, they can't help but exclaim, "I want to eat that with my face!" Silly? Yes. But it gets the point across, don't you think? The nuttiness of the Asiago cheese and the savory flavor of the sage balance out the sweetness of the squash—making one harmonious dish! Serve along with a simple green salad with our Balsamic Vinaigrette (page 262) and a side of our Braised Endive Gratin (page 211). Delish!

1. Preheat the oven to 375°F. Grease a 9 x 13-inch casserole dish with 1 tablespoon of the butter.

2. Put the butternut squash and olive oil in a large bowl, sprinkle with the 1 teaspoon of salt and the ½ teaspoon of pepper, and toss to coat. Spread the squash out on a large rimmed baking sheet. Roast, stirring occasionally, for 35 minutes, or until just tender and beginning to brown. Remove the pan from the oven and set aside to cool slightly.

3. In a medium saucepan set over medium-low heat, melt the remaining 3 tablespoons butter, then add the leeks, sage, and salt and pepper to taste. Cook, stirring, until tender, about 10 minutes.

4. Spread half of the leek mixture in the bottom of the prepared casserole dish. Cover with half of the squash and half of the cheese. Repeat the layers of leeks, squash, and cheese.

5. Pour the cream evenly over the casserole and bake for 25 minutes. Pull the casserole out of the oven and sprinkle the top with pine nuts. Return the pan to the oven and bake for 15 more minutes, or until bubbling around the edges.

Shepherdless Pie

Makes 6 servings

Cooking spray

2 teaspoons olive oil

1 onion, chopped

2 celery stalks, diced

1 garlic clove, minced

1 small butternut squash, peeled, seeded, and cut into ¾-inch cubes

3 carrots, chopped

1 cup broccoli, chopped

1 (15.5-ounce) can kidney beans

2 red bell peppers, seeded and chopped

1 (15-ounce) can diced tomatoes

1 teaspoon chopped fresh parsley

2 tablespoons cornstarch

4 sweet potatoes

1 cup vegetable broth, homemade (page 337) or store bought, warmed

We're never sheepish about serving our meatless version of this traditional comfort food, and you shouldn't be either. The kidney beans satisfy meat lovers with their hearty flavor, while sweet potatoes and winter vegetables provide a nice twist on a classic dish. Your flock won't want to stray far from the dinner table when this is on the menu! Serve along with our Dill Bread (page 229) to complete the meal.

1. Preheat the oven to 400°F. Spray a 9 x 13-inch casserole dish with cooking spray.

2. In a large sauté pan set over medium heat, heat the olive oil. Add the onion, celery, and garlic, and cook for 5 minutes. Add the squash, carrots, and broccoli. Cook for 10 minutes, or until the carrots start to soften. Add the beans, peppers, and tomatoes. Bring the mixture to a simmer and cook until the squash is just tender, 15 minutes. Stir in the parsley and cornstarch. Transfer to the prepared casserole dish.

3. Meanwhile, pierce each sweet potato several times with a fork. Bake them for 45 minutes, or until tender. Let cool until they can be handled. Peel the sweet potatoes and put them in a large bowl. Add the warm vegetable broth and whisk until smooth. Spread the mashed sweet potatoes over the stew.

4. Bake for 15 minutes, or until the top is a lovely golden brown.

Farro, Wild Mushroom, and Walnut Casserole

Makes 8 servings

Cooking spray

1½ cups uncooked farro

1 teaspoon salt

2 tablespoons olive oil

2 medium onions, chopped

6 cups sliced fresh shiitake mushroom caps (about 12 ounces)

1 tablespoon chopped fresh thyme

1 tablespoon chopped fresh sage

½ teaspoon freshly ground black pepper

½ cup white wine

⅔ cup dried cranberries

⅔ cup walnuts, chopped

Farro—which is sometimes called spelt or emmer wheat—is one of the first grains ever discovered. It is a unique alternative to pasta and rice because of its distinctive chewy texture and is healthy, tasty, and versatile. Higher in fiber and protein than wheat, farro is also especially rich in magnesium and B vitamins. Its nutty flavor makes it a welcome addition to soups and salads, and it serves as the star of this savory stuffing-type dish.

1. Preheat the oven to 350°F. Spray a 9 x 13-inch casserole dish with cooking spray.

2. In a large pot set over high heat, combine 5 cups of water with the farro and ½ teaspoon salt. Bring the mixture to a boil. Reduce the heat to medium and simmer for 15 minutes, or until the farro is al dente. Drain and set aside.

3. In a large saucepan set over medium heat, heat 1 tablespoon of the oil. Add the onions and cook, stirring, for 2 minutes. Reduce the heat to medium-low and cook until the onions are tender and lightly browned, 15 to 20 minutes.

4. In a large skillet set over medium-high heat, heat the remaining 1 tablespoon oil. Add the mushrooms, thyme, sage, pepper, and the remaining ½ teaspoon salt. Cook, stirring occasionally, for 5 minutes, until the mushrooms have released their juices. Add the wine and cook for 4 to 5 minutes, or until the liquid evaporates. Add the mushroom mixture, onions, and the cranberries to the cooked farro and stir well. Put the mixture into the prepared casserole dish, sprinkle the walnuts over the top, and cover the dish with foil.

5. Bake for 30 minutes, until all the liquid has been absorbed and the farro is tender. Let stand for 5 minutes before serving.

This dish can be made GLUTEN-FREE by substituting a gluten-free wild rice blend, such as Lundberg's, for the farro.

FREEZES WELL For best results, prepare the casserole through step 4. Wrap in foil and freeze for up to 2 months. Thaw the casserole overnight in the refrigerator before baking as stated in the recipe. Note that casseroles that have not been completely thawed may take 15 to 30 minutes longer, so be sure to check for bubbling edges and a hot center.

Sides
That Take Front and Center

Who can think of sides when they're overshadowed by gourmet delicacies? We can. Here are a whole bunch of lip-smacking, stick-to-your-ribs, make-them-go-"mmm" recipes that will leave everyone asking for more. Some recipes may play a support role, while others may try to steal the show. We've learned that the main course doesn't always have to be the main event. Inventive sides like our creamy Cauliflower Gratin (page 212), and our light (yet very flavorful) Herb-Baked Caprese Tomato Stacks (page 200), can transform mealtime standbys into real standouts. They're quick and easy, too—very desirable qualities for those cooks who have a gazillion other things to do besides cook. Enjoy a wide range of dishes that will bring the best to any occasion, including heaping portions of praise.

Lunch Lady Doris's
Spicy Mac & Cheese

Makes 8 servings

- 1½ cups dried elbow macaroni
- 2½ cups fresh or frozen broccoli florets
- ½ cup sun-dried tomatoes
- 2 tablespoons unsalted butter
- ⅓ cup sliced green onions, green parts only
- 2 tablespoons all-purpose flour
- ½ teaspoon cayenne
- 1½ teaspoons dried basil
- 1 teaspoon salt
- 1¾ cups whole milk
- 6 ounces sharp Cheddar cheese, shredded (1½ cups)
- 4 ounces Gruyère cheese, grated (1 cup)
- 4 ounces Gouda cheese, grated (1 cup)

FREEZES WELL
See our freezer tips on page 16.

Who said macaroni and cheese is just for kids? It may have been during our adolescent days in the lunchroom where we fell in love with this all-American comfort dish, but this is not the macaroni and cheese of your childhood! Our version includes savory veggies, a rich medley of grown-up cheeses, and just enough cayenne to take this simple comfort food to a new gourmet delight. Makes a complete meal on its own or is a great side for just about anything, but we suggest serving it with some creamy tomato soup. Delish!

1. Preheat the oven to 350°F.

2. Cook the macaroni according to package instructions. If you are using fresh broccoli, blanch in hot salted water for 5 minutes, then drain. If you are using frozen broccoli, thaw and drain it. Add the broccoli to the macaroni. Set aside.

3. Meanwhile, place the sun-dried tomatoes in a small bowl and add enough warm water to cover. Let stand for 10 minutes or until softened. Drain well, then chop into ¼-inch pieces and set aside.

4. Melt the butter in a medium saucepan set over medium heat. Add the green onions and cook until tender, about 5 minutes. Stir in the flour, cayenne, basil, and salt. Add the milk, and cook, stirring, until slightly thickened and bubbly. Add ¾ cup of the Cheddar, the Gruyère, and Gouda, a little at a time, stirring well after each addition, until the cheeses are melted. Stir in the macaroni and broccoli mixture and the softened sun-dried tomatoes. Transfer to a 9 x 13-inch casserole dish and sprinkle the top of the casserole with the remaining ¾ cup Cheddar cheese.

5. Bake for about 30 minutes or until the cheese is melted and the casserole is heated through.

Broccoli *Cornbread*

Makes 6 to 8 servings

Cooking spray

1 (16-ounce) box corn muffin mix

1½ cups cottage cheese

1 (10-ounce) box frozen broccoli cuts, thawed and well drained

¾ cup (1½ sticks) unsalted butter, melted

3 large eggs

¼ teaspoon salt

Sandy doesn't even like cornbread, and yet this is one of her favorite dishes. If you weren't one before, we'll make a cornbread lover out of you, too. This dish is extremely easy to make and works great when paired with our CQ's Royal Cottage Pie (page 42) or our Shrimply Delicious Shrimp and Grits (page 78). It also can stand proud all on its own, making a great appetizer or a replacement for the rolls in your bread basket!

1. Preheat the oven to 350°F. Lightly coat a 9 x 13-inch casserole dish with cooking spray.

2. Combine the muffin mix, cottage cheese, broccoli, butter, eggs, and salt in a large bowl. Pour into the prepared casserole dish and bake for 30 minutes or until the center is firm and the top is golden brown.

Broccoli Rabe
with Shallots

Makes 6 to 8 servings

- 2 bunches broccoli rabe
- 2 tablespoons extra-virgin olive oil
- 4 medium shallots, minced
- 1 teaspoon salt
- ½ teaspoon red pepper flakes

Broccoli rabe (think "rob" when you say it, not "babe"!) is made up of long, leafy greens with small broccoli-like florets. Although broccoli and broccoli rabe are similarly named and are both rich in vitamins and nutrients, the two vegetables are pretty different. The biggest difference is how they taste. Broccoli rabe is slightly bitter, so we suggest that you blanch it first before you sauté it in the yummy shallot-infused oil. Pair it with our Super-Simple Spinach-Stuffed Shells (page 82) to impress your guests! They will never know that dinner came together in such a flash.

1. Trim the ends off the broccoli rabe. Bring a large pot of salted water to a rapid boil over high heat. Add the broccoli rabe and cook for about 3 minutes. Use a slotted spoon to transfer the broccoli rabe to a large bowl of ice-cold water to stop the cooking. When completely cold, drain it well.

2. Heat the oil in a 12-inch nonstick skillet set over moderate heat. Add the shallots and cook, stirring occasionally, until they have browned slightly, about 5 minutes. Add the broccoli rabe and cook for 8 to 10 minutes, or until the broccoli rabe starts to brown. Season with the salt and red pepper flakes. Serve warm.

Oh Boy!
Broccoli Casserole

Makes 6 to 8 servings

Cooking spray

3 cups cooked long-grain white rice (see page 329)

2 (10-ounce) packages frozen chopped broccoli, thawed and drained

1½ cups Cream of Mushroom Soup (page 339)

8 ounces Cheddar or Monterey Jack cheese, shredded (2 cups)

½ cup chopped onion

¼ cup whole milk

2 tablespoons unsalted butter, softened

Helping kids everywhere learn to love broccoli! This classic broccoli, cheese, and rice casserole will quickly become a favorite in your family. (Maybe they'll forget to complain about eating something green.)

1. Preheat the oven to 350°F. Coat a 2-quart casserole dish with cooking spray.

2. Combine the cooked rice, the broccoli, soup, cheese, onion, milk, and butter in a large bowl. Spoon the mixture into the prepared casserole dish. Bake for 45 minutes, or until the cheese has melted and the casserole is heated through.

This dish can be made GLUTEN-FREE by using gluten-free Cream of Mushroom Soup in place of our recipe (see page 21 for recommendations of our favorite brands).

FREEZES WELL
See our freezer tips on page 16.

Brussels Sprouts
with Bacon, Garlic, and Shallots

Makes 8 servings

6 slices bacon, chopped

1½ pounds Brussels sprouts, trimmed and halved

½ cup sliced shallots (about 1 large)

6 garlic cloves, thinly sliced

¾ cup Chicken Broth (page 335) or store bought

⅛ teaspoon salt

⅛ teaspoon freshly ground black pepper

Brussels sprouts are a food that seldom elicits a cheer from dinner guests. But when you serve them like this, you're gonna get a "Heck, yeah!" Brussels sprouts are pleasingly bitter when sautéed and are perfect for pairing with bacon. Your guests may start doing cartwheels and backflips and try to form themselves into a pyramid. Don't say we didn't warn you! Serve with our Chicken with 40 Cloves of Garlic (page 65).

1. Heat a large nonstick skillet over medium heat. Add the bacon and cook for 5 minutes, or until it begins to brown. Transfer the bacon to a paper towel–lined plate.

2. Increase the heat to medium-high. Add the Brussels sprouts and shallots to the bacon fat and cook for 4 minutes. Add the garlic and cook for 4 more minutes, stirring frequently, or until the garlic begins to brown. Add the chicken broth and bring the mixture to a boil. Cook for 5 minutes, or until the stock mostly evaporates and the sprouts are crisp-tender, stirring occasionally. Remove the pan from the heat. Season with the salt and pepper. Stir in the bacon and serve.

Onion Surprise
Casserole

Makes 6 to 8 servings

- ¼ cup plus 2 tablespoons (¾ stick) unsalted butter
- 3 medium Texas 1015 or Vidalia onions, chopped
- 8 ounces Swiss cheese, grated (2 cups)
- 1 cup crushed saltine crackers
- 2 large eggs
- ¾ cup heavy cream
- 1 teaspoon salt
- ⅛ teaspoon freshly ground black pepper

One day, when thumbing through her mom's recipe box, Sandy found this recipe from her Aunt Estelle. On the recipe card, Aunt Estelle had simply written the comment: "This is really good." Knowing the caliber of cook that Estelle is, Sandy and her mom decided to try it, even though an onion casserole didn't really sound like much. To their surprise, this is an absolutely amazing side dish.

This recipe features the delicious 1015 onion. Created in Weslaco (just down the road from where Sandy grew up) by Leonard Pike, at the Texas A&M University Extension Service, Texas 1015 onions are known for their mild, juicy, and sweet characteristics, as well as the fact that they contain very little pyruvate (the chemical that causes strong flavor and leads to tears). So, no more crying in the kitchen—cooking is supposed to be fun!

1. Preheat the oven to 350°F.

2. Melt ¼ cup (4 tablespoons) of the butter in a large skillet set over medium-high heat. Add the onions and sauté until tender and translucent, about 8 minutes. Put half of the onions into a 9 x 13-inch casserole dish. Sprinkle with 1 cup of the cheese and ½ cup of the cracker crumbs. Repeat the layers of onion and cheese.

3. In a medium bowl, lightly beat the eggs, then add the cream, salt, and pepper. Pour the mixture evenly over the casserole.

4. Melt the remaining 2 tablespoons of butter in a small skillet and stir in the remaining ½ cup cracker crumbs. Toast the crumbs until they are lightly brown, about 10 minutes, then sprinkle over the casserole.

5. Bake for 25 minutes, or until the onions have softened and the cracker crust is golden brown.

Herb-Baked Caprese
Tomato Stacks

Makes 8 servings

Cooking spray

3 medium tomatoes, cut into
   ¼-inch-thick slices

Salt and freshly ground
black pepper

8 (¼-inch-thick) slices fresh
   mozzarella

1 tablespoon chopped fresh
   basil

⅓ cup Seasoned Bread Crumbs
   (page 330)

2 teaspoons unsalted butter,
   melted

This dish is so simply prepared, yet yields amazingly complex flavors. Sandy was inspired to make these tasty stacks from ingredients that seemed always to be on hand in her and Michael's home. Because there are so few ingredients in this dish, it is imperative that your ingredients are quality. We also recommend that you take the time to make your bread crumbs from scratch, as it adds that extra something to the dish. And don't worry about any extra bread crumbs getting stale; just store them in the freezer and they will stay fresh for months. If you find yourself with extra basil, don't waste it! Use it to make some tasty Pesto (opposite page).

1. Preheat the oven to 425°F. Coat a 9 x 13-inch casserole dish with cooking spray.

2. Arrange one layer of tomatoes (do not overlap) in the bottom of the casserole dish. Season the tomatoes with salt and pepper. Put a slice of fresh mozzarella on top of each tomato, then top each with basil. Top each stack with another slice of tomato, and season with salt and pepper.

3. Combine the bread crumbs and butter in a small bowl. Sprinkle the crumbs over the stacks.

4. Bake for 5 to 10 minutes or until the tomatoes are heated through, the bread crumbs are lightly browned, and the mozzarella just starts to melt. Serve hot.

Pesto

When a recipe calls for just a bit of fresh basil, don't let the rest go to waste—in fact, buy a little extra (three bunches total) and make a delicious pesto. It's easy!

Makes 1½ cups

- 4 large garlic cloves
- ¾ cup toasted pine nuts
- ¾ cup grated Parmesan cheese (3 ounces)
- 1½ teaspoons salt
- ½ teaspoon freshly ground black pepper
- 3 cups loosely packed fresh basil
- ⅔ cup extra-virgin olive oil

Place ingredients in a food processor and blend. If not using immediately, put the pesto in a zip-top plastic bag and freeze for up to 2 months.

Creamed Carrot Crunch Casserole

Makes 6 to 8 servings

Cooking spray

4 tablespoons (½ stick) unsalted butter

2 pounds carrots, peeled and cut into ¼-inch-thick pieces

1 tablespoon salt, plus more to taste

1 teaspoon freshly ground black pepper

½ teaspoon dried marjoram

2 tablespoons all-purpose flour

1½ cups heavy cream

3 medium garlic cloves, minced

1½ cups panko bread crumbs

Say that three times fast! It'll cook up even faster. This dish is easy to whip up, amazingly creamy and rich, and versatile. We particularly love it with our Damn Skinny Yankee Pot Roast (page 151) and our Tuna Noodle Casserole (page 72).

1. Preheat the oven to 350°F. Lightly coat a 9 x 13-inch casserole dish with cooking spray.

2. Melt 2 tablespoons of the butter in a large skillet set over medium-high heat. Add the carrots, salt, pepper, and marjoram. Cook, stirring occasionally, until the carrots just start to brown, about 7 minutes. Sprinkle the flour over the carrots, stirring constantly. Cook until flour turns golden, 1 to 2 minutes. Slowly pour in the cream while stirring constantly. Bring to a boil, then remove the pan from the heat.

3. Pour the mixture into the prepared casserole dish and cover with aluminum foil. Bake until the cream is bubbling and the carrots just give way when pierced with a knife, 20 to 25 minutes.

4. Meanwhile, melt the remaining 2 tablespoons of butter in a medium skillet set over medium heat. Add the garlic and cook until the butter just begins to brown, about 3 minutes. Add the bread crumbs and season with salt and pepper. Cook, stirring occasionally, until the bread crumbs are lightly browned, about 5 minutes. Transfer to a medium bowl and set aside.

5. When casserole has finished cooking, remove the foil and allow it to sit for about 10 minutes. Sprinkle the toasted bread crumbs evenly over the top before serving.

Asparagus Bundles
Wrapped in Prosciutto

Makes 8 servings

Cooking spray

1 (8-ounce) package whipped cream cheese, at room temperature

3 garlic cloves, minced

3 tablespoons finely chopped fresh chives

1 tablespoon finely chopped fresh flat-leaf parsley

½ teaspoon salt

¼ teaspoon freshly ground black pepper

3 pounds asparagus spears, trimmed to 4- to 5-inch-long tips

Extra-virgin olive oil, for drizzling

8 slices prosciutto

This delicious side dish makes an appearance at Crystal's sister Cindy's holiday table every year. There is just something so elegant about the presentation of the neatly wrapped bundles. Crystal and her sister prefer the texture of the whipped cream cheese because it makes it much easier to fold in the herbs and spread the cheese onto the prosciutto without tearing it. If you can't find whipped cream cheese, regular will do—just let it soften before adding the garlic and herbs. Crystal and her sister also prefer the taste of prosciutto, but you can easily substitute pancetta if need be.

1. Preheat the oven to 400°F. Spray a slotted broiler pan with cooking spray.

2. In a medium bowl, combine the cream cheese, garlic, 2 tablespoons of the chives, and the parsley, salt, and pepper, and stir well. Set aside.

3. Lightly coat asparagus spears in the oil. Divide the asparagus into 8 piles. Take a slice of prosciutto and spread a thin layer of the cream cheese mixture on one side. Take one pile of asparagus and put it on a short end of the prosciutto. Roll the asparagus up in the prosciutto and set the bundle on the prepared broiler pan, seam side down. Repeat with the remaining ingredients.

4. Bake for 10 to 12 minutes, until the asparagus is crisp-tender and the prosciutto has browned. Put on a serving dish and garnish with the remaining 1 tablespoon of chives. Serve warm.

Carrot Soufflé

Makes 8 servings

Cooking spray

1¾ pounds carrots, peeled and chopped

1 teaspoon salt

¼ teaspoon freshly ground black pepper

2 tablespoons unsalted butter

2 tablespoons all-purpose flour

½ cup warm milk

½ cup roasted unsalted almonds, finely chopped

4 large eggs, separated

Sandy always makes this savory, light, and airy carrot soufflé at Thanksgiving. The fall season and root vegetables are a natural combination. For a more elegant presentation, try crowning your soufflé. (After all, we are Queens, ya know!) What does that mean, you ask? Soufflés are most impressive when they rise dramatically over the rim of the baking dish. To create this beautiful crown on your own soufflé, fill the dish about three-quarters full. If it's less full, the soufflé may not rise over the rim; if it's more full, the soufflé may spill over unless you wrap the dish with a collar. Make a "collar" on the rim of the dish with a double layer of parchment paper or aluminum foil that extends 3 inches above the dish. If using foil, coat one side of the foil strip generously with melted butter, and wrap the buttered side of the foil around the outside of dish. Tie the collar securely with kitchen twine.

1. Preheat the oven to 350°F. Spray an 8 x 8-inch casserole dish with cooking spray.

2. Put the carrots in a large pot of lightly salted water. Bring to a boil and cook until the carrots are tender, about 20 minutes. Drain and return the carrots to the pot. Add ½ teaspoon of the salt and the pepper. Mash the carrots with a fork or put them through a potato ricer.

3. In a large saucepan set over medium heat, melt the butter. Add the flour and whisk to combine. Gradually add the milk and the remaining ¹/₂ teaspoon of salt. Bring to a simmer and cook for 5 minutes, or until slightly thickened. Stir in the carrots and almonds. Remove the pan from the heat. Beat the egg yolks together, then stir them into the carrot mixture. Let cool until the mixture is lukewarm.

4. Meanwhile, beat the egg whites until stiff but not dry, about 4 minutes. Fold the egg whites into the carrot mixture. Gently pour the mixture into the prepared dish. Bake for 50 to 60 minutes, until the soufflé feels firm at the center, or until a sharp knife inserted in the center comes out clean. Serve immediately, scooping out portions with a large spoon.

This dish can be made GLUTEN-FREE by replacing the flour with a gluten-free all-purpose mix, either store bought (see page 21 for recommendations of our favorite brands) or homemade (see page 322 for our recipe).

Corn Pudding

Makes 6 to 8 servings

Cooking spray

2 tablespoons olive oil

½ green bell pepper, finely chopped

1 small onion, finely chopped

1 tablespoon all-purpose flour

1 (16-ounce) can creamed corn

1 cup Seasoned Bread Crumbs (page 330) or store bought

1 cup whole milk

1 large egg

1 teaspoon salt

Summers wouldn't be complete without fresh, sweet corn! When Crystal first moved to Austin, Sandy introduced her to a type of Mexican street food that very well may have changed the way she viewed life: gigantic ears of roasted corn smothered in Mexican *crema* and sprinkled with lots of spice and lime juice. They call it *elote*, but we call it delish! It is the perfect treat, the sweetness of the corn blending so perfectly with the southwestern spices.

Another one of our favorite ways to enjoy summer corn is in this pudding. Our love of *elote* made us realize that this sweet, velvety dish is an ideal match for some of our spicier fare. Try serving it with Yvonne's Unstuffed Poblano Casserole (page 108) for a real fiesta!

1. Preheat the oven to 350°F. Spray a 9 x 13-inch casserole dish with cooking spray.

2. In a large skillet set over medium-high heat, heat the olive oil. Add the bell pepper and onion and cook for 6 minutes, or until they are soft. Add the flour and stir to coat the veggies. Cook for 1 minute more, to cook out the raw-flour taste.

3. In a large bowl, combine the corn, ½ cup of the bread crumbs, the milk, egg, and salt. Add the onion mixture to the bowl and mix well. Pour the mixture into the prepared casserole dish. Sprinkle the remaining ½ cup of bread crumbs on top.

4. Bake for 30 minutes, or until browned and set. Serve hot.

This dish can be made GLUTEN-FREE by replacing the flour with a gluten-free all-purpose mix, either store bought (see page 21 for recommendations of our favorite brands) or homemade (see page 322 for our recipe). You can also purchase gluten-free bread crumbs (see page 21 for brands) or make your own.

FREEZES WELL For best results, prepare the casserole through step 3. Wrap in foil and freeze for up to 2 months. Thaw the casserole overnight in the refrigerator before baking as stated in the recipe. Note that casseroles that have not been completely thawed may take 15 to 30 minutes longer, so be sure to check for bubbling edges and a hot center.

A+ Asparagus

Makes 6 to 8 servings

Cooking spray

2 pounds fresh asparagus

7 tablespoons unsalted butter

2 shallots, minced

2 garlic cloves, minced

1 (12-ounce) jar marinated artichoke hearts, drained and rinsed

1 pound baby portobello mushrooms, thickly sliced

½ teaspoon salt

½ teaspoon freshly ground black pepper

1 cup Ritz cracker crumbs

2 tablespoons all-purpose flour

1¾ cups heavy cream

¼ teaspoon cayenne

1 teaspoon smoked paprika

4 ounces Cheddar cheese, grated (1 cup)

Every Christmas, Crystal's family (the Cook side) gets together for a holiday party at her Aunt Mary Ann's. Since the family is so large, it's the one time of year that everyone makes the effort to be there to visit with one another. Everyone brings a dish for the buffet, and we all eat like kings and queens. Crystal's Aunt Sonja is known as one of the family's best cooks. Always aiming to impress her guests, she relies on this side dish to do just that. And if you ever thought asparagus was boring, you'll change your mind once you taste it all dolled up with shallots, artichokes, and baby portobello mushrooms. It's a real showstopper.

1. Preheat the oven to 350°F. Coat a 9 x 13-inch casserole dish with cooking spray.

2. Hold an asparagus spear with both hands, about 2 inches from the end. Gently bend the asparagus until it snaps. It will break at the point where the stem is too tough to be enjoyable; discard the stem. Repeat for all your asparagus. Cook the asparagus in boiling water until crisp-tender, 2 to 3 minutes. Drain and set aside.

3. Melt 3 tablespoons of the butter in a medium sauté pan set over medium-high heat. Add the shallots and garlic, and sauté until soft, about 5 minutes. Add the artichoke hearts and mushrooms, and cook until tender, about 10 minutes. Season with ¼ teaspoon of the salt and ¼ teaspoon of the pepper. Set aside.

4. Melt 2 tablespoons of the butter in a small bowl. Add the cracker crumbs and stir well. Put three-quarters of the cracker crumbs into the prepared casserole dish. Spoon the artichoke mixture on top of the crumbs and top with the asparagus.

5. Melt the remaining 2 tablespoons of the butter in a saucepan set over medium heat. Add the flour and cook until it turns light brown and forms a paste. Slowly stir in the cream, cayenne, paprika, remaining ¼ teaspoon salt, and remaining ¼ teaspoon pepper. Cook, stirring, until the mixture thickens, about 10 minutes. Pour the sauce over the vegetables, and sprinkle with the cheese and the remaining cracker crumbs.

6. Bake 25 to 30 minutes or until the sauce is bubbly and the cheese is melted.

Paprika is made from ground dried bell peppers or chilies. It can range from sweet to spicy, depending on the kind of pepper used. Smoked paprika is generally harder to find than regular mild paprika, but take it from Crystal—it's worth the effort. This dish benefits from the added rich, smoky flavor.

Sweet Potato
Casserole

Makes 6 to 8 servings

- 8 large sweet potatoes
- 2/3 cup packed light brown sugar
- 2/3 cup pecans, toasted
- 1/2 cup all-purpose flour
- 5 tablespoons unsalted butter, plus more for greasing the casserole dish
- 3/4 cup heavy cream
- 1/2 cup pure maple syrup
- 1 large egg, beaten
- 2 teaspoons vanilla extract
- 1 teaspoon salt

Wham bam, thank you, yam! Even if you've never been a sweet potato fan, you will love this seriously delicious casserole. No marshmallows needed here—brown sugar, pecans, and maple syrup make this dish so irresistibly tempting that seconds are rarely turned down.

1. Preheat the oven to 400°F.

2. Wash the sweet potatoes, dry well, and put on a baking sheet. Bake for about 1 hour or until soft. Remove the potatoes from the oven.

3. Reduce the oven temperature to 375°F.

4. Put the brown sugar, pecans, flour, and 5 tablespoons butter in the bowl of a food processor. Pulse until crumbly. Transfer the mixture to a bowl and put in the refrigerator until ready to use.

5. In the bowl of a stand mixer, fitted with the paddle attachment, add the cream, maple syrup, egg, vanilla, and salt. Peel the baked sweet potatoes, and add the flesh to the bowl. Beat the sweet potato mixture on medium-high speed until smooth.

6. Grease a 9 x 13-inch casserole dish with some butter. Pour the sweet potato mixture into the dish and smooth the top with the back of a spoon. Sprinkle the pecan topping evenly over the dish. Bake for 40 minutes or until heated through and the top has browned.

To quickly toast nuts and seeds without your constant attention, place 1/4 cup of nuts or seeds in a microwave dish and add 1 teaspoon butter. Microwave on high for about 5 minutes, stirring once after 2 minutes. While the nuts or seeds are toasting, you can be doing something else, like pouring yourself a glass of wine!

Braised Endive
Gratin

Makes 8 servings

Cooking spray

¼ cup (½ stick) unsalted butter

3 tablespoons fresh lemon juice

1 tablespoon granulated sugar

½ teaspoon salt

8 endive, cut in half

2 cups bread crumbs (page 330) or store bought

1 cup shredded Parmesan cheese (4 ounces)

2 tablespoons chopped fresh parsley

Cooking endive in a bit of butter and lemon juice transforms its otherwise crisp and bitter leaves into tender, luscious, almost sweet bundles. This recipe is great as a side dish for our "Like a Good Neighbor" Ham and Gruyère Strata (page 62), as well as just for snacking! Tasty!

1. Preheat the oven to 350°F. Spray a 9 x 13-inch casserole dish with cooking spray.

2. In a large sauté pan set over medium heat, melt 2 tablespoons of the butter. Add the lemon juice, sugar, and salt, and stir well. Put the endive, cut side down, into the butter and cook for 5 minutes. Flip the endive over and cook the second side for 5 minutes, or until the endive start to brown. Put the endive, cut side down, into the prepared casserole dish. Cover the dish and bake for 15 minutes, or until a knife can be easily inserted in the endive.

3. Meanwhile, in a small saucepan set over medium heat, melt the remaining 2 tablespoons of butter. Add the bread crumbs and stir. Pour the bread crumbs into a bowl, add the cheese and parsley, and toss to combine.

4. Remove the dish from the oven and sprinkle the top of the endive with the bread crumb mixture. Return the dish to the oven and bake for 5 more minutes to brown the bread crumbs. Serve hot.

This dish can be made GLUTEN-FREE by using gluten-free bread crumbs, either store bought (see page 21 for recommendations of our favorite brands) or homemade (see page 330 for our recipe).

This recipe can be made DIABETIC-FRIENDLY by substituting a pinch of stevia for the sugar. Note that you only need a pinch, as stevia is about 300 times sweeter than sugar.

Cauliflower
Gratin

Makes 6 to 8 servings

- 8 tablespoons (1 stick) unsalted butter
- 2 heads of cauliflower, cut into florets
- Salt
- ½ cup finely chopped onion
- 2 garlic cloves, minced
- ½ cup all-purpose flour
- 3 cups whole milk
- 14 ounces Gruyère cheese, grated (3½ cups)
- 3 tablespoons chopped fresh flat-leaf parsley
- Freshly ground black pepper
- ⅔ cup panko bread crumbs
- 2 tablespoons chopped fresh chives

We even made cauliflower taste amazing. This dish is a standout, with roasted cauliflower smothered in a rich, creamy Gruyère sauce. The cauliflower develops a nice, deep browning from roasting that gives the gratin a fantastic sweet, nutty flavor. We like to serve this with our Charlotte's Prime Rib (page 96) or our Mandarin Meatloaf (page 160).

1. Preheat the oven to 400°F.

2. Melt 4 tablespoons of the butter. Put the cauliflower in a large roasting pan, drizzle the melted butter over the cauliflower, and toss well. Season liberally with salt, and roast in the oven for 30 minutes or until soft and slightly browned. Remove the pan from the oven, and set aside. Reduce the oven temperature to 350°F.

3. In a medium saucepan set over medium heat, melt 2 tablespoons of the butter. Add the onion and sauté until tender, about 8 minutes. Add the garlic and sauté for 1 minute. Add the flour and cook, whisking constantly, for 1 minute. Gradually add the milk while whisking constantly. Bring the mixture to a boil. Reduce the heat to low and simmer, stirring constantly, until the mixture has thickened, about 10 minutes.

4. Remove the pan from the heat, and add 2 cups of the Gruyère and the parsley. Stir until the cheese is melted and the sauce is smooth. Season with salt and pepper to taste. Add the roasted cauliflower and stir to coat. Pour the mixture into a 9 x 13-inch casserole dish.

5. Melt the remaining 2 tablespoons of the butter. In a small mixing bowl, combine the melted butter and the bread crumbs. Add the remaining 1½ cups cheese and the chives, and stir to combine. Sprinkle the topping evenly over the gratin.

6. Bake for 30 minutes or until bubbly and browned on top. Let the gratin cool for 10 minutes before serving.

Zucchini
Delight

Makes 6 to 8 servings

Cooking spray

8 cups sliced zucchini (about 2½ pounds)

1 cup chopped onion

½ cup Chicken Broth (page 335)

2 cups cooked long-grain white rice (see page 329)

1 cup sour cream

4 ounces sharp Cheddar cheese, shredded (1 cup)

¼ cup grated Parmesan cheese (1 ounce)

¼ cup Seasoned Bread Crumbs (page 330)

2 large eggs, lightly beaten

1 teaspoon salt

¼ teaspoon freshly ground black pepper

Our zucchini casserole tastes just as good as Mom's, but we've trimmed out many of the calories. Rich in flavor, this dish is a perfect partner for our Mamaw's Stuffed Peppers (page 48), Jayne's Baked Spaghetti (page 88), and Chicken Penne Pasta with Pink Sauce (page 116).

1. Preheat the oven to 350°F. Coat a 9 x 13-inch baking dish with cooking spray.

2. Combine the zucchini, onion, and chicken broth in a large pot set over medium-high heat, and bring to a boil. Cover, reduce the heat to low, and simmer for 20 minutes or until the vegetables are tender. Drain well, transfer to a large bowl, and partially mash the vegetables. Add the rice, sour cream, Cheddar cheese, 2 tablespoons of the Parmesan cheese, the bread crumbs, eggs, salt, and pepper to the vegetables, and stir gently to combine. Spoon the zucchini mixture into the prepared baking dish. Sprinkle the top with the remaining 2 tablespoons Parmesan cheese.

3. Bake for 30 minutes or until the top is golden brown.

This dish can easily be made VEGETARIAN-FRIENDLY by substituting vegetable broth for the chicken broth.

FREEZES WELL
See our freezer tips on page 16.

Aunt Fannie's
Cabin Squash Casserole

Makes 6 to 8 servings

Cooking spray

3 pounds yellow summer squash, chopped

1 small onion, chopped

2 large eggs

½ cup (1 stick) unsalted butter

1 tablespoon granulated sugar

1 teaspoon salt

1 teaspoon freshly ground black pepper

½ cup saltine crackers, crushed

Crystal has been fortunate enough to live in the same state as her sister Cindy for quite some time now, while the rest of her family is still in Georgia. So when times are tough and it's difficult to financially swing two back-to-back holiday trips, Crystal is lucky enough to get to have Thanksgiving dinner with her sister. Cindy is an amazing cook, and she allows all her family guests a side dish or dessert request. Crystal always asks for the Asparagus Bundles Wrapped in Prosciutto (page 203); Colin requests pumpkin pie; Keely gets mashed potatoes, sweet potato soufflé, and rolls (apparently she has a lot to be thankful about!); and Kris always asks for this squash casserole. Crystal's aunt Joan got the recipe from one of her favorite restaurants, Aunt Fannie's Cabin, in Smyrna, Georgia. The restaurant is now closed, but its squash casserole lives on.

1. Preheat the oven to 375°F. Spray a 9 x 13-inch casserole dish with cooking spray.

2. In a large saucepan set over high heat, combine 3 cups of water and the squash and bring to a boil. Boil until squash is fork-tender, about 15 minutes. Drain the squash in a colander, transfer to a bowl, and mash it with a fork. Add the onion, eggs, ¼ cup of the butter, the sugar, salt, and pepper, and stir well. Pour the mixture into the prepared casserole dish.

3. Melt the remaining ¼ cup of butter and pour it over the top of the casserole. Sprinkle with the crushed crackers. Bake for about 1 hour, or until brown on top. Serve hot.

This dish can be made GLUTEN-FREE by using gluten-free saltines.

This recipe can be made DIABETIC-FRIENDLY by substituting a pinch of stevia for the sugar. Note that you only need a pinch, as stevia is about 300 times sweeter than sugar. You should also replace the saltine cracker topping with a low-carb bread crumb, or simply omit it.

The story around this recipe reminds us that we all have our favorite casseroles and comfort dishes from our childhood. So the next time you plan to have friends over, why not make it a potluck where everyone shares their favorite recipe from their youth? What's interesting about this party idea is that it lets everyone bring something unique to the table. During dinner, guests can explain how their dish came about and tell any favorite family stories associated with it, such as the Thanksgiving when Aunt Ida pulled out her famous congealed salad from her fridge and it slid across the floor. Extra points go to guests who bring their recipes with them or a special childhood photo from the time during which they typically ate their famed family dish. And the grand prize goes to the story that gets everyone rolling on the floor, just like Aunt Ida's congealed salad!

Royal Ratatouille

Makes 8 servings

½ cup olive oil

1 medium eggplant, cut into ¼-inch-thick slices

1 large yellow onion, cut into ¼-inch-thick slices

1 green bell pepper, cut into rings

4 Roma tomatoes, sliced into ¼-inch-thick slices

2 garlic cloves, thinly sliced

2 jalapeño peppers, seeded and finely chopped

Salt and freshly ground black pepper

½ teaspoon granulated sugar

1 teaspoon dried basil

3 small zucchini, cut into ¼-inch-thick slices

½ cup chopped fresh parsley

3 yellow squash, cut into ¼-inch-thick slices

1 teaspoon dried oregano

Ratatouille is the French term for "all the healthy and delicious veggies you need in one scrumptious serving." Well, not really, but that's how we think of it. A hearty dish of stewed vegetables, it's a perfect accompaniment to heavier meats like beef and lamb, but it's also great as a side dish to eggs. We love it alongside our The "Sitch" Chicken Parmesan (page 114). It's the kind of dish whose leftovers taste even better the next day when the flavors have had more of a chance to develop. Ratatouille sounds and tastes complicated, but it really comes down to chopping, seasoning, and layering. Easy, and the results are *magnifique!*

1. Preheat the oven to 350°F.

2. Put 2 tablespoons of the oil in the bottom of a 9 x 13-inch casserole dish. Make one layer of each of the ingredients, in the following order: all of the eggplant and a third of the onions, bell peppers, tomatoes, garlic, and jalapeño peppers. Sprinkle with salt, pepper, and a pinch of the sugar. Drizzle 2 tablespoons of oil over the layer and sprinkle with the basil.

3. Make a second layer of each of the ingredients, in the following order: all of the zucchini and a third of the onions, bell peppers, tomatoes, garlic, and jalapeños. Sprinkle with salt, pepper, and another pinch of the sugar. Drizzle 2 tablespoons of oil over the layer and sprinkle with parsley.

4. Make a final layer of each of the ingredients, in the following order: all of the yellow squash and the remaining onions, bell peppers, tomatoes, garlic, and jalapeño peppers. Sprinkle with salt, pepper, and the remaining sugar. Drizzle the remaining 2 tablespoons of oil over the top and sprinkle with the oregano.

5. Cover and bake until the vegetables are tender, about 1 hour. Serve hot.

This recipe can be made DIABETIC-FRIENDLY by substituting a pinch of stevia for the sugar. Note that you only need a pinch, as stevia is about 300 times sweeter than sugar.

Ratatouille does involve a lot of chopping, but if you want to cut the prep work in half, simply remember your kitchen appliances! Most kitchen tools are created to make tasks easier. So why are they sitting there taking up space and collecting dust? Remember, folks, you registered for them for a reason, so let's put them to work! One of the Queens' most trusted appliances is the food processor. Food processers can do all of your slicing, dicing, shredding, and pureeing in seconds, and with all the cooking you'll be doing from this book (subtle hint), it's not only important to save time in the kitchen, it's also important to save your wrists!

Spinach and Spice and Everything Nice

Makes 6 to 8 servings

- 3 tablespoons olive oil
- ¼ cup chopped pickled jalapeños (about 20 slices)
- 4 garlic cloves, minced
- 1 pound fresh spinach
- ¼ cup pickled jalapeño juice (from the jar)
- 2 tablespoons fresh lemon juice
- ¼ teaspoon salt
- ¼ teaspoon freshly ground black pepper

The spiciness of this dish comes from pickled jalapeños. Sandy always has pickled jalapeños in her fridge, and they are perhaps her favorite condiment. She will add them to sandwiches, eggs, tacos, quesadillas . . . you name it! In fact, she would never dream of letting a single jalapeño go to waste. She even uses the pickling liquid to flavor stir-fries and veggies. Spinach prepared the way we do here makes a nice side for our BBQ Pork Ribs (page 52) and Chicken Paprikash (page 122). Crystal prefers to leave out the jalapeños, adding a little more lemon juice instead to brighten it up. Prepared that way, it pairs nicely with dishes such as our Gnocchi Bake (page 146).

1. In a sauté pan set over medium heat, heat the olive oil.
2. Add the jalapeños and garlic and cook for about 2 minutes, or until the garlic just begins to brown.
3. Add the spinach and sauté for 2 minutes.
4. Add the jalapeño juice, lemon juice, salt, and pepper, and stir well. Serve hot.

Rockin' Tomatoes
Rockefeller

Makes 6 to 8 servings

Cooking spray

6 tablespoons (¾ stick) unsalted butter

1 medium onion, finely chopped

2 (10-ounce) packages frozen spinach, thawed and drained

1 cup lightly crushed herbed croutons

1 cup grated Parmesan cheese (4 ounces)

2 large eggs, beaten

2 teaspoons Tabasco sauce

1 teaspoon garlic powder

½ teaspoon salt, plus more to taste

½ teaspoon freshly ground black pepper, plus more to taste

2 large ripe tomatoes

The next time you have company, make sure to treat them to this! This relatively simple side will have your family and friends thinking you've cooked all day. And if you can get little Johnny to eat spinach, then that's a plus, too! This creamy, rich spinach dish graces the plate and stands up to any meat pairing, making it a perfect side for your next dinner party. When serving, use an ice cream scoop to make neat, perfectly shaped mounds. Try pairing it with our Savory Salmon Turnovers (page 134) or our Greek Pastitsio (page 102).

1. Preheat the oven to 350°F. Coat a 9 x 13-inch casserole dish with cooking spray.

2. In a medium sauté pan set over medium heat, melt the butter. Add the onion and sauté for 8 minutes or until it starts to soften. Reduce the heat to low and add the spinach, croutons, ½ cup of the cheese, the eggs, Tabasco, garlic powder, salt, and pepper. Cook, stirring occasionally, for around 20 minutes, or until eggs are no longer runny.

3. Cut the tomatoes into 6 thick slices. Arrange the slices in the bottom of the prepared casserole dish. Season with salt and pepper. Bake the tomato slices for 8 to 10 minutes or until they begin to soften.

4. Preheat the broiler.

5. Divide the spinach mixture evenly over the tomato slices. Sprinkle the remaining ½ cup Parmesan on top of the spinach mixture. Return the casserole to the oven and broil for 2 minutes or until the cheese is golden brown. Serve immediately.

Rosemary Parmesan
Scalloped Potatoes

Makes 8 to 10 servings

- ¾ cup (1½ sticks) unsalted butter, plus more for greasing pan
- 3 to 4 pounds russet potatoes, peeled and sliced in ⅛-inch-thick slices
- 1½ teaspoons salt
- 1½ teaspoons freshly ground black pepper
- 1½ teaspoons finely chopped fresh rosemary
- 3½ cups whole milk
- 1 cup grated Parmesan cheese (4 ounces)

There were certain food pairings in the Pollock house that never varied. When meatloaf was on the table, it was a given that these scalloped potatoes and green beans were faithfully by its side. No, maybe not a given—a guarantee, something you could bet the farm on. Today we serve these potatoes with more than just meatloaf. In fact, they're a great sidekick for Beef Burgundy (page 98) and our Coq au Vin (page 120).

1. Preheat the oven to 350°F. Grease a 9 x 13-inch casserole dish with some butter.

2. Layer one-third of the potato slices in the bottom of the casserole dish, overlapping slightly, so that the dish is completely covered. Dot the top of the potatoes with 4 tablespoons of the butter, then season with ½ teaspoon of the salt, ½ teaspoon of the pepper, and ½ teaspoon of the rosemary. Repeat these layers two more times. Pour the milk over the top of the potatoes.

3. Place the casserole dish in the oven and bake for 1 hour. Remove from the oven and evenly sprinkle the Parmesan cheese over the potatoes. Bake for 30 more minutes or until the top is golden brown and the potatoes can be pierced with a knife easily.

Mamaw's
Potato Casserole

Makes 6 servings

Cooking spray

2 russet potatoes, peeled and thinly sliced

1 teaspoon salt

½ teaspoon freshly ground black pepper

1½ cups Cream of Chicken Soup (page 338)

½ cup evaporated milk

1 medium onion, thinly sliced

¼ cup (½ stick) unsalted butter, cut into small pieces

Simple ingredients and preparation, but always warm and comforting, this is just one of those dishes that reminds you of home. Crystal stayed with her Mamaw Cook often when growing up, and Mamaw always served this dish alongside a variety of entrées. Maybe it was because she always had the dish's affordable and readily available staples on hand, or maybe it was because it tasted so good. Either way, it makes quite a satisfying meal when paired with a roasted chicken (page 340) and a simple side dish like our Spinach and Spice and Everything Nice (page 218).

1. Preheat the oven to 350°F. Spray a 9 x 13-inch casserole dish with cooking spray.

2. Put the potatoes in the prepared casserole dish, season with the salt and pepper, and toss well.

3. In a large bowl, combine the soup, evaporated milk, and ⅓ cup water. Pour the mixture over the potatoes. Lay the onion slices on top of the casserole and dot with the butter.

4. Bake for 1 hour, until potatoes are fork-tender.

FREEZES WELL For best results, prepare the casserole through step 3. Wrap in foil and freeze for up to 2 months. Thaw the casserole overnight in the refrigerator before baking as stated in the recipe. Note that casseroles that have not been completely thawed may take 15 to 30 minutes longer, so be sure to check for bubbling edges and a hot center.

Potatoes Two Times with a Kick
Casserole

Makes 10 servings

- 10 large russet potatoes
- 4 cups shredded Colby Jack cheese (16 ounces)
- 1 pound bacon, cooked and crumbled
- 1 bunch green onions, green parts only, chopped
- ½ cup pickled jalapeños, chopped
- 3 large eggs, lightly beaten
- 1½ cups sour cream
- ½ cup (1 stick) plus 1 tablespoon unsalted butter, at room temperature
- 2 teaspoons salt
- 1 teaspoon freshly ground black pepper
- 10 dashes Tabasco sauce (or more if you like)
- Cooking spray

Crystal's nieces, Alexis and Cassie, are like most sisters close in age: they are the best of friends and mortal enemies at the same time. Even though they love each other dearly, neither of them is so gracious as to offer the last twice-baked potato to the other. Instead, they wage an all-out war over who eats the last one. In hopes of creating some world peace, we have transformed twice-baked potatoes into a large, filling casserole. This way, there should be plenty for all!

1. Preheat the oven to 400°F.

2. Poke the potatoes with a fork all over. Bake the potatoes on a rimmed baking sheet for about 1 hour, or until tender. Remove from the oven and let cool.

3. Once the potatoes are cool, scrape off all of the skins and discard. Put the inside of the potatoes in a large bowl and mash until semi-smooth. Add 2½ cups of the cheese, the bacon, green onions, jalapeños, eggs, sour cream, butter, salt, pepper, and Tabasco sauce. Mix well.

4. Reduce the oven temperature to 375°F. Spray a 9 x 13-inch casserole dish with cooking spray.

5. Pour the potato mixture into the prepared casserole dish and top with the remaining 1½ cups cheese. Bake for 35 to 40 minutes, or until the mixture is heated through and bubbling around the edges.

Simple Herb-Roasted Vegetables

Makes 8 servings

Cooking spray

1 bunch fresh parsley, chopped

1 bunch fresh basil, chopped

3 garlic cloves, minced

½ teaspoon red pepper flakes

1 cup vegetable oil

2 pounds red potatoes, quartered

1 red bell pepper, chopped

1 zucchini, chopped

1 pound carrots, peeled and chopped

1 teaspoon salt

½ teaspoon freshly ground black pepper

This recipe reminds Crystal of her college days in Boston. During the long, cold winter months (which seemed to last until early May), she loved nothing more than loading up her plate with some warm and filling roasted vegetables. Pair this with our BBQ Pork Ribs (page 52) or our Awesome Aussie Meat Pies (page 100) and a big ol' glass of ale, and you'll be able to brave the cold another day.

1. Preheat the oven to 425°F. Spray an 8 x 13-inch rimmed baking sheet (half sheet pan) with cooking spray.

2. In a blender, pulse the parsley, basil, garlic, red pepper flakes, and oil until smooth. You're looking for the consistency of Italian vinaigrette, so add more oil if the mixture needs thinning.

3. In a large bowl, combine the potatoes, bell pepper, zucchini, and carrots. Add the blended herb sauce, salt, and black pepper. Toss well to coat. Spread the vegetables in a single layer on the prepared baking sheet.

4. Roast for about 40 minutes, or until the vegetables are tender and a bit browned. Serve right away.

Cook Family
Pineapple Casserole

Makes 6 to 8 servings

Cooking spray

6 tablespoons all-purpose flour

1 cup granulated sugar

2 (20-ounce) cans unsweetened pineapple chunks

8 ounces mild Cheddar cheese, grated (2 cups)

35 butter Ritz crackers, crushed

¾ cup (1½ sticks) unsalted butter, melted

Sounds strange, but it is really delicious. (Crystal had to convince Sandy, too.) There's something about the sweet-salty combination of pineapple, Cheddar cheese, and Ritz crackers that's irresistible. This casserole is generally served as a side, but it's sweet enough for dessert.

1. Preheat the oven to 350°F. Lightly coat a 9 x 13-inch casserole dish with cooking spray.

2. In a medium bowl, combine the flour and sugar. Drain the pineapple, reserving 6 tablespoons of the juice. Add the juice to the flour and sugar, and stir to combine. Add the pineapple and cheese. Stir well, and pour into the prepared casserole dish.

3. In a separate bowl, combine the cracker crumbs and butter. Sprinkle the crumbs on top of the casserole. Bake for 20 to 30 minutes or until the crumb topping is golden brown and the casserole is heated through.

Risotto with Asparagus and Lemon

Makes 8 servings

- 1 pound asparagus, trimmed and cut into 1-inch pieces
- ¼ cup olive oil
- 1 teaspoon salt
- ½ teaspoon freshly ground black pepper
- 6 cups Chicken Broth (page 335) or store bought
- 3 shallots, chopped (about ½ cup)
- ½ teaspoon red pepper flakes
- 1¼ cups Arborio rice
- 2 tablespoons unsalted butter
- ½ cup grated Asiago cheese (2 ounces)
- 2 tablespoons grated lemon zest
- 2 tablespoons lemon juice
- 1 tablespoon chopped fresh parsley

Risotto is one of those foods that is very impressive and seems difficult, but the secrets to mastering it are very easy. You just have to pay attention and stir! Paired with savory yet sweet roasted asparagus and tart lemon, this risotto makes an ordinary dinner seem like a gourmet experience. Go with the ambience and light a few candles. Instant date night!

1. Preheat the oven to 450°F.

2. On a baking sheet, toss the asparagus with 1 tablespoon of the oil. Spread the asparagus in an even layer and season with ½ teaspoon salt and ¼ teaspoon black pepper. Roast until tender, 7 to 10 minutes, depending on the width of the asparagus.

3. In a medium saucepan set over medium-high heat, bring the chicken broth to a simmer. Reduce the heat and keep the stock warm over low heat.

4. In a large saucepan set over medium-high heat, heat the remaining 3 tablespoons of oil. Add the shallots and red pepper flakes and sauté until the shallots begin to soften, 5 to 7 minutes.

5. Add the rice to the saucepan, and cook, stirring, for 4 minutes, until the rice is coated in oil and starts to toast. Add the warm stock, a little at a time and stirring often, until all the liquid has been absorbed into the rice, making it tender but not mushy, about 18 minutes.

6. Stir in the butter, cheese, lemon zest, lemon juice, and parsley. Remove the pan from the heat and fold in the asparagus. Season with remaining salt and black pepper.

This dish can be made **VEGETARIAN-FRIENDLY** by substituting Veggie Broth (page 337) for the Chicken Broth.

Nene's
Spanish Rice

Makes 8 servings

- 3 cups Chicken Broth (page 335) or store bought
- 3 tablespoons vegetable oil
- 1½ cups long-grain white rice
- ½ red bell pepper, chopped
- ½ large onion, chopped
- 3 garlic cloves, chopped
- 1 teaspoon ground cumin
- 1 teaspoon salt
- ½ teaspoon freshly ground black pepper
- ½ cup tomato sauce
- Cooking spray

Sandy loves her brother-in-law, but she loves his mother, Irene, the best! Everyone calls her Nene, and she makes the best Spanish rice in the Rio Grande Valley. There's a lot of Spanish rice in the Valley, but this recipe puts the others to shame. And it's simple! Fresh bell peppers, onions, and tomato sauce make this dish lively. Serve it with our Chicken Enchiladas (page 110) and Red, Red Wine Sangria (page 26), and any day can be Cinco de Mayo!

1. In a medium saucepan set over medium-high heat, heat the chicken stock. Keep it warm over low heat.

2. In a large sauté pan set over medium heat, heat the oil. Add the rice and cook for about 5 minutes, stirring occasionally, until it browns. Add the red bell pepper, onion, and garlic, and cook for 2 minutes. Add the cumin, salt, and black pepper, and stir well.

3. Add 2½ cups of the warm chicken broth and the tomato sauce to the rice mixture. Reduce the heat to low, cover the pan, and simmer for 15 minutes, or until the liquid has completely absorbed. If the rice is too dry, add more chicken stock, ¼ cup at a time.

This dish can be made **VEGETARIAN-FRIENDLY** by substituting Veggie Broth (page 337) for the Chicken Broth.

Green Rice
Hot Dish

Makes 6 to 8 servings

Cooking spray

2 cups cooked long-grain white rice (see page 329)

12 ounces sharp Cheddar cheese, grated (3 cups)

1 (12-ounce) can evaporated milk

1 medium onion, chopped

1 cup chopped fresh flat-leaf parsley

2 large eggs, beaten

1 garlic clove, minced

2 tablespoons olive oil

2 teaspoons salt

½ teaspoon freshly ground black pepper

You betcha it's a hot dish! The history of the "hotdish" goes back to when budget-conscious farm wives needed to feed their own families as well as congregations of the first Minnesota churches. This filling side resembles a quiche and is packed full of flavor. Evaporated milk, which is thicker and richer than regular milk, helps give this dish its creamy texture. Perfect for cold winters, when you just need something warm and tasty in your belly.

1. Preheat the oven to 350°F. Coat a 9 x 13-inch casserole dish with cooking spray.

2. Put the rice, cheese, evaporated milk, onion, parsley, eggs, garlic, olive oil, salt, and pepper into a large mixing bowl and stir well. Pour the mixture into the prepared casserole dish. Bake for 50 minutes or until the casserole is set and the top is brown and a little crunchy.

Wild Rice

Makes 8 servings

- 9 tablespoons unsalted butter
- 1 cup wild rice
- 2 (10½-ounce) cans beef consommé
- 1 pound button mushrooms, sliced
- ½ medium red bell pepper, chopped
- 1 bunch green onions, green parts only, sliced
- ¼ cup chopped fresh parsley
- 1 teaspoon salt
- ½ teaspoon freshly ground black pepper
- ½ cup slivered almonds, toasted

Chock-full of hearty mushrooms and tasty vegetables, this recipe turns boring rice into something wild! A flavorful and savory dish with the nutty accent of toasted almonds, it's truly something to roar about. We think this dish perfectly complements our Chicken with 40 Cloves of Garlic (page 65)!

1. Rinse the rice well under running water and drain. In a large saucepan set over medium heat, combine the rice with 2 cups of the consommé. Bring the mixture to a boil. Reduce the heat to low, cover the pan, and simmer until the liquid is absorbed, about 30 minutes.

2. In a large skillet set over medium-high heat, melt 4 tablespoons of butter. Add the mushrooms, bell pepper, and green onions and cook for 5 minutes, until tender. Add the parsley, salt, pepper, and almonds and stir well. Pour the vegetable mixture into the pan of cooked rice and stir well. Pour the mixture into the prepared casserole dish. Refrigerate, covered, for at least 2 hours and up to 2 days.

3. Preheat the oven to 350°F. Grease a 9 x 13-inch casserole dish with 1 tablespoon of the butter.

4. Take the dish out of the refrigerator, dot with the remaining 4 tablespoons of butter, and add the remaining consommé. Cover the dish with foil and bake for 30 to 40 minutes, or until the consommé has been absorbed. Serve hot. If not serving immediately, let the rice cool completely and store in an airtight container in the refrigerator for up to 1 week.

Dill Bread

Makes 8 servings

Cooking spray

¼ cup (½ stick) unsalted butter

2 cups small-curd cottage cheese

½ cup whole milk

2 (¼-ounce) packages dry yeast

4 to 4½ cups all-purpose flour

¼ cup granulated sugar

1 small onion, finely chopped

2 large eggs

4 teaspoons dill seed

2 teaspoons salt

½ teaspoon baking soda

The recipe calls for a casserole dish, but we love using our cast-iron skillet. It gives the bread a more rustic feel—so homey and comforting. The incorporation of dill seed gives each wedge a delightfully herbal pop, making it a nice complement to most any meal. We particularly love it with our Shepherdless Pie (page 189) and Chicken Casserole: A Cook Family Favorite (page 66).

1. Spray a 9 x 13-inch casserole dish with cooking spray.

2. In a medium saucepan set over medium heat, melt the butter. Remove the pan from the heat and stir in the cottage cheese and milk. Sprinkle the yeast over the mixture and gently stir to dissolve. Let sit for 10 minutes.

3. In a large bowl, mix together 2 cups flour, sugar, onion, eggs, dill seed, salt, and baking soda. Add the yeast mixture to the flour mixture and mix just until incorporated. Don't overwork. Gently stir in remaining 2 to 2½ cups flour until it forms a stiff batter. Cover the bowl with a damp towel and let the dough rise for 1 hour.

4. Punch down the dough and transfer it to the prepared casserole dish. Cover and let rise for 40 minutes. Preheat the oven to 350°F.

5. Uncover the dish and bake the bread for 30 to 40 minutes, or until golden brown.

This dish can be made GLUTEN-FREE by replacing the flour with a gluten-free all-purpose mix, either store bought (see page 21 for recommendations of our favorite brands) or homemade (see page 322 for our recipe).

Curried Rice
Veggie Bake

Makes 6 to 8 servings

Cooking spray

1 tablespoon vegetable oil

1 onion, chopped

1 garlic clove, crushed

2 tablespoons curry powder

3 sweet potatoes, peeled and diced

1 red bell pepper, chopped

1 (15-ounce) can diced tomatoes

1 (8-ounce) bag fresh spinach

2 cups cooked rice (see page 329)

1 large egg, beaten

2 cups grated Gruyère cheese (8 ounces)

2 cups Seasoned Bread Crumbs (page 330) or store bought

¼ cup chopped fresh cilantro

¼ teaspoon ground turmeric

The Queens have long been believers in the healing power of curry, but lately they've been hearing a lot of good things about the health benefits of turmeric. This bright yellow-orange spice has been used as a powerful anti-inflammatory in traditional Chinese and Indian medicine for centuries. Recently, it has proven to be beneficial in the treatment of many health conditions, including Alzheimer's disease and arthritis. We like it because it adds a warm, peppery flavor and a beautiful color to this dish.

1. Preheat the oven to 400°F. Spray a 9 x 13-inch casserole dish with cooking spray.

2. In a medium sauté pan set over medium-high heat, heat the oil. Add the onion and garlic and cook, stirring, until slightly browned, about 5 minutes. Add the curry powder and cook for 2 more minutes. If the onion starts to dry out, add a couple of tablespoons of water to the pan. Add the sweet potatoes, bell pepper, and tomatoes, cover, and simmer for 10 minutes, until the veggies start to soften. Remove the lid and stir in the spinach. Cook for 5 more minutes, or until the sauce has reduced and thickened.

3. Put the rice in a bowl and add the egg and 1 cup of the cheese. Stir well and scoop out into the prepared casserole dish. Press the rice down into the dish, then pour the vegetable mixture on top.

4. In a medium bowl, combine the remaining 1 cup of cheese and the bread crumbs, cilantro, and turmeric. Sprinkle the mixture over the top of the vegetables. Bake for 20 minutes, or until the top is brown and crispy.

This dish can be made GLUTEN-FREE by using gluten-free bread crumbs, either store bought (see page 21 for recommendations of our favorite brands) or homemade (see page 330 for our recipe).

FREEZES WELL For best results, prepare the casserole through step 3. Wrap in foil and freeze for up to 2 months. Thaw the casserole overnight in the refrigerator. The next day, prepare the bread crumb topping (step 4) and bake as stated in the recipe. Note that casseroles that have not been completely thawed may take 15 to 30 minutes longer, so be sure to check for bubbling edges and a hot center.

Rise and Shine!

Casseroles to Start the Day

For the majority of us, breakfast doesn't play a big enough role in our busy and hectic lifestyles. And if we do find the time in our morning schedules, it sadly consists of a cup of coffee and a bowl of cold cereal. (Shame, shame!) For us, breakfast really is the most important meal of the day—and it's one that should be fully appreciated and enjoyed. With these easy casserole recipes—and a few make-ahead ones, too—breakfast can be something special, as it should be. So whether you're planning a brunch get-together with friends or just want to surprise the kids, here are some tried-and-true recipes that will have them jumping out of bed in no time. Sweet or savory, these delightful dishes are not your average breakfast fare. They make breakfast a brighter occasion and could just turn you into a morning person.

Frenchy Toast
Casserole

Makes 6 to 8 servings

- ¾ cup (1½ sticks) unsalted butter
- 1½ cups packed light brown sugar
- 2 teaspoons ground cinnamon
- 1 loaf extra-thick sliced white bread, such as Texas Toast, crusts removed
- 2 cups whole milk
- 6 large eggs
- 1 cup your favorite berries

There are no grumpy faces when it's a Frenchy Toast Casserole morning. This dish puts the "sweet" in "home sweet home." Add your kids' favorite berries, and you've got yourself one tasty treat.

1. Preheat the oven to 350°F.

2. Melt the butter in a small saucepan set over medium heat. Add the brown sugar and 1 teaspoon of the cinnamon and stir to make a paste. Spread the paste in the bottom of a 9 x 13-inch casserole dish. Lay the bread on top of the paste in two layers.

3. In a separate bowl, combine the milk, eggs, and remaining 1 teaspoon cinnamon. Pour the mixture over the bread in the dish. Bake for 30 minutes, or until top has risen a little and is golden brown. Top with berries when serving.

FREEZES WELL
See our freezer tips on page 16.

This casserole can be made the night before and kept chilled in the fridge overnight. All you'll have to do the next morning is pop it in the oven.

Citrus Blintz

Makes 8 to 10 servings

Cooking spray

6 large eggs

2 egg whites

1½ cups sour cream

2 teaspoons finely grated grapefruit zest

½ cup fresh orange juice

¼ cup (½ stick) unsalted butter, softened

1 cup all-purpose flour

½ cup plus 2 tablespoons granulated sugar

2 teaspoons baking powder

2 cups cottage cheese

1 (8-ounce) package cream cheese, softened

2 egg yolks

2 teaspoons vanilla extract

1 teaspoon fresh lemon juice

½ cup orange marmalade

2 tablespoons water

The area where Sandy grew up in the Rio Grande Valley is one of the best places in the nation for growing citrus. There is something about the soil, climate, and constant sunshine that lends itself to perfect citrus farming. Sandy's dad, Max, worked the citrus farms, and every year Sandy would go out with her dad to the farms to help him harvest and to sample the goods! It's only natural that when developing recipes, Sandy wanted to pull from this fond memory. This wonderfully delicious spin on traditional blintzes has all the great taste but without all the work. Forget the trial and error; use this surefire recipe to woo your crowd.

1. Preheat the oven to 350°F. Coat a 9 x 13-inch casserole dish with cooking spray.

2. In a blender, combine the eggs, egg whites, sour cream, grapefruit zest, orange juice, and butter. Cover and blend until smooth. Add the flour, ½ cup of the sugar, and the baking powder. Cover and blend again until smooth. Transfer the batter to a medium bowl.

3. In a clean blender, combine the cottage cheese, cream cheese, egg yolks, vanilla, lemon juice, and remaining 2 tablespoons sugar. Cover and blend until smooth.

4. Pour 2 cups of the batter into the prepared casserole dish. Spoon the cottage cheese mixture over the batter and swirl the filling into the batter with the tip of a knife. Pour the remaining batter evenly over the mixture in the dish. Bake for 45 minutes or until puffed and golden. Cool for 30 minutes on a wire rack before serving.

5. To serve, heat the marmalade with the water in a small saucepan set over medium heat until melted. Drizzle the blintz with the melted marmalade and spread to cover.

Bed and Breakfast Casserole

Makes 6 to 8 servings

Cooking spray

1 (8-ounce) round Brie cheese

1 pound ground hot pork sausage

12 thin slices white bread, crusts removed

1½ cups grated Parmesan cheese (6 ounces)

7 large eggs

3 cups heavy cream

2 cups whole milk

1½ tablespoons dried sage

1½ teaspoons dry mustard

1 teaspoon seasoned salt

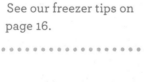

FREEZES WELL
See our freezer tips on page 16.

Bed and breakfast inns are very popular in the areas surrounding Austin, Texas, which is known as the "Hill Country." Around here, B&Bs are usually historic homes that have been in the innkeepers' families for years. One of the best aspects of staying at a B&B is breakfast! The innkeeper traditionally gets up early and prepares a lovely morning spread for the guests. The richness of Brie, sausage, and egg reminds us of days well spent relaxing around a perfect breakfast with other guests at our favorite B&Bs.

1. Preheat the oven to 350°F. Lightly coat a 9 x 13-inch casserole dish with cooking spray.

2. Trim the rind from the Brie. (Place the cheese in the freezer for about 30 minutes before trimming to make it easier to work with.) Cut the cheese into ¼-inch cubes; set aside.

3. Cook the sausage in a large skillet set over medium-high heat, breaking up any lumps with the back of a spoon, until browned throughout, about 6 minutes. Drain well.

4. Layer the bread in the bottom of the prepared casserole dish. Scatter the sausage, Brie, and Parmesan cheese over the bread.

5. In a large bowl, lightly whisk the eggs, then add the cream, milk, sage, dry mustard, and seasoned salt. Whisk to combine and pour evenly over the casserole. Bake for 50 minutes, or until the egg mixture is set. Serve hot.

This casserole can be made the night before and kept chilled in the fridge overnight. All you'll have to do the next morning is pop it in the oven.

Smokin'
Strata

Makes 6 to 8 servings

Cooking spray

2 tablespoons unsalted butter

1½ medium red bell peppers, finely chopped

2 leeks, thinly sliced, white and light green parts only

1 (10-ounce) loaf focaccia bread, cut into ½-inch cubes

4 ounces mild smoked Gouda cheese, grated (1 cup)

1½ cups whole milk

1½ cups half-and-half

9 large eggs, lightly beaten

2 tablespoons Dijon mustard

½ teaspoon salt

½ teaspoon freshly ground black pepper

In the words of Crystal's dad, Jody, "Sometimes you just want breakfast for dinner." We couldn't agree more. This egg masterpiece is not only great for breakfast but also ideal for a savory dinner any night of the week. Aside from the taste, the beautiful thing about stratas is how filling they are. At the heart of any great strata you will find a dense, rustic bread (we use focaccia) layered with an egg mixture and cheese. In this particular recipe we add leeks and red bell peppers for a touch of sweetness and color, but the real standout is the smoky flavor provided by the Gouda cheese. Hence, the strata's name. Enjoy!

1. Preheat oven to 375°F. Coat a 9 x 13-inch casserole dish with cooking spray.

2. In a medium sauté pan set over medium-high heat, melt the butter. Add the bell peppers and leeks and sauté until soft, about 8 minutes. Set aside.

3. Spread half of the bread cubes in the prepared casserole dish. Top with three-fourths of the cheese and three-fourths of the red pepper mixture. Repeat the layers.

4. In a medium bowl, whisk together the milk, half-and-half, eggs, mustard, salt, and pepper. Pour over the strata layers. Bake for 1 hour, or until the eggs are firm and set in the center and the top of the casserole is golden brown.

Texas Migas

Makes 8 to 10 servings

Cooking spray

6 corn tortillas

Vegetable oil, for frying

12 large eggs

2 tablespoons heavy cream

¼ cup (½ stick) unsalted butter

½ cup chopped onion

1 cup chopped green bell pepper

1 (10-ounce) can Rotel tomatoes or diced tomatoes with green chilies

¼ cup chopped fresh cilantro

1 teaspoon salt

1 teaspoon freshly ground black pepper

¼ cup chopped pickled jalapeño peppers

8 ounces Cheddar or Monterey Jack, grated (2 cups)

If you have ever had breakfast in Texas, then odds are you've experienced a plate of delicious migas, a mixture of fluffy eggs, spices, cheese, and fried tortillas. For Sandy, migas present somewhat of a love-hate relationship. You see, Michael (her main squeeze for over 12 years) loves migas so much she sometimes feels he loves them more than her. He's tried them in every restaurant in Austin, always noting the subtle differences and what would make the perfect combination of flavors. She took note and developed this recipe in attempts of satisfying her "migas man." And let's just say there is no longer any doubt who Michael loves more. Serve these with a side of refried beans and your choice of corn, flour, or whole-wheat tortillas to enfold all of the ingredients into tasty tacos. And if you're feeling spicy, try making your own Pickled Jalapeños (opposite page).

1. Preheat the oven to 350°F. Coat a 9 x 13-inch casserole dish with cooking spray.

2. Cut the tortillas into ¼-inch-thick strips. Heat the vegetable oil in a wide skillet set over medium-high heat until it reaches 350°F on a deep-fry thermometer. Working in small batches, lay the tortilla strips in the oil and fry, turning occasionally, for about 1 minute. Look for the strips to become golden brown and crunchy. Remove the strips from the oil and let drain on a paper towel. Set aside.

3. In a large bowl, whisk together the eggs and cream. Set aside.

4. In a medium sauté pan set over medium-high heat, melt the butter. Add the onion and bell pepper, and sauté until the onion is translucent and the pepper starts to soften, about 8 minutes. Transfer the mixture to the bowl with the eggs, then add the tomatoes, cilantro, salt, and pepper. Mix well.

5. Pour the egg mixture into the prepared casserole dish. Place the casserole in the oven and bake for 30 minutes, or until the eggs are just set in the center. Remove the casserole from the oven and sprinkle the jalapeños, cheese, and fried tortilla strips evenly over the top. Return the casserole to the oven and continue to cook for 5 to 8 minutes or until the cheese melts. Remove from the oven and let sit for 5 minutes before serving.

Pickled Jalapeños

Makes 3 pints

- 2 pounds fresh jalapeño peppers
- 5 cups white vinegar
- 4 teaspoons pickling salt
- 2 teaspoons granulated sugar

1. Wash the peppers and cut them into $1/4$-inch-thick slices. Tightly pack the jalapeños into 3 pint jars, being careful not to crush them. Set aside.

2. In a medium saucepan, combine the vinegar, salt, and sugar with 1 cup of water. Bring the mixture to a boil over high heat and pour it over the peppers in the jars. Clean the rim of the jars with a clean towel and screw the canning lids securely on the jars. Process pints in a boiling water bath for 10 minutes. Place the jars in large pot and add enough water to cover the jars by 1 to 2 inches. Cover the pot and bring the water to a boil. Boil for 10 minutes. Turn off the heat, then carefully lift the jars out of the water and place on an absorbent towel. Let the jars cool completely. They can be stored for up to one year.

The "Pile High" Frittata

Makes 6 to 8 servings

- 3 tablespoons unsalted butter, plus more for pan
- 3 tablespoons canola oil
- 4 cups frozen shredded hash brown potatoes
- 1 medium onion, thinly sliced
- ½ cup chopped green bell pepper
- 1 cup sliced green onions
- ⅛ teaspoon cayenne
- 2 teaspoons seasoning salt
- Freshly ground black pepper
- 1 pound cooked ham, cubed
- 12 large eggs
- ¼ cup heavy cream
- Pinch of Italian seasoning
- 8 ounces sharp Cheddar cheese, grated (2 cups)

Ever had a Denver omelet? If not, you are missing out on a real treat. A Denver omelet (sometimes also referred to as a western omelet) is a tasty egg concoction typically prepared with Cheddar cheese, diced ham, onions, green bell peppers, and sometimes scattered hash browns. Its origins remain as scattered as the hash browns, but our best guess is that it probably originated one morning out on the range, cooked up by some hungry cowboys trying to fill their bellies. Inspired by their tasty creation, this recipe is the Queens' casserole version of the popular dish. Pile your diced ham, green bell peppers, onions, cheese, and hash browns a mile high and watch it bake to a beautiful golden brown. We added a kick of cayenne pepper to spice it up a bit.

1. Place an oven rack in the bottom third of the oven. Preheat the oven to 375°F. Grease a 9 x 13-inch casserole dish with butter.

2. Heat the oil and 3 tablespoons butter in a skillet set over medium heat. Add the potatoes, onion, bell pepper, green onions, cayenne, 1 teaspoon of the seasoned salt, and black pepper to taste. Cook for about 8 minutes or until the vegetables are very lightly browned. Add the ham and cook for 3 more minutes, stirring every once in a while with a wooden spoon or spatula. Transfer the mixture to the prepared baking dish.

3. In a bowl, whisk together the eggs, cream, Italian seasoning, and remaining 1 teaspoon seasoned salt. Pour the egg mixture into the baking dish and toss with the potatoes. Bake for 25 minutes. Sprinkle the top of the casserole with the cheese, and bake for 8 to 10 minutes more, until the cheese is melted and the eggs are set. Cool for about 10 minutes before serving.

Did you know that green bell peppers are just immature red bell peppers? Well, neither did we—until Sandy discovered this fact. Green and red bell peppers have the same caloric content, but due to a longer maturation time, the red bells have much higher levels of vitamin C (almost twice as much) and tons more beta-carotene! So, if you are feeling low on vitamin C, feel free to substitute your green bell with a nutrition-packed red!

Sunday's Best
Crab and Cheese Quiche

Makes 8 servings

2 large eggs, lightly beaten

½ cup whole milk

½ cup mayonnaise

1 teaspoon cornstarch

½ teaspoon smoked paprika

½ teaspoon salt

½ teaspoon freshly ground black pepper

½ pound lump crab meat, flaked

6 ounces Swiss cheese, shredded (1½ cups)

1 (9-inch) unbaked pie crust (page 323)

Dress up this quiche and show it off for breakfast. Yes, we're talking about your quiche. You dress yourself in your Sunday best, so why not dress up your breakfast? Don't be fooled by its outer appearance; this quiche will surprise and delight as your family and guests discover surprising ingredients, such as fresh crab and smoked paprika, in their first bite.

1. Preheat the oven to 350°F.

2. In a medium bowl, combine the eggs, milk, mayonnaise, cornstarch, paprika, salt, and pepper. Stir in the crab and cheese. Pour the mixture into the pie shell. Bake for 30 to 40 minutes, or until a knife inserted into center of the quiche comes out clean.

A Side of Hash Brown
Casserole, Please!

Makes 6 to 8 servings

Cooking spray

1 (2-pound) package frozen hash brown potatoes, thawed

¾ cup (1½ sticks) unsalted butter, melted

1½ cups homemade Cream of Chicken Soup (page 338)

1 (8-ounce) container sour cream

½ cup chopped onion

8 ounces Cheddar cheese, shredded (2 cups)

1 teaspoon salt

¼ teaspoon freshly ground black pepper

2 cups crushed cornflake cereal

Your morning eggs will find their perfect partner in this cheesy and delicious casserole. It's baked with a crunchy, buttery topping that will bring you back for seconds—and thirds! This casserole is a good alternative to mashed or baked potatoes at dinnertime, too. Try serving it with fried chicken for a true comfort feast.

1. Preheat oven to 350°F. Lightly coat a 9 x 13-inch casserole dish with cooking spray.

2. In a large bowl, combine the hash browns, ½ cup of the melted butter, the soup, sour cream, onion, cheese, salt, and pepper. Spoon the mixture into the prepared casserole dish.

3. In a medium saucepan set over medium heat, sauté the cornflake crumbs in the remaining ¼ cup melted butter until the cornflakes start to brown, about 4 minutes. Sprinkle the cornflakes over the top of the casserole. Cover the casserole with foil and bake for 40 minutes or until the top is golden brown and the edges are bubbling. Serve immediately.

This dish can be made VEGETARIAN-FRIENDLY by using Cream of Mushroom Soup (page 339) instead of chicken soup. Now, isn't that easy?

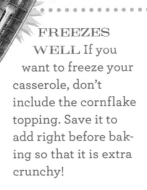

FREEZES WELL If you want to freeze your casserole, don't include the cornflake topping. Save it to add right before baking so that it is extra crunchy!

Ham and Cheese
Skillet Casserole

Makes 6 to 8 servings

- 1 large russet potato, peeled and cut into ½-inch pieces
- 2 tablespoons vegetable oil
- ¾ teaspoon salt
- ½ teaspoon freshly ground black pepper
- 2 large eggs
- 1 cup whole milk
- 1 tablespoon unsalted butter, melted
- 1 cup all-purpose flour
- 2 green onions, thinly sliced, green parts only
- 12 ounces thick-sliced deli ham, cut into ½-inch pieces
- 2 ounces sharp Cheddar cheese, shredded (½ cup)

One of the very few items Crystal has of her Mamaw Maggie's is her cast-iron skillet. Until recently she used the skillet only for making cornbread, but she has now discovered the pan's varied talents. If you are not familiar with cast-iron pans, they can seem intimidating. All that talk of properly seasoning them, how to wash them (or not wash), seems like too much work. But trust us, the benefits of the cast-iron pan far outweigh any care concerns. They heat evenly and beautifully, and when properly cared for, they will last a lifetime. Crystal's pan has lasted several lifetimes! This breakfast recipe will work with any oven-safe skillet, but when using a cast-iron skillet, your bottom layer of potatoes will get a nice crispness to it.

1. Place an oven rack in the upper third of the oven. Preheat the oven to 450°F.

2. Toss the potatoes with 1 tablespoon of the vegetable oil, ¼ teaspoon of the salt, and ¼ teaspoon of pepper in a microwave-safe bowl. Cover the bowl with a paper towel and microwave on high, stirring the potatoes halfway through cooking, until the potatoes begin to soften, 5 to 7 minutes. Drain the potatoes well and set aside.

3. In a separate large bowl, whisk together the eggs, milk, butter, remaining ½ teaspoon of salt, and ¼ teaspoon of pepper. Stir in the flour and green onions until just incorporated but still a bit lumpy, and set aside.

4. Heat the remaining 1 tablespoon of oil in a 10-inch oven-safe skillet set over medium-high heat until shimmering. Add the ham and potatoes; cover the skillet with foil and cook until the potatoes start to brown, about 10 minutes. Uncover the skillet, pour in the egg mixture, and sprinkle the cheese over the top. Bake for 25 to 30 minutes, or until puffed and golden. Transfer the skillet to a wire rack and let cool for 5 minutes. Use a rubber spatula to loosen the casserole from the skillet, then slide it onto a cutting board, slice into wedges, and serve.

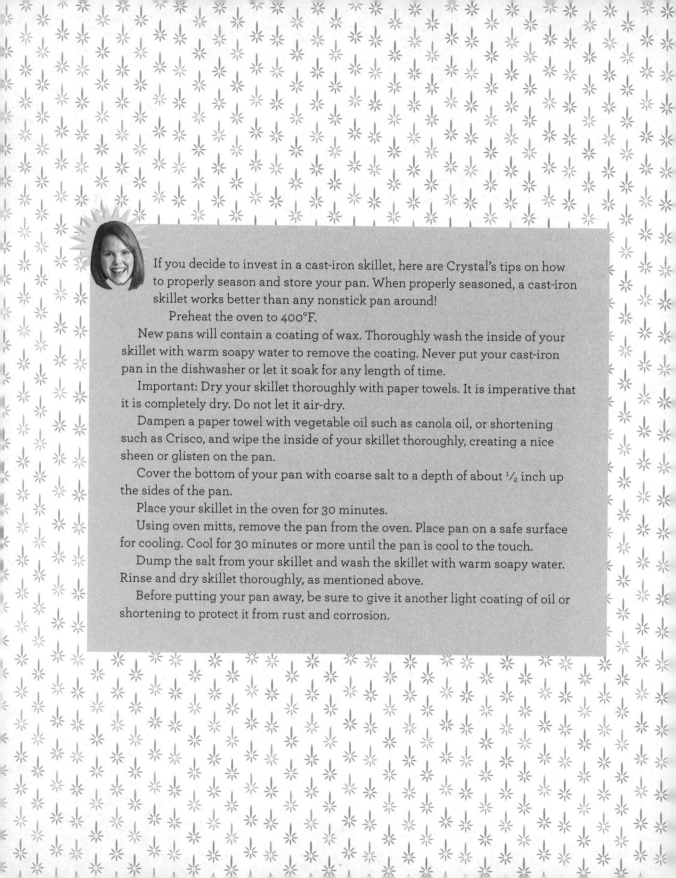

If you decide to invest in a cast-iron skillet, here are Crystal's tips on how to properly season and store your pan. When properly seasoned, a cast-iron skillet works better than any nonstick pan around!

Preheat the oven to 400°F.

New pans will contain a coating of wax. Thoroughly wash the inside of your skillet with warm soapy water to remove the coating. Never put your cast-iron pan in the dishwasher or let it soak for any length of time.

Important: Dry your skillet thoroughly with paper towels. It is imperative that it is completely dry. Do not let it air-dry.

Dampen a paper towel with vegetable oil such as canola oil, or shortening such as Crisco, and wipe the inside of your skillet thoroughly, creating a nice sheen or glisten on the pan.

Cover the bottom of your pan with coarse salt to a depth of about $\frac{1}{2}$ inch up the sides of the pan.

Place your skillet in the oven for 30 minutes.

Using oven mitts, remove the pan from the oven. Place pan on a safe surface for cooling. Cool for 30 minutes or more until the pan is cool to the touch.

Dump the salt from your skillet and wash the skillet with warm soapy water. Rinse and dry skillet thoroughly, as mentioned above.

Before putting your pan away, be sure to give it another light coating of oil or shortening to protect it from rust and corrosion.

Not-Just-for-Breakfast
Garlic Cheese Grits

Makes 6 to 8 servings

Cooking spray

Salt and freshly ground black pepper

4 garlic cloves, minced

2 cups quick-cooking grits

8 ounces sharp Cheddar cheese, grated (2 cups)

4 large eggs, beaten

20 dashes Tabasco sauce

Some things are like clockwork. For Crystal, her weekly routine during her high school years consisted of getting up and making herself grits and toast for breakfast. Oh, how she loved her grits! Some mornings she had them with sugar and butter; other days she simply salt-and-peppered them. It didn't really matter how they were prepared. You can imagine, then, how sad she was when she couldn't find grits while at college in Boston (that and her sweet tea). Determined to get her college friends on track, Crystal had her mother ship her care packages loaded with containers of grits. She served them at every opportunity and explored different ways of preparing them in order to impress her guests. One of the most popular recipes was this delicious take, which adds the right amount of garlic and cheese. Forget cold cereal—mornings should be all about grits.

1. Preheat the oven to 375°F. Coat a 9 x 13-inch baking dish with cooking spray.

2. Bring 8 cups of water, 2 teaspoons salt, and garlic to a boil in a medium saucepan set over high heat. Once boiling, gradually add the grits, whisking constantly to break up any lumps. Reduce the heat to a simmer and cook, stirring occasionally, for 10 minutes, until the grits are thick.

3. Remove the pan from the heat and stir in 1½ cups of the cheese and the eggs. Add the Tabasco (less if you are not a fan of heat) and salt and pepper to taste. Pour the grits into the prepared baking dish. Bake for 45 minutes.

4. Sprinkle the remaining ½ cup cheese over the top, and bake for 15 more minutes, or until the grits are set and the cheese on top is melted. Let rest for 10 minutes before serving.

Granola Oatmeal
Bake

Makes 6 to 8 servings

Cooking spray

1¾ cups whole milk

2 tablespoons unsalted butter

1 cup old-fashioned rolled oats

⅓ cup chopped dried apricots

⅓ cup dried tart cherries

⅓ cup golden raisins

5 tablespoons packed light brown sugar

½ teaspoon vanilla extract

¼ teaspoon salt

½ cup coarsely chopped walnuts

Oatmeal is one of the healthiest and most energy-packed breakfast foods around. To give our loved ones a great start to their day while keeping a lazy weekend morning—well—lazy, we created this casserole. The three kinds of dried fruit and touch of vanilla dress it up just enough so that it still feels like a treat.

1. Preheat the oven to 350°F. Lightly coat a 9 x 13-inch casserole dish with cooking spray.

2. In a medium saucepan set over medium heat, bring the milk and butter to a boil. Slowly stir in the oats, apricots, cherries, golden raisins, 3 tablespoons of the brown sugar, the vanilla, and salt. Cook, stirring, for 1 minute. Pour the mixture into the prepared casserole dish.

3. Bake for 15 minutes. Sprinkle with the remaining 2 tablespoons brown sugar and the walnuts. Bake for 5 more minutes, or until bubbly. Cool slightly before serving.

Freakin' Insane Chocolate-Chip Applesauce Quick Bread

Makes 6 to 8 servings

Vegetable shortening, such as Crisco

2 cups all-purpose flour, plus more for dusting the pan

1½ cups applesauce

½ cup (1 stick) unsalted butter, melted

1 teaspoon vanilla extract

1 cup granulated sugar

2 teaspoons baking soda

1 teaspoon ground allspice

1 teaspoon ground cloves

1 teaspoon ground cinnamon

½ teaspoon salt

1 cup semi-sweet chocolate chips

This outrageous breakfast bread was introduced to Crystal when she was at her dear friend Amy's home. It was one of those scenarios where you have room for only one piece, yet end up taking the loaf home! Amy told Crystal that her mom and her mom's friend Janie made this recipe often when Amy was growing up. When they had passed, Amy inherited her mom's recipe book, which included several copies of this recipe, in both her mom's and Janie's handwriting. Amy has taken to making it every holiday for her family and friends. Baking and sharing this delicious bread with the rest of the family is the ultimate way to honor their memories and their special friendship.

1. Preheat the oven to 350°F. Grease an 8½ x 4½ x 2½-inch loaf pan with shortening and dust with flour.

2. In a large mixing bowl, combine the applesauce, butter, and vanilla. In a separate medium mixing bowl, combine the 2 cups flour, the sugar, baking soda, allspice, cloves, cinnamon, and salt. Gradually add the dry ingredients to the wet ingredients, stirring until just incorporated. Stir in the chocolate chips. Pour the batter into the prepared pan. The pan should be about half full. Bake for 45 minutes, or until a toothpick inserted in the center comes out clean. Let cool completely before cutting and serving.

Caramel Cinnamon
Sweet Rolls

Makes 12 servings

1 package active dry yeast (2½ teaspoons)

½ cup warm water

8 tablespoons (1 stick) unsalted butter, softened

3 cups all-purpose flour

1¼ cups plus 3 tablespoons granulated sugar

2 large eggs

1½ teaspoons ground cinnamon

Caramel Sauce (opposite page)

Anyone would get right out of bed if he or she smelled these rolls rising in the oven—even on a Saturday! We believe the magic lies in the homemade caramel sauce. The caramel is rarely something we consider making from scratch, yet it is surprisingly easy to do. Double the sauce recipe and store the extra goodness in a plastic squeeze bottle in the fridge. The squeeze bottle is the perfect tool for drizzling this rich caramel over ice cream or apple slices.

1. In the bowl of an electric mixer fitted with a paddle attachment, dissolve the yeast in the warm water. Add 6 tablespoons of butter, the flour, ½ cup of the sugar, and the eggs to the bowl. Beat for 2 minutes, then add the remaining 1¼ cups of flour and beat until smooth, about 2 minutes. Scrape the batter from the sides of the bowl. Transfer the dough to a clean bowl. Cover the bowl with a clean kitchen towel and let the dough rise in a warm place (about 85°F) until doubled in size, about 1 hour.

2. Turn the dough out onto a well-floured counter. Roll into a 12 x 16-inch rectangle. Gently spread the remaining 2 tablespoons of the butter on the dough. In a small bowl, combine the cinnamon and remaining 3 tablespoons sugar; sprinkle onto the dough, leaving a ½-inch border around the dough. Roll the dough up like a jelly roll, starting from the larger side. Cut the dough into 12 equal pieces.

3. Place the rolls in a 9 x 13-inch casserole dish that has been greased with the other tablespoon of softened butter, tucking the loose ends of the dough under each roll so they'll hold together when baked. Cover the pan with a clean kitchen towel and let the rolls rise in a warm place (about 85°F) until doubled in size, about 1 hour.

4. Preheat the oven to 350°F. Bake the rolls for 15 to 20 minutes, or until light golden brown. Pour the hot caramel sauce on the rolls while still hot.

Caramel Sauce

Makes 2 cups

- ½ cup (1 stick) unsalted butter
- ½ cup packed light brown sugar
- ¼ cup granulated sugar
- 2 tablespoons honey
- ¼ cup heavy cream

In a large pot set over medium-high heat, melt the butter. Add the brown sugar, granulated sugar, and honey. Bring to a boil, and cook for 4 to 5 minutes, stirring once or twice (watch carefully to avoid scorching). Remove the pot from the heat and swirl in the cream until it is fully incorporated. Be very careful when adding the cream because the mixture will bubble up.

Sandy's Granny Haley made the best cinnamon rolls in the world. It seemed so effortless and magical to her grandkids. The smell of cinnamon wafting through the house stopped people in their tracks. As Sandy grew older and really began to appreciate the lessons given by her family, she started taking note when Granny would cook. Unfortunately for Sandy, one of her biggest regrets was not getting the exact measurements for the cinnamon rolls. When Sandy graduated from culinary school, one of the first tasks given to her by her mother was to re-create Granny's cinnamon rolls. Sandy was able to locate an old hand-written recipe card with the general method, but the problem was that the recipe said things like a "drop" of this and a "handful" of that. Sandy has worked diligently on these cinnamon rolls. She feels like hers have gotten really close to Granny's, but she thinks Granny's hands must have been much smaller. Her laughter and tiny hands are missed.

Blueberry Coffee Cake

Makes 6 to 8 servings

Cooking spray

2 cups all-purpose flour

1 cup granulated sugar

2 teaspoons baking powder

1½ teaspoons grated lemon zest

1 teaspoon salt

½ cup (1 stick) unsalted butter, softened

1 cup plus 3 to 5 teaspoons whole milk

2 large eggs, slightly beaten

1 teaspoon vanilla extract

1½ cups fresh or thawed frozen blueberries

1 cup confectioners' sugar

¼ teaspoon almond extract

Ever heard of "loafering"? Obviously, this is a Southern version of "loafing," a favorite Sunday afternoon occupation. "Loafering" was a term used often in Crystal's childhood—a word Crystal's mom used to describe their Sunday afternoon drives and visits with friends and family. Every Sunday, Crystal would climb into the family car with her mom and off they would go. One of their favorite stops was at Crystal's Great Aunt Cricket and Aunt Doc's house. (Yep, that is not a typo. When Crystal was a tiny red-haired child, she mistakenly called her Great Uncle Doc "Aunt Doc," and it stuck! Everyone called him Aunt Doc, and he didn't mind at all!) Aunt Cricket was the epitome of the Southern hostess, and she always had a pot of coffee brewed and a freshly baked cake on hand. The family would sit around her kitchen table and listen to Aunt Doc tell his outrageous stories, and the cake would always make the tales that much sweeter. This blueberry cake reminds Crystal of those afternoons and "loafering" around with her mom!

1. Preheat the oven to 375°F. Coat a 9 x 13-inch baking dish with cooking spray.

2. In a large bowl, combine the flour, granulated sugar, baking powder, lemon zest, and salt. Using a pastry blender or fork, cut in the butter until the mixture resembles coarse crumbs. Add 1 cup of the milk, the eggs, and vanilla, and stir well. Pour three-fourths of the batter into the prepared pan. Top with the blueberries, then spoon the remaining batter over the blueberries. Bake for 35 minutes, until a toothpick when inserted in the center of the cake comes out clean. Transfer to a wire rack and let cool 30 minutes.

3. In small bowl, whisk together the confectioners' sugar, almond extract, and 3 tablespoons of the milk. Add more milk as needed for the icing to be thin and easy to drizzle. Drizzle over the cake. Cut into squares and serve.

Maybe blueberries aren't your thing. If that is the case, simply substitute with your favorite berry. Sandy loves making this recipe with blackberries and cherries, too. It really just depends on what is in season and what mood you're in!

Lettuce Discuss Our Options

Iceberg! Straight Ahead!

Casseroles can be chock-full of yummy, nutritious veggies, but sometimes there's just no substitute for fresh, leafy greens. And salads can be just as delicious and tempting as a heaping dish of our signature pot pie. Or at least a really close second. To get the most out of this chapter, make sure to look for our pairing tips. Our Tomato and Feta Salad (page 265) goes great with our Moussaka (page 104). Try the Panzanella Salad (page 274) with an Italian casserole. The combinations of flavorful goodness seem endless!

Dress It Up!

Some casseroles are more complex than others, but overall, the main goal of a casserole is to make weeknight dinners or entertaining easier on you. That way, you have more time to enjoy dinner with your friends and family. Most casseroles are a meal on their own, so pairing them with a simple salad and some bread is always an easy solution! The Queens suggest that you keep a bag of your favorite mixed greens on hand and take flavor cues from your casserole to match your dressings! Having something Italian? Serve it with a Lemon Parmesan Dressing (page 257). Having Mexican? Go for a Creamy Chipotle Ranch Dressing (page 258). It's that easy! Whether you like vinaigrette or the creamy stuff, you only need a few simple ingredients on hand (and a couple of minutes) to make some yourself. Here are a few of our favorites.

Lemon Parmesan Dressing

Makes 1 cup

- ¾ cup vegetable oil
- ¼ cup fresh lemon juice
- 2 tablespoons grated Parmigiano Reggiano cheese
- 1 garlic clove, minced
- ¼ teaspoon granulated sugar
- ¾ teaspoon salt

This simple dressing is great paired with most Italian fare or with delicate dishes, such as seafood. The fresh flavor of lemon and the heartiness of the Parmesan is what makes this dressing sing. If possible, use a very finely grated Parmigiano Reggiano, as it will dissolve better. We also love this dressing when brushed on grilled vegetables, tossed in pasta salad, or drizzled over roasted new potatoes.

1. In a jar with a tight-fitting lid, combine the oil, lemon juice, cheese, garlic, sugar, and salt. Shake well to blend thoroughly.

2. The dressing will keep in the refrigerator for up to 2 weeks. Shake well before serving.

This dressing can be made DIABETIC-FRIENDLY by substituting a pinch of stevia for the sugar. Note that you only need a pinch, as stevia is about 300 times sweeter than sugar.

Creamy Chipotle Ranch Dressing

Makes 2 cups

- ½ cup mayonnaise
- ½ cup buttermilk
- 2 chipotle peppers in adobo sauce, minced
- 4 garlic cloves, minced
- ¼ cup chopped fresh cilantro leaves
- 1 teaspoon salt

Sandy's nephews, John and David, have called this spicy version of ranch dressing "gravy" since they were very small boys, and they add that gravy to just about anything! They not only put it on their salads, they also use it as a dip for raw veggies, as a dip for their pizza, and as a sauce on their mom's fish tacos. The chipotle peppers bring the heat, and the mayo can easily be replaced with plain nonfat yogurt if you want to cut some calories! That is the beauty of making your own dressing—you're in control of your ingredients!

1. In a blender, combine the mayonnaise, buttermilk, peppers, garlic, cilantro, and salt. Pulse until the dressing is smooth. If you prefer a chunkier dressing, you can combine the ingredients in a jar with a tight-fitting lid and shake well.

2. The dressing will keep in the refrigerator for up to 2 weeks. Shake well before serving.

Fiesta French
Dressing

Makes 1 cup

- ¾ cup corn oil (you can also use olive oil)
- ¼ cup cider vinegar
- 2 teaspoons mustard
- 2 teaspoons paprika
- 1 teaspoon granulated sugar
- 2 teaspoons salt
- ¼ teaspoon freshly ground black pepper

The tanginess of the mustard and vinegar makes this dressing a zesty addition to sandwiches or for perking up a simple green salad. In fact, this dressing is so lively, it's like having a fiesta of flavors in your mouth! When we created this recipe, we found that corn oil worked best. It lends a nice, smooth flavor to the dressing.

1. In a blender or food processor, combine the oil, vinegar, mustard, paprika, sugar, salt, and pepper. Blend until well combined.

2. The dressing will keep in the refrigerator for up to 2 weeks. Shake well before serving.

This dressing can be made DIABETIC-FRIENDLY by substituting a pinch of stevia for the sugar. Note that you only need a pinch, as stevia is about 300 times sweeter than sugar.

Do you know where the name Thousand Island dressing comes from? It was named after a large cluster of islands (over 1,800 of them) that are scattered on the northern part of Lake Ontario and along the Saint Lawrence River. Once controlled by pirates and bootleggers, the islands later became a popular vacation destination for the rich and famous. While we know the dressing was named for the place where it was created, the origin of the dressing itself is a little more controversial. There are two main stories about the formulation of this popular condiment.

One version states that it was created on the yacht belonging to George Boldt, the proprietor of New York City's Waldorf-Astoria Hotel. According to legend, a resourceful steward mixed it up when he realized that none of the usual ingredients for salad dressing were aboard the yacht. Boldt so enjoyed its distinctive taste that he named it after the area in which they were traveling and added it to the menu at the restaurant of the famed hotel.

The other version is that Sophia LaLonde, the wife of a Thousand Islands fishing guide, came up with the dressing and served it to visiting fishermen who went on excursions led by her husband. When visiting vaudeville star May Irwin tried the dressing, she was so impressed that she asked for the recipe. Mrs. LaLonde shared it with her, as well as with the Herald House, where Miss Irwin was staying, and they, too, began serving it to the public. Miss Irwin named the dressing after her vacation spot and claimed to have later shared the recipe with George Boldt so that he could add it to the menu of the Waldorf-Astoria.

To this day, nobody knows which (if either) of these stories is true. But whether you're Team Boldt or Team LaLonde, we can all agree that this ingenious creation changed salad dressing forever.

Thousand Island Dressing

Makes 1 cup

- ½ cup mayonnaise
- 2 tablespoons ketchup
- 1 tablespoon Heinz chili sauce
- ½ teaspoon Worcestershire sauce
- 1 tablespoon finely chopped onion
- 2 teaspoons sweet pickle relish
- 1 tablespoon granulated sugar
- ½ teaspoon garlic powder
- ¼ teaspoon salt
- ⅛ teaspoon freshly ground black pepper

Sandy's dad, Max, is a huge fan of this traditional Thousand Island dressing. Much like his grandsons and their "gravy" (see page 258), he dips everything in it. His favorite use for this dressing is for dipping his fries! When Crystal lived in Utah, she saw that restaurants made a similar dressing, which they called "fry sauce."

1. In a large bowl, combine the mayonnaise, ketchup, chili sauce, Worcestershire sauce, onion, relish, sugar, garlic powder, salt, and pepper. Whisk well.

2. Chill in the refrigerator for at least 30 minutes to allow the flavors to combine. Store in an airtight container for up to 2 weeks. Whisk well before serving.

This dish is GLUTEN-FREE as long as you use a gluten-free brand of Worcestershire sauce.

This dish is also VEGETARIAN-FRIENDLY as long as your Worcestershire sauce doesn't contain anchovies.

Balsamic Vinaigrette

Makes ⅔ cup

- ¼ cup balsamic vinegar
- 1 tablespoon Dijon mustard
- 1 garlic clove, minced
- 6 tablespoons olive oil
- 1 teaspoon salt
- ½ teaspoon freshly ground black pepper

Crystal's go-to favorite, Balsamic Vinaigrette, is low in fat and quite versatile. When drizzled over ripe garden tomatoes, fresh mozzarella, and basil, you have the summer's best salad. This dressing also makes a sweet marinade for grilled chicken breast or pork tenderloin. Crystal especially likes this with our Savory French Onion Tart (page 143).

1. In a small bowl, whisk together the balsamic vinegar, mustard, and garlic. Add the oil in a slow, steady stream, whisking constantly until well blended. Season with salt and pepper.

2. Store in an airtight container in the refrigerator for up to 2 weeks. Whisk well before serving.

Greek *Dressing*

Makes 1 cup

- ½ cup extra-virgin olive oil
- 5 tablespoons red wine vinegar
- 2 tablespoons fresh lemon juice
- 1½ teaspoons Dijon mustard
- 2 garlic cloves, minced
- ¼ teaspoon granulated sugar
- 1 teaspoon dried oregano
- ¼ teaspoon salt

This delicious and mildly tart dressing is amazing served over a Greek-style salad of lettuce, tomatoes, Kalamata olives, and feta cheese. It's also delicious in a sandwich wrap and even over pasta. Much like the Balsamic Vinaigrette (page 262), this makes a great marinade for chicken and fish, too.

1. In a medium bowl, whisk together the olive oil, vinegar, lemon juice, mustard, garlic, sugar, oregano, and salt. Whisk well to blend thoroughly.

2. Store in an airtight container in the refrigerator for up to 2 weeks. Whisk well before serving.

Crystal's Wedge Salad
with Bacon and Blue Cheese Dressing

Makes 8 servings

- 1 cup mayonnaise
- 1 (8-ounce) container sour cream
- 2 tablespoons Worcestershire sauce
- 2 teaspoons fresh lemon juice
- 1 cup crumbled blue cheese (4 ounces)
- 12 slices bacon, cooked and crumbled
- ½ cup shredded Parmesan cheese (2 ounces)
- 1 garlic clove, minced
- 1 teaspoon salt
- ½ teaspoon freshly ground black pepper
- 1 head iceberg lettuce, cut into 8 wedges

Crystal *loves* a wedge salad. When we were on a book tour, we'd get back to the hotel some nights completely pooped and starving, and all she wanted was a big wedge salad. A wedge salad may seem like an odd choice, but Crystal is on a personal mission to bring iceberg back! The sometimes-forgotten lettuce can be quite masterful in this setting. The ingredient list is small, but the textures and flavors really pack a punch. From the chilled crispness of the iceberg to the creamy tang of the blue cheese dressing—it is simply divine. Personally, we think the secret to a well-crafted wedge is that each serving should have a density conducive to eating it with a fork and knife. We kept our recipe straightforward, but feel free to top off your creation with crumbled bacon, chopped cherry tomatoes, hard-boiled egg, candied pecans, and even more blue cheese, of course.

1. In a medium bowl, combine the mayonnaise, sour cream, Worcestershire sauce, lemon juice, blue cheese, bacon, Parmesan cheese, garlic, salt, and pepper. Stir well.

2. Put the lettuce wedges on 8 plates. Drizzle ¼ cup of the dressing over each wedge and serve.

This dish is GLUTEN-FREE as long as your Worcestershire sauce is a gluten-free brand.

Tomato and Feta Salad

Makes 8 servings

- 1 pound ripe plum tomatoes, chopped
- 1 cucumber, seeded and chopped
- ½ teaspoon oregano
- 1 cup feta cheese, drained and cut into cubes (8 ounces)
- ½ cup pitted Kalamata olives, chopped
- Juice of ½ lemon
- ¼ cup extra-virgin olive oil
- 1 teaspoon salt
- ½ teaspoon freshly ground black pepper
- 8 basil leaves, torn into pieces

Tomato salads are a fresh addition to any meal. This particular salad has a Mediterranean flair, which makes it the perfect accompaniment to a white, flaky fish dish or our Moussaka (page 104). But with a few simple ingredient swaps, the tomato salad can take on an entirely different flavor. Check out our Pint-Size Caprese Salad (page 266) and our Tomato and Avocado Salad (page 267), which lend flavors to complement some of our Italian and Mexican casseroles. Who knew the tomato was so well traveled?

In a large bowl, combine the tomatoes, cucumber, oregano, cheese, and olives. Add the lemon juice, oil, salt, and pepper, and toss. Add the basil, toss again, and serve.

Pint-Size
Caprese Salad

Makes 6 servings

- 1 tablespoon lemon juice
- 1 cup fresh basil leaves (about 20), plus a few for garnish
- 1 small garlic clove, minced
- 1/3 cup extra-virgin olive oil
- 1 pint cherry tomatoes, halved
- 1 cup bocconcini, drained and halved
- 1/2 teaspoon salt
- 1/4 teaspoon freshly ground black pepper
- 2 tablespoons aged balsamic vinegar

This petite variation of the classic Caprese calls for cherry tomatoes and bocconcini (bite-size fresh mozzarella balls), but don't let the pint-size ingredients fool you—they pack the same flavorful punch. The flavors are brightened here with lemon juice and fresh basil, while the balsamic vinegar adds acidity. Serve with red pepper flakes on the side if you want to spice things up even more!

1. In a food processor or blender, blend together the lemon juice, basil, and garlic. With the machine running, gradually pour in the olive oil, blending to form a smooth dressing.

2. Pour the dressing into a medium bowl and add the tomatoes and cheese. Season with the salt and pepper, and toss well. Garnish with a few torn basil leaves and the balsamic vinegar.

Tomato and Avocado *Salad*

Makes 6 servings

2 Roma tomatoes, chopped

1 avocado, chopped

1 red onion, sliced

2 tablespoons fresh lemon juice

½ teaspoon salt

¼ teaspoon freshly ground black pepper

10 fresh cilantro leaves, for garnish

When making a salad, sometimes less is more. The undeniable stars of this simple salad are the tomato and the avocado, and in our opinion, this may be one of the best-tasting combinations that nature has ever produced! Try this salad with a Mexican dish, as its clean flavors balance out the spice and heavy cheese most Mexican recipes call for. It pairs especially well with our Chicken Enchiladas (page 110) and Yvonne's Unstuffed Poblano Casserole (page 108).

Put the tomatoes and the avocado in a medium bowl. Add the onion, lemon juice, salt, and pepper, and toss well. Garnish with the cilantro and serve.

Jayne's Marinated Vegetable Salad

Makes 10 servings

- 1 cup cider vinegar
- ¾ cup granulated sugar
- ½ cup vegetable oil
- 1 (15-ounce) can corn, drained
- 1 (9-ounce) box frozen baby peas, thawed and drained
- 1 (14.5-ounce) can French-style green beans, drained
- ½ onion, chopped
- 2 celery stalks, chopped
- 1 green bell pepper, chopped
- 1 (4-ounce) jar pimentos, chopped, drained
- 1 teaspoon salt
- ½ teaspoon freshly ground black pepper

This salad always reminds Sandy and her husband, Michael, of his family gatherings in his parents' backyard. Everyone is lounging around by the pool sipping cocktails and watching Michael's dad, Mike, prepare the grill. On warm Austin days, nothing is as refreshing as Jayne's (Michael's mom) marinated salad. It is cool, crisp, and has the perfect amount of crunch. Since it is best made beforehand and chilled overnight, you, too, can look like Jayne, the effortlessly fabulous hostess. Kick back with a glass of wine before guests arrive—the salad is ready!

1. In a small saucepan set over medium-high heat, bring the vinegar to a boil. Add the sugar, reduce the heat to medium, and simmer for 5 minutes, until the sugar is dissolved. Remove the pan from the heat and add the oil.

2. In a large bowl, combine the corn, peas, green beans, onion, celery, green pepper, pimentos, salt, and pepper. Pour the vinegar mixture over the vegetables. Chill the salad for 8 hours or overnight. Serve cold.

This recipe can be made DIABETIC-FRIENDLY by substituting garbanzo beans for the corn. Diabetics need to be mindful of corn because of its high sugar content. Also, substitute 1 teaspoon stevia for the sugar. Note that you need far less stevia, as it is about 300 times sweeter than sugar.

Hargill's Bunco Club
Seven-Layer Salad

Makes 10 servings

- 2 cups spring salad mix
- 1 bunch green onions, green parts only, chopped
- 1 green bell pepper, chopped
- 1 (16-ounce) bag frozen peas
- 2 cups mayonnaise
- 1 tablespoon granulated sugar
- 2 cups shredded sharp Cheddar cheese (8 ounces)
- 12 slices bacon, cooked and crumbled

My, oh my, this is a Hargill, Texas, classic recipe. This seven-layer salad has made an appearance at pretty much every Bunco party, church supper, baby shower, picnic, and family reunion Sandy can think of. Sealing the top of the salad with mayo is the key to its freshness and creaminess. Give it a try. It will be a favorite for your family, too!

1. In a 9 x 13-inch casserole dish, layer the salad in this order: spring salad mix, green onions, green bell peppers, and frozen peas.

2. In a small bowl, combine the mayonnaise and the sugar. Spread the mayonnaise over the top of the veggies, completely sealing in the goodies below. Top the mayonnaise with the cheese and the bacon. Chill in the refrigerator for 1 hour before serving.

This recipe can be made DIABETIC-FRIENDLY by substituting a pinch of stevia for the sugar. Note that you only need a pinch, as stevia is about 300 times sweeter than sugar.

Crystal's May-I-Have-More-Mayo Potato Salad

Makes 8 servings

- 3 pounds red potatoes
- 1 teaspoon salt
- ½ teaspoon freshly ground black pepper
- ½ cup mayonnaise
- ½ cup Greek yogurt
- 3 tablespoons rice vinegar
- 3 green onions, green parts only, thinly sliced
- 3 celery stalks, chopped
- ½ cup chopped fresh parsley
- ½ cup chopped fresh basil
- 3 tablespoons chopped fresh dill
- 2 teaspoons finely grated lemon zest

Potato salad is like wine in that it is very much about personal taste. Some like a mustard-based salad, some like a mayo-based one, and some like a combination of both. For Crystal, it has to be mayo, and she likes to add a little Greek yogurt for some tang. Mixed up with tons of fresh herbs, this potato salad is amazingly light and refreshing! Make it ahead of time, 'cause again (like wine), it is better after it has aged.

1. Put the potatoes in a large pot of heavily salted water. Bring to a boil, reduce the heat to medium-low, and simmer until the potatoes are tender, about 17 minutes. Drain and let cool.

2. Cut potatoes into ¾-inch pieces, put them in a large bowl, and season with the salt and pepper. In a separate bowl, combine the mayonnaise, yogurt, and vinegar, and pour the mixture over the potatoes. Add the green onions, celery, parsley, basil, dill, and lemon zest, and toss well. Cover and refrigerate overnight before serving (if you can wait that long). The salad will keep in the refrigerator for up to 5 days.

Community-Building
Warm Bacon Spinach Salad

Makes 8 servings

- ¼ cup olive oil
- 1 medium onion, thinly sliced
- 1 tablespoon all-purpose flour
- 1 tablespoon granulated sugar
- 1 teaspoon dry mustard
- ¼ cup sherry vinegar
- 1 teaspoon salt
- ½ teaspoon freshly ground black pepper
- 1 (10-ounce) bag fresh spinach
- 3 slices bacon, cooked and crumbled
- 1 large hard-boiled egg, sliced
- 2 cups croutons

Hargill—the town where Sandy grew up—is not large by any means. There is a single community building in town where folks hold family reunions, the annual Hargill cook-off, and many wedding celebrations. At the center of most events is a potluck dinner, and this salad is a community staple and almost always makes an appearance. This salad simply bursts with flavor, most notably from the bacon, as well as the great balance of the sweet sautéed onions and tangy vinegar. Delish!

1. In a medium skillet set over medium-high heat, add the oil and onion and cook until the onion begins to soften, about 6 minutes.

2. In a small bowl, combine the flour, sugar, and dry mustard. Add the mixture to the onion mixture. Gradually add the vinegar and 1 cup of water to the pan and cook, stirring constantly, until thickened, about 5 minutes. Season with the salt and pepper.

3. Divide the spinach among 8 plates. Pour the warm dressing over the spinach and garnish with the crumbled bacon, egg slices, and croutons.

This dish can be made GLUTEN-FREE by replacing the flour with a gluten-free all-purpose mix, either store bought (see page 21 for recommendations of our favorite brands) or homemade (see page 322 for our recipe), and using gluten-free croutons.

This recipe can be made DIABETIC-FRIENDLY by substituting a pinch of stevia for the sugar. Note that you only need a pinch, as stevia is about 300 times sweeter than sugar.

Jayne's
Seafood Pasta Salad

Makes 4 to 6 servings

1 (8-ounce) package orecchiette pasta

2 tablespoons olive oil

6 large hard-boiled eggs, chopped

1 cup mayonnaise

1/3 cup Heinz chili sauce

1/4 cup sour cream

1 tablespoon fresh lemon juice

1 1/2 teaspoons salt

12 ounces crab meat

2 pounds fresh shrimp, boiled, chilled, peeled, and deveined

1 celery stalk, chopped

1/2 cup chopped broccoli, lightly steamed

1/4 cup sliced green onions, green parts only

Sandy's mother-in-law, Jayne, is one of our favorite people in the world. You would be hard pressed to find someone kinder and more supportive than she is. This recipe is her specialty, and she is given much grief if a family event comes and goes without its appearance. Do yourself a favor and make it today!

1. In a large pot of boiling salted water, cook the pasta until al dente, about 12 minutes. Drain and rinse the pasta under cold water. Put the pasta in a large bowl, add the olive oil, and toss to coat. Cover the bowl and chill in the refrigerator for at least 1 hour.

2. In another large bowl, combine the eggs, mayonnaise, chili sauce, sour cream, lemon juice, and salt, and mix well. Add the crab meat, shrimp, celery, broccoli, and green onions, and stir well. Cover the bowl and chill for at least 3 hours.

3. Add the chilled pasta to the crabmeat mixture and mix well. The salad will keep in the refrigerator for up to 3 days.

This dish can be made GLUTEN-FREE by using a gluten-free pasta. See page 21 for recommendations of our favorite brands.

There is enough protein in this recipe to make the dish DIABETIC-FRIENDLY, as long as you replace the orecchiette with a whole-wheat pasta that is high in fiber.

Broccoli Salad

Makes 8 servings

- 6 cups fresh broccoli florets, chopped
- 8 slices bacon, cooked and crumbled
- 3 green onions, green parts only, chopped
- ½ cup dried cranberries or raisins
- ½ cup chopped pecans
- 1 cup mayonnaise
- 2 tablespoons cider vinegar
- ½ cup granulated sugar

You'll be surprised how this tasty salad tricks many picky eaters into dining on veggies! Crystal's sister-in-law Ramona employs this salad to get her daughter Chloe to eat her broccoli. The trick lies in the combination of the flavors—the raw broccoli pairs beautifully with salty bacon and a sweet and creamy dressing.

1. In a large bowl, combine the broccoli, bacon, green onions, cranberries, and pecans.
2. In a separate bowl, combine the mayonnaise, vinegar, and sugar to make a dressing. Pour the dressing over the broccoli mixture and toss well. Serve room temperature or cold.

This dish can be made DIABETIC-FRIENDLY by omitting the dried fruit and substituting a sugar substitute like stevia for the sugar. Take a look at the guidelines on the sweetener package to know how much to put in the salad, since something like Splenda is much sweeter than sugar.

Panzanella
Salad

Makes 8 servings

- 6 cups day-old Italian bread, torn into bite-size pieces
- ⅓ cup plus 3 tablespoons olive oil
- 3 garlic cloves, minced
- 2 teaspoons salt
- 1 teaspoon freshly ground black pepper
- ¼ cup fresh lemon juice
- 2 tablespoons red wine vinegar
- 1 teaspoon granulated sugar
- 4 Roma tomatoes, chopped
- 1 cucumber, seeded and chopped
- 1 cup cubed fontina cheese (4 ounces)
- ½ cup Kalamata olives, pitted and halved
- 10 fresh basil leaves, shredded

If you've ever tried traditional panzanella, then you know it's basically a bread salad made with lots of fresh vegetables. Our version includes the usual tomatoes and basil, along with cucumbers for crunch, Kalamata olives for a little salty goodness, and some creamy fontina cheese, because cheese makes everything even better! This is a great summer salad to bring to a cookout.

1. Preheat the oven to 400°F.

2. On a baking sheet, toss the bread with ⅓ cup of the oil, the garlic, ½ teaspoon of the salt, and ¼ teaspoon of the pepper. Spread into a single layer and bake for 5 to 10 minutes, or until crispy, stirring a few times to ensure that it toasts evenly.

3. In a small bowl, whisk together the lemon juice, vinegar, sugar, 1 teaspoon of the salt, and ½ teaspoon of the pepper. Drizzle in the remaining 3 tablespoons of oil, whisking until blended.

4. In a bowl, toss the toasted bread with the tomatoes, cucumber, cheese, olives, and basil. Drizzle with the dressing and season with the remaining ½ teaspoon of salt and the remaining ¼ teaspoon pepper. Let sit for 10 minutes before serving.

This recipe can be made GLUTEN-FREE by using a gluten-free bread. See page 21 for recommendations of our favorite brands.

A Few of Sandy's Favorite Things
Orzo Pasta Salad

Makes 8 servings

- 1 pound orzo pasta
- 2 garlic cloves, minced
- 1 teaspoon olive oil
- 1 leek, white and pale green parts only, thinly sliced
- 1 teaspoon salt plus more for pasta water
- 1 cup baby arugula
- 1½ cups pine nuts
- Juice of 1 lemon
- 1 teaspoon salt
- ½ teaspoon freshly ground black pepper
- 1 cup grated Parmesan cheese (4 ounces)

Pasta tossed with peppery arugula and leeks (yum!)
Engagement and marriage to computer geeks (just one!)
Memories like these carry my mind to Spring
'Cause these are a few of my favorite things

When the dog bites! (never a pug, they are angels)
When the bee stings (bastard!)
When I'm feeling sad (out of wine)
I simply remember (to eat) my favorite things
And then I don't feel so bad!!!!! ('nuff said!)

1. In a medium saucepan set over high heat, cook the orzo in boiling salted water until tender, about 10 minutes. Drain the pasta and set aside to cool.

2. In a small saucepan set over medium-high heat, sauté the garlic in the olive oil. Add the leek and 1 teaspoon salt, and cook for about 3 minutes. Stir in the arugula and cook until wilted, about 3 minutes.

3. Put the orzo in a medium bowl and add the pine nuts, lemon juice, the remaining 1 teaspoon salt, and pepper. Toss well. Sprinkle the cheese over the top of the salad. Serve warm or cold.

This recipe can be made GLUTEN-FREE by substituting quinoa for the orzo.

Cornbread Salad
Two Ways

Even though we Queens grew up in different states, we have eerily similar lives—so similar, in fact, that we are still trying to figure out how we're related. Both of us come from large families with parents who have been married over 50 years; both have four siblings; both are the youngest child. Crystal's mother's middle name is Irene; Sandy had a grandmother named Irene. We even have the same birthday. But most important, we grew up eating similar foods, but with regional twists. Here is the Pollock version of Cornbread Salad, and the Cook version follows.

Pollock Family Version

Makes 6 servings

- 5 cups crumbled Mexican Cornbread (page 327)
- 1 pound bacon, cooked and crumbled
- 1 red bell pepper, seeded and chopped
- 1 cucumber, seeded and chopped
- 2 large beefsteak tomatoes, diced
- 1 bunch green onions, green parts only, sliced
- 1 cup Creamy Chipotle Ranch Dressing (page 258), or store-bought ranch dressing

1. In a large bowl, combine the cornbread, bacon, red bell pepper, cucumber, tomatoes, and green onions.
2. Pour the salad dressing over the salad and toss to coat. Serve immediately.

Cook Family Version

Makes 6 servings

- 1 recipe Cook's Cornbread, crumbled (page 328)
- 2 (15.5-ounce) cans pinto beans, rinsed and drained
- 1 onion, chopped
- 1 green bell pepper, seeded and chopped
- 1 beefsteak tomato, chopped
- 1 cup mayonnaise
- ½ cup sweet gherkins pickle juice
- 1 pound bacon, cooked and crumbled

In a 9 x 13-inch casserole dish, layer the ingredients as follows: cornbread, beans, onion, bell pepper, tomato, mayonnaise, pickle juice, and bacon. Cover and chill overnight. Serve cold.

These dishes can be made GLUTEN-FREE if you use a gluten-free cornbread mix to make your cornbread. We recommend Bob's Red Mill Gluten Free Cornbread Mix.

Tomato, Goat Cheese, and Quinoa Salad

Makes 6 to 8 servings

- 1 cup quinoa
- 1 teaspoon salt
- 2 tablespoons olive oil
- 2 garlic cloves, minced
- ¼ cup balsamic vinegar
- 1 pint cherry tomatoes, halved
- 1 (5.3-ounce) container goat cheese, crumbled
- ½ cup fresh basil, thinly sliced, plus more for garnish

This warm quinoa salad makes a powerful sidekick for any entrée. It has a similar texture to that of couscous or rice, with a slight crunch and a somewhat nutty flavor. Quinoa is considered a super food because it contains more protein than any other grain. And this protein is complete, containing all nine essential amino acids—talk about a boost! Mix it with tomato and garlic and goat cheese for a delicious dish that packs quite a nutritional punch.

1. Put the quinoa in a strainer and rinse it under warm water until the water runs clear.

2. Bring 3 cups of water and the salt to a boil in a medium saucepan. Add the quinoa and bring it back to a boil. Reduce the heat to low, cover the pan, and simmer for 15 minutes, or until the quinoa is tender and translucent. Drain off the water and put the quinoa in a bowl.

3. Heat the olive oil in a medium sauté pan set over medium-high heat. Add the garlic and cook for 1 minute. Add the balsamic vinegar and tomatoes and toss to coat.

4. Cook, stirring occasionally, until the mixture has reduced and become syrupy, 15 to 20 minutes. Pour the tomato mixture into the bowl of quinoa and toss to mix. Add the goat cheese and basil and toss well. Garnish with more basil and serve warm.

Desserts
Fit for a Queen

Blame it on our Southern roots, but we find the end of a meal is just another necessary excuse for a sweet indulgence. Gooey, rich chocolate, buttery pastry, fresh fruits, and other quality ingredients are essential to Casserole Queens desserts. From indulgent and decadent (try the Peanut Butter Freezer Pie with Chocolate and Bananas, page 302) to light and fluffy (Chu Chu's Tropical Trifle, page 316), these treats are easy to prepare and will win the hearts of even the most discriminating dessert aficionados! The Queens aren't afraid to love dessert, and we have gone the extra mile to bring you an array of cakes, pies, cobblers, and other goodies to delight your family and guests.

Gooey Apple Butter Cake

Makes 6 to 8 servings

- 3 Granny Smith apples
- 1 tablespoon fresh lemon juice
- 1 (15 to 18.6-ounce) box yellow cake mix
- 1 cup (2 sticks) unsalted butter, melted
- 3 large eggs
- 1 (8-ounce) package cream cheese, softened
- 1½ teaspoons vanilla extract
- 1½ teaspoons ground cinnamon
- 3 cups confectioners' sugar

Crystal's nieces have nicknamed their mother "Butter." This term of endearment for Karen stems from the fact that she cooks everything with butter. One of her specialties is this cake, and—you guessed it—there's lots of butter! A cream cheese and apple mixture bakes up nice and gooey on top of a soft cake layer. Served warm, it just doesn't get any butter—we mean, better.

1. Preheat the oven to 350°F.

2. Peel and slice the apples, then toss them in a bowl with the lemon juice to keep them from turning brown. Set aside.

3. In the bowl of a standing mixer fitted with the whisk attachment, add the cake mix, ½ cup of the melted butter, and one of the eggs. Mix for 2 minutes at medium-low speed. The batter should easily come together into a ball. Transfer the batter to a 9 x 13-inch baking dish and smooth the top with a spatula.

4. In the same bowl used for the batter, beat the cream cheese at medium-low speed for 30 seconds, until fluffy. Add the remaining ½ cup butter, the remaining 2 eggs, vanilla, and cinnamon. Beat on medium speed for 1 minute. Add the sugar and beat for 1 more minute.

5. Fold the apple slices into the cream cheese mixture, and spread the mixture over the cake mix in the baking dish.

6. Bake for 45 minutes or until the cake jiggles slightly when gently shaken and is somewhat solidified in the center. (The cream cheese mixture will not solidify completely.) Remove the cake from the oven and allow it to cool in the pan for 30 minutes.

7. Stored in the refrigerator, the cake will keep for 3 to 4 days, but it will never last that long!

FREEZES WELL See our freezer tips on page 16.

Chilled
Coconut Cake

Makes 8 to 10 servings

Vegetable shortening, such as Crisco

All-purpose flour

1 (15 to 18.6-ounce) box yellow cake mix

1 cup granulated sugar

1 cup whole milk

1½ cups heavy cream, whipped

1 (7-ounce) bag sweetened coconut flakes

This cake is an everyday favorite at Crystal's mom's house. Any time Crystal's family gets together for a Sunday dinner, she has this tasty treat to look forward to. It got the nickname "Rice Cake" from Crystal's niece, Alexis, when she was little because she thought the coconut flakes were little pieces of rice.

1. Grease and flour a 9 x 13-inch metal casserole dish.

2. Follow the package instructions to mix the cake batter and bake the cake in the prepared casserole dish. While cake is still warm, poke holes in the top of it with a fork.

3. In a saucepan set over medium-low heat, combine the sugar and milk. Heat the mixture, stirring, until the sugar is dissolved; do not let boil. Pour the mixture over the cake, and let the cake cool completely.

4. Once the cake is cool, spread the whipped cream over the top of the cake. Cover the top of the cake with coconut flakes. Place the cake in the refrigerator and let it chill overnight.

5. Store any leftovers in the fridge for up to 1 week—the longer this cake is in the refrigerator, the better it gets!

FREEZES WELL See our freezer tips on page 16.

Buttermilk Cake
with Malted Chocolate Frosting

Makes 12 servings

- 1½ cups (3 sticks) unsalted butter, softened, plus more for the dish
- 4 cups cake flour
- 1 teaspoon baking soda
- ½ teaspoon baking powder
- 1 teaspoon salt
- 3 cups granulated sugar
- 3 teaspoons vanilla extract
- 2 cups buttermilk
- 6 large egg whites
- 4 teaspoons light corn syrup
- ¼ cup unsweetened cocoa powder
- ½ cup malted milk powder
- 1½ cups confectioners' sugar
- 3 to 4 tablespoons heavy cream

Crystal's friend Martha is known for stealing all of the malt balls out of her children's Halloween treat bags. Though she tries not to do it, she finds them so deliciously sweet and addictive, she simply can't help herself. She spends the day after Halloween with a toothache, a remorseful conscience, and three angry boys. Thanks to this cake, she no longer has to resort to petty theft to get her malty fix. Don't worry; this rich cake won't cause a toothache . . . and you don't have to wait until Halloween to try it!

1. Preheat the oven to 350°F. Butter a 9 x13-inch casserole dish.

2. Sift together the flour, baking soda, baking powder, and ½ teaspoon of the salt.

3. In the bowl of an electric mixer fitted with the whisk attachment, cream 1 cup of the butter with the granulated sugar until light and fluffy, about 3 minutes. Beat in 1½ teaspoons of the vanilla. Add the flour mixture to the creamed butter and sugar alternately with the buttermilk, beating well after each addition. Add the egg whites and beat at medium speed for about 1 minute. Pour the batter into the prepared dish. Bake for 20 minutes. Reduce the heat to 325°F and bake for 25 more minutes. Let the cake cool in the dish.

4. Meanwhile, in small bowl, whisk the remaining ½ cup of butter, the corn syrup, and the remaining 1½ teaspoons of vanilla. Add the cocoa powder, the remaining ½ teaspoon of salt, and the malted milk powder, and whisk until well blended. Add the confectioners' sugar and 3 tablespoons of the heavy cream. If the frosting is too thick, add more cream until you reach a good spreading consistency. Frost the top of the cake.

Yvette's Pineapple Upside-Down Cake

Makes 8 to 10 servings

- ½ cup (1 stick) unsalted butter
- 1 cup packed light brown sugar
- 1 (20-ounce) can sliced pineapple in heavy syrup
- 1 (16-ounce) jar whole maraschino cherries
- 1 cup granulated sugar
- 3 large egg yolks
- ½ cup pineapple juice
- 3 large egg whites, lightly beaten
- 1 teaspoon baking powder
- 1 cup all-purpose flour

Yvette, Sandy's sister, is known all over the Valley for this cake. In fact, it's her claim to fame in those parts: "Oh, honey, you know Yvette. She's the one that makes that ridiculously tasty upside-down cake." Want in on her secret? She uses a cast-iron skillet to bake it, versus transferring it to a cake pan! This keeps the top of the cake extra crunchy and gives it a little extra caramelized flavor that people go crazy for.

1. Preheat the oven to 325°F.

2. In a small saucepan set over medium heat, melt the butter. Add the brown sugar and cook until bubbly, about 10 minutes. Pour the caramel into a 9-inch cast-iron skillet. (Not to worry if you don't have a cast-iron skillet on-hand—you can use a metal 9 x 13-inch casserole dish instead.) Lay the pineapple slices evenly over the caramel, but don't overlap. Place a cherry in the center of each pineapple ring.

3. Beat together the granulated sugar and egg yolks until pale yellow. Add the pineapple juice, egg whites, baking powder, and flour. Pour the mixture over the pineapples. Bake for about 30 minutes or until a toothpick inserted into the center of the cake comes out clean. If the cake starts to brown too much, lay a piece of foil loosely over the cake while it finishes cooking.

4. Transfer the pan to a wire rack and let cool for 15 minutes. Invert the cake onto a serving platter. Serve while warm.

Apple Crunch
Coffee Cake

Makes 10 servings

- ½ tablespoon butter, for buttering the dish
- 2 cups all-purpose flour, plus more for dusting
- 2 cups Golden Delicious apples, peeled, cored, and chopped
- 2 cups granulated sugar
- 1 cup vegetable oil
- 2 large eggs
- 2 teaspoons ground cinnamon
- 2 teaspoons baking powder
- ½ teaspoon salt
- 1 cup chopped walnuts

Cake for breakfast? Sure! If it's wrong, do you really want to be right? We didn't think so. Full of apples and nuts, this versatile cake can be breakfast, dessert, or an afternoon snack. It's all you need to make anytime special.

1. Preheat the oven to 350°F. Butter and flour a 9 x 13-inch casserole dish.

2. In a large bowl, combine the apples, flour, sugar, oil, eggs, cinnamon, baking powder, salt, and nuts and stir well. The batter will be thick.

3. Spread the batter in the prepared casserole dish. Bake for 55 minutes, or until a toothpick inserted in the center of the cake comes out clean. Let cool for 5 minutes before serving.

4. Store in an airtight container in the refrigerator for up to 1 week.

This dish can be made GLUTEN-FREE by replacing the flour with a gluten-free all-purpose mix, either store bought (see page 21 for recommendations of our favorite brands) or homemade (see page 322 for our recipe). Also, be sure to use a gluten-free baking powder.

Hot Fudge Sundae Cake

Makes 10 servings

- 1 cup all-purpose flour
- ¾ cup granulated sugar
- ¼ cup plus 2 tablespoons Dutch-processed cocoa powder
- 2 teaspoons baking powder
- ¼ teaspoon salt
- ½ cup whole milk
- 2 tablespoons vegetable oil
- 1 teaspoon vanilla extract
- 1 cup chopped pecans
- 1 cup packed dark brown sugar
- 1¾ cups hot water
- Vanilla ice cream

It's a question we've all asked ourselves at one time or another: do I treat myself to a sundae, or am I more in the mood for a piece of cake? But why decide between two limiting options when you can have the best of both worlds? Sunday may be fun day, but this decadent cake served with vanilla ice cream is a treat for any day of the week.

1. Preheat the oven to 350°F.

2. In an ungreased 9 x 13-inch casserole dish, stir together the flour, granulated sugar, 2 tablespoons of the cocoa powder, the baking powder, and salt.

3. In a medium bowl, combine the milk, oil, and vanilla. Pour the liquid mixture into the casserole dish and stir well with a fork. Stir in the pecans and spread the mixture, pressing evenly into the casserole dish. Sprinkle the top with the brown sugar and the remaining ¼ cup of cocoa powder. Pour the hot water evenly over the batter.

4. Bake for 40 minutes, or until a toothpick inserted into the center of the cake comes out clean. Remove the dish from the oven and let cool for 15 minutes. Serve with a scoop of vanilla ice cream.

5. Store the cake in an airtight container in the refrigerator for up to a week.

This dish can be made GLUTEN-FREE by replacing the flour with a gluten-free all-purpose mix, either store bought (see page 21 for recommendations of our favorite brands) or homemade (see page 322 for our recipe). Also, be sure to use a gluten-free baking powder.

Bailey's Drug Store
Chocolate Cake

Makes 8 to 10 servings

- ½ cup vegetable shortening, such as Crisco, plus more for greasing the dish
- 2 cups all-purpose flour, plus more for dusting the dish
- 2 cups granulated sugar
- 2 large eggs
- 6 tablespoons unsweetened cocoa powder
- 2 teaspoons baking powder
- 1 teaspoon salt
- 1½ cups whole milk
- 1 teaspoon vanilla extract
- Chocolate Frosting (opposite page)

Bailey's Drug Store, in Blue Ridge, Georgia, is long gone, but the cake lives on. Crystal's Aunt Mary Ann and Aunt Thelma used to love eating this cake with ice cream during their lunch break at work. Both were hardworking women in the 1950s and they needed this daily treat to keep them going. Every now and then, couldn't you also use a little noontime sweet to get you through the day? Don't cheat yourself. It is better with ice cream, so make sure and give yourself a big scoop! We suggest good ol' vanilla!

1. Preheat the oven to 350°F. Grease and flour a 9 x 13-inch casserole dish.

2. Using a whisk, beat together the sugar and ½ cup shortening. Add the eggs, and whisk until light in color. Add the 2 cups flour and stir until combined.

3. In a separate bowl, combine the cocoa powder, baking powder, and salt. Add the dry ingredients to the sugar mixture alternately with the milk, stirring to combine after each addition. Add the vanilla and stir until combined.

4. Pour the batter into the prepared casserole dish. Bake for 45 minutes or until a toothpick inserted in the center comes out clean. Transfer the baking dish to a wire rack and let the cake cool completely.

5. Spread the chocolate frosting over the top of the cake. The cake will keep in the refrigerator, wrapped in plastic wrap, for 5 days.

Chocolate Frosting

Makes about 2½ cups

- ½ cup (1 stick) unsalted butter
- 2 cups granulated sugar
- ¼ teaspoon salt
- 2 teaspoons vanilla extract
- ¼ cup unsweetened cocoa powder
- 1 (5-ounce) can evaporated milk

1. In a saucepan set over medium-high heat, combine the butter, sugar, salt, vanilla, cocoa powder, and evaporated milk. Bring to a boil and cook, stirring constantly, for 4 minutes.

2. Transfer the frosting to the bowl of a standing mixer fitted with the whisk attachment, and beat for 1 to 2 minutes, or until it is thick enough to spread.

3. The frosting can be made ahead and stored in an airtight container in the refrigerator for up to 5 days.

Granny Haley's
Angel Food Cake with
Vanilla Strawberry Sauce

Makes 8 servings

- 1 cup cake flour
- 1¾ cups granulated sugar
- 12 egg whites, at room temperature
- 1½ teaspoons cream of tartar
- ¼ teaspoon salt
- 2 teaspoons vanilla extract
- 1 pint strawberries, washed, hulled, and sliced
- 1 tablespoon cornstarch
- 1 tablespoon unsalted butter
- 8 mint leaves for garnish

Sandy's Granny Haley kept a glass Coke bottle in her cabinet for the times she made angel cake. When the cake would come out of the oven, she would flip it over and let it hang on the neck of the Coke bottle to cool. She did this all the time, but the first time Sandy and her sister Kellye saw it, they must have looked very confused, which made Granny Haley giggle like no one's business. Granny Haley's giggle was legendary: her entire body would shimmy and shake, and she would get all flustered, turning fifty different shades of pink and red. Man, she was darling.

1. Preheat the oven to 375°F.

2. Sift together the flour and ¾ cup of the sugar.

3. In a large bowl, beat the egg whites with the cream of tartar, salt, and 1½ teaspoons of the vanilla until stiff enough to hold soft peaks, but still moist and glossy, about 5 minutes. While beating, add ¾ cup of the sugar, 2 teaspoons at a time. Continue to beat until the meringue holds stiff peaks.

4. Sift about a quarter of the flour mixture over the meringue, and using a rubber spatula, gently fold in the flour. Fold in the remaining flour, a quarter at a time.

5. Pour the batter into an ungreased Bundt pan. Bake for 35 to 40 minutes, until a toothpick inserted in the center comes out clean.

6. Meanwhile, put the strawberries in a bowl and sprinkle them with the remaining $\frac{1}{4}$ cup of sugar. Let them stand for 15 minutes. Stir occasionally. Drain the berries, reserving the juice. Add enough water to the juice to make 1 cup of liquid. In a medium saucepan set over medium heat, combine the cornstarch and the juice and cook, stirring constantly, until the mixture thickens, about 7 minutes. Stir in the butter, and then fold in the berries and the remaining $\frac{1}{2}$ teaspoon of vanilla.

7. Let the cake cool completely in the pan. Then invert the pan onto a cutting board to release the cake, and slice the cake into 8 wedges. Garnish with the mint leaves and extra strawberries, if desired. Serve with the strawberry sauce.

This dish can be made GLUTEN-FREE by eliminating the regular cake flour and substituting a gluten-free cake flour mix. We recommend Pamela's brand. Also, be sure to use a gluten-free cornstarch.

Granny Haley's
Orange Date Cake

Makes 8 to 10 servings

Vegetable shortening, such as Crisco

2 cups all-purpose flour, plus more for dusting the dish

1 cup chopped dates

¼ cup (½ stick) unsalted butter

1 cup granulated sugar

2 large eggs

½ teaspoon baking powder

½ teaspoon baking soda

⅔ cup sour milk (see headnote)

2 tablespoons grated orange zest

½ cup chopped pecans

1 cup confectioners' sugar

2 tablespoons orange juice

This recipe was a favorite of Sandy's Granny Haley. Sandy remembers how Granny Haley would serve this cake whenever anyone would come by for a Sunday afternoon visit over coffee or tea. The subtly sweet cake was the perfect snack and accompaniment to their ever sweeter conversation.

Most people don't have sour milk on hand, so here's a simple way to make some. Combine ⅔ cup milk and ⅔ teaspoon white vinegar or lemon juice, and let it sit for 10 minutes before using.

1. Preheat the oven to 350°F. Grease and flour a 9 x 13-inch casserole dish.

2. Put the dates in a bowl and cover them with hot water. Let them soak for 1 hour.

3. In a separate bowl, cream together the butter, granulated sugar, and eggs.

4. Sift the 2 cups flour, the baking powder, and baking soda into a medium bowl. Add the dry ingredients to the butter and sugar mixture alternately with milk, adding a third of each at a time and mixing thoroughly before adding the next. Drain the dates and stir them in with the orange zest and nuts. Pour the batter into the prepared casserole dish. Bake for 40 to 50 minutes or until a toothpick inserted into the center of the cake comes out clean.

5. Meanwhile, whisk together the confectioners' sugar and orange juice, making sure to break up any lumps. The consistency should be such that it can be easily drizzled or poured over the cake. If it's too thick, thin it with a little more orange juice; if it's too thin, add more confectioners' sugar, a teaspoon at a time, making sure to mix thoroughly before adding more. Drizzle the orange glaze over the cake while it is still warm. Cut into squares and serve while warm.

6. Store leftover pieces in an airtight container at room temperature for up to 5 days.

There were many funny stories that came out of these visits at Granny Haley's, but this one takes the cake—literally! Sandy's Uncle Dale and his friend Kiefer were cooks in the army. One day, they discovered that their kitchen was being raided every night by hungry soldiers with a sweet tooth. To teach the thieves a lesson, Kiefer made a special cake full of shrimp shells. But in an unexpected turn of events, some high-ranked officers stopped by for a special meeting and the cakes meant for the thieves got served to the VIPs. Kiefer and Dale just knew they were going to be discharged, but not one word was ever mentioned. Maybe the officers were simply used to eating bad mess-hall food.

Mom's
Glazed Oatmeal Cake

Makes 8 to 10 servings

- ½ cup vegetable shortening, such as Crisco, plus more for greasing the dish
- 1⅓ cups all-purpose flour, plus more for dusting the dish
- 1¼ cups hot water
- 1 cup old-fashioned rolled oats
- 1¾ cups packed light brown sugar
- 1 cup granulated sugar
- 2 large eggs
- 1 teaspoon baking soda
- 1 teaspoon ground cinnamon
- ½ teaspoon salt
- 6 tablespoons (¾ stick) unsalted butter
- 1 tablespoon evaporated milk
- 1 cup chopped pecans
- 1 cup sweetened coconut flakes

Both Sandy and Crystal's love for cooking stems from their mothers. This particular recipe is one that Sandy and her mother, Marge, shared throughout her youth, and it signifies that mother-daughter bond. What better place to get to know your kids than through cooking your favorite recipes in the kitchen?

1. Preheat the oven to 350°F. Lightly grease and flour a 9 x 13-inch casserole dish.

2. In a small bowl, pour the hot water over the oats and let sit for 10 minutes for the oats to absorb the water.

3. Cream together 1 cup of the brown sugar, granulated sugar, and ½ cup of the shortening in a large bowl. Add the eggs and stir well.

4. In a separate bowl, sift together the 1⅓ cups flour, baking soda, cinnamon, and salt. Add the dry ingredients to the shortening mixture, and stir well. Add the softened oats a little at a time, stirring after each addition, until all of the oats are incorporated.

5. Pour the batter into the prepared casserole dish. Bake for 30 minutes or until a toothpick inserted into the center of the cake comes out clean. Transfer the cake to a wire rack and let cool completely.

6. Preheat the broiler.

7. For the icing, put the remaining ¾ cup brown sugar, the butter, evaporated milk, and nuts in a saucepan set over medium-high heat and bring to a boil. Boil for 1 minute. Remove the pan from the heat and add the coconut.

8. Ice the cake, transfer it to the oven, and broil for 3 to 5 minutes or until the icing is golden brown. Watch the cake very carefully as the icing can burn easily. Cut into square pieces and serve immediately.

9. Store any leftover pieces in an airtight container and refrigerate for up to 5 days.

Clementine
Cake

Makes 8 to 10 servings

Vegetable shortening, such as Crisco

All-purpose flour

¾ cup water

1 (15 to 18.6-ounce) box white cake mix

4 large egg whites, lightly beaten

½ cup plus 5 to 6 teaspoons clementine juice (from about 7 clementines)

¼ cup canola oil

1½ teaspoons grated clementine zest

4 clementines, peeled, sectioned, and membranes removed

⅓ cup unsalted butter, softened

3 cups confectioners' sugar

¾ cup semi-sweet chocolate chips, for garnish

24 clementine sections with membranes removed (about 2½ clementines), for garnish

"Oh, my darling, oh, my darling"—you'll be singing this sweet, sweet song until you bite into this, one of our favorite cakes. Then you'll forget all about singing and focus your attention on the delicious citrus flavor mixed ever so delicately in a moist white cake. A cross between sweet oranges and Chinese mandarins, clementines add a touch of unexpected sweetness—and are what make the cake, in our opinion. Pun intended.

1. Preheat the oven to 350°F. Grease and flour a 9 x 13-inch casserole dish.

2. In the bowl of a standing electric mixer fitted with the whisk attachment, combine the water, cake mix, egg whites, ½ cup of the clementine juice, the canola oil, and 1 teaspoon of the clementine zest. Beat on low speed for 30 seconds. Increase the speed to medium and beat for 2 minutes. Pour the batter into the prepared casserole dish. Place the sections from 2 clementines evenly across the top of the batter; gently press down into batter. Chop the remaining 2 clementines' sections and sprinkle over the batter. Bake for 15 to 20 minutes or until a toothpick inserted in the center comes out clean. Cool for 10 minutes, then remove the cake from the pan and set it on a wire rack to cool completely.

3. To make the frosting, in a small bowl, beat the butter until light and fluffy. Add the confectioners' sugar, remaining $\frac{1}{2}$ teaspoon clementine zest, and 5 teaspoons of clementine juice, and beat with a wire whisk until combined. If the frosting is too thick to spread, thin it by adding more juice. Frost the cooled cake.

4. In a small microwave-safe bowl, melt the chocolate chips and stir until smooth. Dip the clementine sections for the garnish halfway into the chocolate and allow the excess to drip off. Place on a wax paper–lined baking sheet; refrigerate until set.

5. To serve, cut the cake into slices and place 1 chocolate-dipped clementine section on each slice.

Pretzel Nut
Nilla Cake

Makes 10 servings

Cooking spray

1 cup granulated sugar

1 cup packed dark brown sugar

¾ cup (1½ sticks) unsalted butter, softened

6 large eggs

½ cup whole milk

1 teaspoon vanilla extract

20 vanilla wafers, crushed

1 cup unsalted peanuts, chopped

1 cup thin pretzel rods, coarsely chopped

In the South, we call vanilla wafers *'nilla* wafers. Just like we call pudding *puddin.'* Hmm . . . come to think of it, bet the person who invented Nilla wafers was from the South, as we Southerners tend to lose the extra parts of words so we can get right to the good stuff. This cake is all kinds of good stuff—vanilla wafers, peanuts, and pretzels—in one delicious dessert. Try it and you just may start droppin' letters and syllables like a Southerner. Who needs them, anyhow, when your mouth is full of cake?

1. Preheat the oven to 350°F. Spray a 9 x 13-inch casserole dish with cooking spray.

2. In a large bowl, cream together the granulated sugar, brown sugar, and butter. Add the eggs, milk, vanilla, vanilla wafers, peanuts, and pretzels. Mix thoroughly. Pour the mixture into the prepared casserole dish.

3. Bake for 1 hour, or until a toothpick inserted into the center comes out clean. Let cool for 5 minutes before serving.

4. Store the cake in an airtight container in the refrigerator for up to 1 week.

Pollock's
Peach Cobbler

Makes 6 to 8 servings

- ½ cup (1 stick) unsalted butter, melted
- 2 cups granulated sugar
- 1 cup all-purpose flour
- 2 teaspoons baking powder
- ¼ teaspoon salt
- ⅔ cup whole milk, at room temperature
- 1 large egg, at room temperature
- 1 (28-ounce) can sliced peaches, drained
- 2 teaspoons ground cinnamon
- ½ teaspoon ground nutmeg
- Confectioners' sugar

Always a hit! Sandy's version of peach cobbler starts with a layer of cakelike pastry: moist and delicious—never dry! It's spiced with nutmeg and cinnamon to accentuate the warm flavor of the peaches and simply can't be beat when accompanied by a scoop of ice cream. We recommend trying cinnamon ice cream for the ultimate flavor combination!

1. Preheat the oven to 350°F. Pour the melted butter into a 9 x 13-inch casserole dish and set aside.

2. In a large bowl, combine 1 cup of the granulated sugar, the flour, baking powder, and salt. Stir in the milk and egg. Pour the mixture evenly over melted butter in the pan.

3. In a separate medium bowl, combine the remaining 1 cup granulated sugar, the peaches, cinnamon, and nutmeg. Spread the peaches over the batter. Bake for 35 to 45 minutes, until the crust is golden brown and the edges are bubbling.

4. Let the cobbler cool for 5 minutes before dusting lightly with confectioners' sugar.

FREEZES WELL
See our freezer tips on page 16.

Marge-Approved
Caramel Bread Pudding

Makes 10 servings

- 8 large eggs
- 3 cups granulated sugar
- 2 cups whole milk
- 2 cups heavy cream
- ¼ cup brandy
- ¼ teaspoon salt
- 1 vanilla bean
- 1 baguette, cut into 1-inch pieces
- ½ teaspoon white vinegar
- 3 tablespoons unsalted butter

Sandy's mom, Margie (aka Marge), has a passion for bread pudding and is a self-proclaimed connoisseur. This is the only bread pudding out of a pile of test recipes that Marge gave her stamp of approval, noting it was the richness of the vanilla custard that won her over. Go ahead and try it. Marge approves!

1. In a large bowl, whisk the eggs. Add 2 cups of the sugar, the milk, cream, brandy, and salt. Split the vanilla bean lengthwise, scrape the seeds into the bowl, and whisk well. Add bread, then place bowl in the refrigerator and let soak for 45 minutes to 1 hour, pushing bread down occasionally to submerge it, until most of the liquid has been absorbed.

2. Meanwhile, in a medium saucepan set over high heat, combine the remaining 1 cup sugar, the vinegar, and ½ cup water and stir until the sugar has dissolved. Cook, without stirring, until the sugar is dark amber in color, 7 to 10 minutes. Remove the pan from the heat and carefully add ¼ cup water (mixture will spatter). Swirl the pot until combined.

3. Working quickly, pour the very hot caramel into a 9 x 13-inch metal casserole dish (a glass pan can crack with extreme high temperatures), carefully rotating the pan so that the caramel covers the bottom and some of the sides; let set aside until cool.

4. Preheat the oven to 350°F. Put a kettle of water on to boil.

5. Rub the cooled caramel sauce and the sides of casserole dish with the butter, and spoon in the bread mixture, packing tightly to fit. Cover the top of the bread with parchment paper.

6. Place the casserole dish in a large roasting pan and pour hot water into the roasting pan until it comes halfway up the sides of the dish. Bake the pudding 1¼ hours or until a knife inserted into the center comes out barely clean. Do not overbake. Let stand for 5 minutes. Serve warm.

7. Store leftovers in an airtight container in the refrigerator for up to 5 days.

S'more Pie

Makes 10 servings

Cooking spray

8 graham crackers

⅓ cup packed dark brown sugar

2½ tablespoons unsalted butter, melted

¾ teaspoon salt

14 ounces semi-sweet chocolate, finely chopped

2 cups heavy cream

2 large eggs, at room temperature

1 (10-ounce) bag mini marshmallows

In Texas, the camping months are rather limited for those of us who do not enjoy sleeping in a steam room. But everyone knows that the best part of a camping trip is the dessert! Now you can avoid all the bug spray and sleeping on the ground and get your chocolate-marshmallow-graham fix in a pie you make at home. May I get s'more, please?

1. Preheat the oven to 350°F. Spray a 9 x 13-inch casserole dish with cooking spray.

2. In a food processor, pulse the graham crackers until finely ground. Add the brown sugar, butter, and ½ teaspoon of the salt, and process until well combined. Press the crumb mixture into the bottom and up the sides of the prepared casserole dish. Bake for 10 minutes, then let cool completely.

3. Put the chocolate in a large, heatproof bowl and set aside. In a large, heavy saucepan set over medium-high heat, bring the cream just to a boil, about 5 minutes. Pour the hot cream over the chocolate. Let it stand for 1 minute, then gently whisk until the chocolate is melted and the mixture is smooth. Gently whisk in the eggs and the remaining ¼ teaspoon of salt until combined. Pour the filling into the graham cracker crust (it will fill the crust about halfway).

4. Bake for about 25 minutes, or just until the center becomes slightly firm. Let cool for 10 minutes.

5. Preheat the oven to Broil.

6. Cover the entire top of the casserole with the marshmallows. Don't let any brown peek through! Put the marshmallow-covered casserole back in the oven 3 to 4 inches from the heat and broil, rotating casserole as necessary, until the marshmallows are golden brown, about 3 minutes. Watch this step very closely, as they can go from browned to burned in a second. Allow to cool for 10 minutes before serving.

7. Store in an airtight container in the refrigerator for up to 1 week.

This dish can be made GLUTEN-FREE by replacing the regular graham crackers with a gluten-free brand. We recommend Kinni-kinnick S'moreables Graham Style Crackers.

Peanut Butter Freezer Pie
with Chocolate and Bananas

Makes 8 to 10 servings

Cooking spray

1½ cups vanilla wafer cookies
(about 30 cookies)

1½ cups packed light brown sugar

3 tablespoons unsalted butter,
melted

4 ounces cream cheese,
softened

½ cup creamy peanut butter

½ teaspoon vanilla extract

2 cups heavy cream, whipped

2 cups sliced banana
(about 2 bananas)

½ cup chocolate syrup

It's bananas how good this dessert is! Seriously, it doesn't get much better than this. A creamy peanut butter topping covers layers of fresh bananas and a tasty vanilla-wafer crust. Drizzled with a rich chocolate sauce, we think it's the best in the bunch!

1. Coat a 9 x 13-inch casserole dish with cooking spray.

2. Pulse the cookies in a food processor until finely ground. Add ½ cup of the brown sugar and the butter; pulse two or three times or just until combined. Press the crumb mixture into the bottom of the prepared casserole dish. Set aside.

3. Put the remaining 1 cup brown sugar, the cream cheese, peanut butter, and vanilla in the bowl of a standing mixer fitted with a whisk attachment. Beat at medium speed until smooth. Fold in the whipped cream.

4. Lay the banana slices on the prepared crust and drizzle with the chocolate syrup. Spread the peanut butter mixture over the bananas and drizzle again with the chocolate syrup. Cover with plastic wrap and freeze until frozen through, about 5 hours. Let stand at room temperature for about 10 minutes before serving.

5. To store, cover with plastic wrap and refrigerate for up to 2 days.

Easy Maple Sopapilla Casserole

Makes 16 servings

Cooking spray

2 sheets frozen puff pastry, thawed

Flour for work surface

¼ cup maple syrup

3 (8-ounce) packages cream cheese, softened

1 cup packed brown sugar

3 tablespoons unsalted butter, melted

¼ cup granulated sugar

1 teaspoon ground cinnamon

Although this makes a great dessert, these sweet puffs are also great with a cup of joe for breakfast. Think of sopapillas as the Tex-Mex alternative to coffee cake or beignets!

Sopapillas are a damn-tasty deep-fried pastry drizzled in honey or syrup, or sprinkled with powdered sugar or cinnamon. They are a popular dessert in South America and New Mexico, as well as in many of Austin's wonderful Tex-Mex restaurants. Our version is not deep fried and combines the sweet pastry goodness of the sopapilla with the creamy decadence of cheesecake. *¡Muy delicioso!*

1. Preheat the oven to 350°F. Spray a 9 x 13-inch casserole dish with cooking spray.

2. Take 1 sheet of the puff pastry and lay it out on a floured work surface. Roll it out to fit in the prepared casserole dish. Lay the pastry in the bottom of the prepared casserole dish. Using a fork, poke holes in the pastry, and then bake for 10 minutes to partially cook the pastry. Remove the dish from the oven and let cool.

3. In a large bowl, whisk together the maple syrup, cream cheese, and brown sugar. Spread the mixture over the cooled puff pastry.

4. Take the second sheet of puff pastry and lay it out on a floured work surface. Roll it out to fit in the casserole dish. Lay the dough on top of the cream cheese mixture and cut slits into the top so that the pastry won't puff too high when baking. Pour the melted butter over the top.

5. In a small bowl, combine the granulated sugar with the ground cinnamon. Sprinkle the cinnamon-sugar mixture evenly over the top of the casserole.

6. Bake for 30 to 35 minutes. Remove from the oven and let cool for 10 minutes before serving.

Not-So-Square Lemon Bars

Makes 10 to 12 servings

- 2 cups plus 6 tablespoons all-purpose flour
- 1 cup (2 sticks) unsalted butter, softened
- ½ cup sifted confectioners' sugar, plus more for sprinkling
- Pinch of salt
- 4 large eggs
- 2 cups granulated sugar
- 6 tablespoons fresh lemon juice
- 1 tablespoon lemon zest

Tart and tangy, lemon bars are one of those amazing desserts that seem to please everyone. Maybe it's because bars are easy to serve and highly portable, a clever cross between a cookie and pie.

The key to a good lemon bar is a strong citrus flavor. You'll want your mouth to pucker in delight! When choosing your lemons, be sure to pick ones that are vibrant in color and feel somewhat heavy in the hand. Also, when zesting, be sure you only get the yellow part, as the white part is very bitter.

1. Preheat the oven to 350°F.

2. Mix 2 cups of the flour, the butter, confectioners' sugar, and salt in a bowl. Press the mixture into the bottom of a 9 x 13-inch baking dish. Bake for 20 minutes or until golden brown. Transfer to a wire rack to cool. Keep oven at 350°F.

3. In the bowl of an electric mixer fitted with the whisk attachment, beat the eggs and granulated sugar until smooth. Add the remaining 6 tablespoons of flour, the lemon juice, and lemon zest and beat until well combined. Pour the filling over the prepared crust, and bake for 25 minutes or until filling has set. Transfer the baking dish to a wire rack and let cool completely. Sprinkle with confectioners' sugar before cutting into bars.

4. Store leftovers in an airtight container in the refrigerator for up to 5 days.

When life gives you lemons, remember Crystal's rule of thumb: 1 medium lemon yields 2 to 4 tablespoons of juice and 1 tablespoon of grated rind.

Crunchy Peanut Butter Chocolate Bars

Makes 12 servings

- 1 cup (2 sticks) unsalted butter
- 6 cups mini marshmallows
- 6 cups Rice Krispies cereal
  Cooking spray
- 1¾ cups confectioners' sugar
- 1 cup creamy peanut butter
- ¾ cup graham cracker crumbs
- ⅔ cup evaporated milk
- 1⅔ cups granulated sugar
- ½ teaspoon salt
- 1½ cups bittersweet chocolate chips
- 1 teaspoon vanilla extract

Rice Krispies? Check. Peanut butter? Check. Chocolate? Check. Delicious on their own, these three flavors will knock your socks off when layered together. The bars are decadent and rich, so be sure to have a glass of milk handy.

1. In a large saucepan set over low heat, melt 4 tablespoons of the butter. Add 4 cups of the marshmallows and stir until melted. Remove the pan from the heat and add the cereal. Stir until the cereal is coated. Press the mixture into the bottom of a 9 x 13-inch casserole dish sprayed with cooking spray. Coat your hands with butter and press the mixture into the pan. Using a chopstick, poke many holes in the layer. Set the pan aside.

2. In a medium saucepan set over low heat, melt ½ cup of the butter. Remove the pan from the heat and stir in the confectioners' sugar. Add the peanut butter and graham cracker crumbs, stirring until well combined. Spread the mixture evenly over the Rice Krispies layer. Using a chopstick, poke many holes in the layer. Let cool completely.

3. In a medium saucepan set over medium heat, combine the remaining 4 tablespoons butter, the evaporated milk, granulated sugar, and salt and bring to a boil; cook 4 to 5 minutes, stirring constantly. Remove from the heat. Stir in the remaining 2 cups marshmallows, the chocolate, and vanilla. Beat for 1 minute until the marshmallows are melted. Pour over the peanut butter fudge, spread evenly, and place in the refrigerator to harden, about 2 hours.

4. To serve, cut into 1-inch squares. Store in an airtight container at room temperature for up to 5 days.

Brownies

Makes 20 brownies

- 1 tablespoon unsalted butter, softened, for buttering the dish
- 2 cups bittersweet chocolate chips (you can use milk chocolate, if you prefer)
- 1⅓ cups vegetable oil
- 2 teaspoons vanilla extract
- 2 cups granulated sugar
- 4 large eggs
- 2 cups all-purpose flour
- 1½ teaspoons salt
- 1 teaspoon baking powder
- 1½ cups chopped pecans
- Caramel Sauce (optional; page 341) or Blackberry Coulis (optional; opposite page)

Early in life, you have to make certain decisions. For example, are you a cookie person or a brownie person? Both of the Queens' men—Tim and Michael—are cookie monsters, but we Queens love ourselves a good brownie! While the recipe calls for serving them with our homemade caramel sauce—which makes them oh-so-decadent—these brownies can stand perfectly on their own. If you're keen on dressing them up, we have included a recipe for our favorite blackberry coulis, too.

1. Preheat the oven to 325°F. Butter a 9 x 13-inch casserole dish.

2. Put a glass bowl over a small saucepan of simmering water. Put the chocolate, oil, and vanilla in the bowl and let them heat gently, stirring constantly until the chocolate melts completely. Set aside until cool to the touch, about 20 minutes.

3. In a large bowl, whisk together the sugar and eggs until the mixture is a light yellow color, about 5 minutes. While whisking, slowly pour in the chocolate mixture and whisk until well combined.

4. In a separate bowl, sift together the flour, salt, and baking powder. Add the dry ingredients to the chocolate mixture and stir well. Stir in the nuts.

5. Spread the batter into the prepared casserole dish. Bake for 35 minutes, or until a toothpick inserted into the center comes out clean. Let cool for 5 minutes before cutting. Serve as is or with Caramel Sauce or Blackberry Coulis. Store in an airtight container in the refrigerator for up to 1 week.

This dish can be made GLUTEN-FREE by replacing the flour with a gluten-free all-purpose mix, either store bought (see page 21 for recommendations of our favorite brands) or homemade (see page 322 for our recipe). Also, be sure to use a gluten-free baking powder.

Blackberry Coulis

Makes 3 cups

- ¾ cup fruity red wine
- 6 tablespoons granulated sugar
- 1 pint blackberries (about 3 cups)

Because what goes better with chocolate than red wine!

In a heavy-bottomed saucepan set over high heat, combine the wine and sugar and bring to a boil. Boil for 2 minutes, until the sugar dissolves. Turn the heat down to medium and simmer for 10 minutes more, to allow the sauce to reduce a bit. Add the berries and bring the mixture back up to a simmer, then cook (don't boil) for 3 minutes. Take the pan off the heat and let the berries cool in the wine syrup.

Pecan Squares

Makes 10 servings

- 1½ cups (3 sticks) unsalted butter, cold, divided, plus more for pan
- 2 cups all-purpose flour
- ⅔ cup confectioners' sugar
- ½ cup firmly packed light brown sugar
- ½ cup honey
- 3 tablespoons heavy cream
- 3½ cups coarsely chopped pecans

A rite of passage for all Southern girls is perfecting the art of the pecan pie. Since Crystal is far from perfect, she found an easier way to showcase her sweet skills. These squares will definitely earn you your Southern-girl kitchen credibility. They are ooey, gooey, and delicious—and a cinch to prepare!

1. Preheat the oven to 350°F. Lightly butter a 9 x 13-inch casserole dish.

2. In a medium bowl, sift together the flour and confectioners' sugar. Using a pastry blender or two forks, cut ¾ cup of the butter into the flour mixture until it resembles a coarse meal. Pat the mixture on the bottom and 1½ inches up the sides of the prepared casserole dish. Bake for 20 minutes, or until golden brown. Remove the dish from the oven and let cool.

3. In a saucepan set over medium-high heat, melt the remaining ¾ cup of butter. Add the brown sugar, honey, and cream, and bring the mixture to a boil. Stir in the pecans and pour the hot filling into the prepared crust. Bake for 25 to 30 minutes, or until golden and bubbly. Let cool for 5 minutes before cutting into 2-inch squares. Store in an airtight container in the refrigerator for up to 1 week.

This dish can be made GLUTEN-FREE by replacing the flour with a gluten-free all-purpose mix, either store bought (see page 21 for recommendations of our favorite brands) or homemade (see page 322 for our recipe).

 Granny Pansy's
Baked Apples

Makes 6 servings

- ½ cup granulated sugar
- 6 Golden Delicious apples
- ⅓ cup packed light brown sugar
- 3 tablespoons unsalted butter, softened
- 1 teaspoon ground cinnamon
- Vanilla ice cream

Even in the Rio Grande Valley of Texas, the temperatures start cooling down in late autumn. This dish always reminds Sandy of spending chilly fall afternoons in her granny Pansy's kitchen. Granny Pansy knew that these were the perfect midday treat when the air started getting crisp and apples were in season. Not too heavy and not involved, just the thing when you're hankering for a little something sweet—just like Granny Pansy!

1. Preheat the oven to 375°F.

2. In a saucepan set over medium heat, combine the granulated sugar with 1 cup of water. Cook until the sugar dissolves, about 4 minutes. Pour the syrup into the bottom of a 9 x 13-inch casserole dish.

3. Core the apples, but don't go all the way through to the bottom. (This will help keep the sugar filling in the apple.) In a medium bowl, mix the brown sugar, butter, and cinnamon thoroughly. Divide the mixture equally among the 6 apples. Put the filled apples in the casserole dish.

4. Bake for 45 minutes to 1 hour, or until a knife can be easily inserted into the apples. Let cool for 5 minutes. Serve with vanilla ice cream.

Austin Chewies

Makes 10 servings

- 2½ cups sweetened coconut flakes
- ¾ cup (1½ sticks) unsalted butter, melted
- 2 cups packed dark brown sugar
- 2 large eggs, beaten
- 4 teaspoons vanilla extract
- 2 cups all-purpose flour
- 1 teaspoon baking soda
- 1 teaspoon salt
- 1 cup pecans, chopped
- 3 cups chocolate chips
- 1 (14-ounce) can sweetened condensed milk
- 6 large egg whites
- 2¼ cups granulated sugar

A little sweet and nutty, just like Austin. If you can't be here, keeping it weird, at least you can make yourself a batch of these. And if you aren't big on chocolate (we suggest you immediately go see a doctor), this recipe will work equally well with butterscotch or peanut butter chips. Heck, you could even do a combination of all three! Just use 1 cup of each instead of 3 cups of chocolate chips.

1. Preheat the oven to 300°F.

2. Spread the coconut in a thin layer on a baking sheet. Bake for about 20 minutes, stirring every 5 minutes to make sure that the coconut browns evenly. Transfer the coconut to a bowl and let cool.

3. Increase the oven temperature to 350°F. Pour the butter into a 9 x 13-inch casserole dish.

4. In a large bowl, combine the brown sugar, eggs, and 1 teaspoon of the vanilla. In a separate bowl, whisk together the flour, baking soda, and salt. Gradually add the flour mixture to the egg mixture and stir until combined. Stir in the pecans. Spread the mixture into the prepared dish. Bake for 25 to 30 minutes, or until browned. Remove the dish from the oven and let cool. Keep the oven on.

5. In a medium saucepan set over medium heat, combine 2½ cups of the chocolate chips with the sweetened condensed milk and heat until chocolate chips melt. Pour over the cooled caramel pecan mix in the casserole dish.

6. In the bowl of a stand mixer fitted with the whisk attachment, beat the egg whites at medium-high speed until soft peaks form. Add the remaining 3 teaspoons of vanilla and beat just to incorporate. With the mixer running on medium speed, gradually add the granulated sugar and beat until the egg whites are firm and glossy, about 3 minutes. Using a large rubber spatula, fold in the toasted coconut. Spread the mixture over the chocolate layer and sprinkle with the remaining ½ cup of chocolate chips.

7. Put the dessert in the oven for 15 minutes to melt the chocolate and heat through. Serve warm.

This dish can be made GLUTEN-FREE by replacing the flour with a gluten-free all-purpose mix, either store bought (see page 21 for recommendations of our favorite brands) or homemade (see page 322 for our recipe). Also, check the label of your chocolate chips to make sure they are gluten-free as well.

Key West
Clafouti

Makes 10 servings

- 2 tablespoons unsalted butter, melted, plus more for the pan
- 2 ripe mangoes, peeled and diced
- ½ cup coconut rum, such as Malibu
- 1 cup sweetened coconut flakes
- 5 large eggs, lightly beaten
- 1¼ cups heavy cream
- 1¼ cups whole milk
- 1 teaspoon grated lime zest
- 1 cup granulated sugar
- ⅔ cup all-purpose flour, sifted
- Confectioners' sugar, for dusting

Clafouti Tootie, Fresh and Fruity! Sorry, we couldn't help ourselves. Traditionally made with cherries, a clafouti is a fluffy, fruit-filled French dessert. The batter is similar to that of pancakes (which makes this dish great for brunch, too), and it is dusted with a layer of powdered sugar for serving. Umm . . . yum! In our version, we have veered away from the traditional tart cherries, opting for tropical fruits like mango, lime, and coconut. The fruit is arranged in the bottom of a baking dish and then covered with a batter spiked with some Malibu rum. This dish is best served straight from the oven, because even though it puffs up nicely, it can deflate rather quickly.

1. Preheat the oven to 325°F. Butter a 9 x 13-inch casserole dish.

2. Put the mangoes and the rum in a large bowl and let sit for 1 hour to allow the mangoes to absorb the liquid.

3. Put the coconut in a single layer on a baking sheet. Toast for 12 to 15 minutes, until golden brown. Transfer to a large plate and let cool.

4. Increase the oven temperature to 350°F.

5. In a large bowl, whisk together the eggs, melted butter, cream, milk, and lime zest.

6. In a separate large bowl, whisk together the granulated sugar and flour, and stir in the coconut. Stir the coconut mixture into the egg mixture.

7. Spread the mango-rum mixture in the bottom of the prepared casserole dish. Top with the batter.

8. Bake for 35 minutes, or until cooked through and golden. Let cool for 5 minutes, sprinkle with the confectioners' sugar, and serve. Store in an airtight container in the refrigerator for up to a week.

This dish can be made GLUTEN-FREE by replacing the flour with a gluten-free all-purpose mix, either store bought (see page 21 for recommendations of our favorite brands) or homemade (see page 322 for our recipe). Also, be sure to look over the ingredients in the rum for any barley, wheat, or rye.

Triple Chocolate Custard

Makes 8 to 10 servings

Cooking spray

1 (16.6-ounce) bag Oreo cookies

¾ cup (1½ sticks) unsalted butter, melted

4 ounces bittersweet chocolate chips

4 ounces milk chocolate chips

4 ounces white chocolate chips

¼ cup water

1 tablespoon unflavored gelatin

5 large egg yolks

¼ cup granulated sugar

1 cup half-and-half

1¾ cups chilled whipping cream

Calling all chocolate lovers! No matter what kind of chocolate you like, this dish is for you. Decadent layers of dark, milk, and white chocolate on an Oreo cookie base—you can close your mouth now.

1. Coat a 9 x 13-inch casserole dish with cooking spray and set aside.

2. Pulse the Oreo cookies in a food processor until roughly ground. Slowly add the butter and pulse until the Oreo crumbs just start to hold together. Pour the mixture into the prepared pan and press into the bottom.

3. Put each of the types of chocolate chips in separate medium bowls.

4. Combine the water and gelatin in a small bowl. Let stand for 10 minutes or until the gelatin softens.

5. Meanwhile, in the bowl of a standing electric mixer fitted with the whisk attachment, beat the egg yolks and sugar for 5 minutes or until the mixture is pale yellow and very thick. Bring the half-and-half just to a simmer in a large, heavy saucepan set over medium-high heat. Gradually whisk the hot half-and-half into the eggs, then pour the egg mixture into the saucepan. Stir over medium heat until the custard thickens and coats the back of a spoon, about 3 minutes (do not boil). Remove the custard from the heat. Add the softened gelatin, and stir until the gelatin dissolves.

6. Strain the gelatin mixture into large glass measuring cup. Immediately pour one-third of the hot custard into each bowl of chocolate chips. Stir each chocolate with a separate spoon until melted and smooth. (If the mixture cools before the chocolate is completely melted, set the bowl over a saucepan of simmering water and stir just until the chocolate melts.) Let the chocolate mixtures cool to room temperature, stirring occasionally, about 30 minutes.

7. In the bowl of a standing electric mixer fitted with the whisk attachment, beat the cream until stiff peaks form. Divide the whipped cream equally among the bowls of chocolate, using about 1 1/3 cups of whipped cream for each. Fold the whipped cream into the chocolates in each bowl with a rubber spatula.

8. Pour the bittersweet chocolate mixture into bottom of the prepared pan. Smooth the top with a spatula, then chill for 10 minutes. Spread the milk chocolate mixture over the bittersweet chocolate layer. Smooth the top with a spatula, then chill for 10 minutes. Spread the white chocolate mixture over the milk chocolate layer. Smooth the top with a spatula, and chill until firm, about 1 hour.

9. To store, cover the pan tightly with plastic wrap and refrigerate for up to 4 days.

Chu Chu's Tropical Trifle

Makes 8 to 10 servings

2 cups whole milk

6 large egg yolks

1½ cups granulated sugar

⅓ cup cornstarch

¼ cup (½ stick) unsalted butter, cut into small pieces

½ cup sweetened coconut flakes

1 cup water

1 teaspoon corn syrup

Seeds scraped from 1 vanilla bean

1 cup fresh pineapple chunks (½ inch)

1 teaspoon dark rum

1 (3-ounce) package store-bought ladyfingers

¼ cup whipped cream

1 cup unsweetened coconut flakes

We know that we wouldn't be where we are today without the continued support and encouragement we receive from our customers. To thank them, we held a recipe contest for which the winner's dish would be featured in our book. Cristiane Diehl (aka Chu Chu), that's you! Take a bow. You deserve it. Your trifle is out of this world! (Well, at least out of this country—it's from Brazil!)

1. Preheat the oven to 350°F.

2. Bring the milk to a boil in a small saucepan set over medium-high heat, stirring constantly to prevent the milk from scalding.

3. In a medium saucepan (no heat), whisk the egg yolks, ½ cup of the sugar, and the cornstarch until the mixture is thick and well blended. While whisking constantly, drizzle in about ¼ cup of the hot milk (this will temper, or warm, the yolks so they won't curdle). Continue whisking and slowly pour in the rest of the milk. Set the pan over medium heat. While whisking vigorously, bring the mixture to a boil, and cook, whisking constantly, for 1 to 2 minutes or until very thick. Remove the pan from the heat. Let the mixture cool for 5 minutes. Whisk in the butter piece by piece, whisking until fully incorporated and the cream is smooth and silky.

4. Meanwhile, toast the sweetened coconut. Spread it out on a sheet pan in an even layer, then place in the oven and bake for about 20 minutes, stirring every 5 minutes to make sure it browns evenly, until it's golden (see Note, opposite). Fold the toasted coconut into the egg mixture. Transfer to a bowl and press a piece of plastic wrap against the surface of the coconut cream to create an airtight seal. Refrigerate until cold, about 2 hours.

5. In a medium saucepan set over medium-high heat, combine the water, remaining 1 cup sugar, the corn syrup, and vanilla seeds. Bring the mixture to a boil. Cook until the sugar is dissolved, after about 2 minutes, then add the pineapple chunks and rum. Reduce the heat to medium and cook until the pineapple is translucent, about 10 minutes. Remove the pan from the heat and set aside to cool. Strain the syrup from the pineapple compote into a shallow dish. Set the compote aside.

6. Dip the ladyfingers one by one into the pineapple syrup and place them in the bottom of a 9 x 13-inch casserole dish. Spread two-thirds of the coconut cream on top of the ladyfingers. Spread the pineapple compote on top of the coconut cream.

7. Whisk together the whipped cream and the remaining coconut cream. Spread the mixture on top of the trifle and scatter the unsweetened coconut flakes over the top to finish. Refrigerate for 3 hours to allow the flavors to blend. Serve cold.

Toasting coconut is not hard, but you have to watch closely, as the coconut can go from almost done to burned in what feels like a matter of seconds. To save time (and for less stress), try toasting the coconut in the microwave. Spread the coconut evenly on a microwave-safe plate. Microwave on high at 30-second intervals and toss until lightly browned.

Frozen Lemon
Dessert

Makes 10 servings

Unsalted butter, softened, for the dish

60 vanilla wafers, crushed (about 3 cups)

½ cup granulated sugar

3 large eggs, separated

3 tablespoons fresh lemon juice (from 2 lemons)

¼ teaspoon salt

1 cup heavy cream

A little slice of sunshine on a plate! Cool and tart, this refreshingly simple dessert packs a ton of lemon flavor that will instantly bring a smile to your face. Take advantage of your sunny disposition by doubling the batch so that you will have an extra on hand to share with surprise guests. That is, unless you are not a fan of the unexpected pop-in. In that case, draw the shades and keep that extra dessert to yourself. We won't tell!

1. Butter a 9 x 13-inch casserole dish. Sprinkle 1½ cups of the crushed vanilla wafers on the bottom of the dish; set aside.

2. In a medium heatproof bowl, combine the granulated sugar, egg yolks, lemon juice, and salt, and whisk until the mixture is light yellow in color, about 6 minutes.

3. Set a medium saucepan over medium heat and pour in ½ inch of water. Bring the water to a simmer. Put the bowl of the sugar–egg yolk mixture over the simmering water and whisk constantly until the sauce is thick enough to coat the back of a metal spoon. Remove the bowl from the pan and let the mixture cool completely.

4. In a separate bowl, beat the egg whites until they hold stiff peaks. Fold them into the cooled sugar–egg yolk mixture.

5. In another separate bowl, whip the heavy cream until it holds stiff peaks. Fold it into the cooled sugar-egg mixture. Pour the mixture into the prepared dish and sprinkle the top with the remaining 1½ cups of crushed vanilla wafers. Freeze until solid, for at least 2 hours.

6. When ready to serve, let it sit at room temperature for 10 minutes before cutting. Store the leftovers in the refrigerator for 2 days.

FREEZES WELL This dessert will keep in the freezer for 2 months.

This dish can be made GLUTEN-FREE by eliminating the vanilla wafer crumbs and substituting gluten-free cookies (see page 21 for recommendations of our favorite gluten-free brands).

From Scratch:
Yes, You Can

So you love cooking and want to take a little more time to make something extra special? Add a little more love? We understand completely. It's all a part of *sophistakitch*—that extra gourmet flair that people will notice. In this chapter, you'll find a number of recipes that will help you create our dishes entirely from scratch. Such as preparing your own soups and broths to give your dish that flavor you crave, without additives or preservatives. And fresh bread crumbs are always tastier than packaged, not to mention an economical way to use leftover bread! We understand that you are pursuing the pinnacle of taste, and we're here to help. When you're done, don't forget to pat yourself on the back. You've just put some extra lovin' in your oven.

Carly's Favorite
Gluten-Free Flour Mix

Makes 5½ cups

- 2 cups brown rice flour
- 1½ cups potato starch
- ½ cup tapioca flour
- ½ cup amaranth flour
- 1 cup quinoa flour

Owner of Nutritional Wisdom, nutritionist Carly Pollack created a perfect gluten-free flour-mix alternative that's just as versatile as traditional flour, plus it is high in fiber! What's not to love?

In a large bowl, combine the brown rice flour, potato starch, tapioca flour, amaranth flour, and quinoa flour. Store in an airtight container for up to 6 months.

Never-Fail
Pie Dough

Makes two 9-inch pie crusts

- 1¼ cups vegetable shortening, such as Crisco
- 3 cups all-purpose flour
- 1 teaspoon salt
- 1 large egg, well beaten
- 1 tablespoon white vinegar
- 5 tablespoons ice water

1. With a pastry cutter or two forks, cut the shortening into the flour and salt in a large bowl, or place in a food processor and pulse until the texture is like sand.

2. In a small bowl, combine the egg, vinegar, and ice water. Pour the wet ingredients into the flour mixture all at once. Stir with a spoon until all of the flour is moistened, or pulse in a food processor until the dough comes together in a ball. Wrap the dough in plastic wrap and chill for 1 hour before using.

Gluten-Free
Pie Crust

Makes one (9-inch) pie crust

- 1⅓ cups Carly's Favorite Gluten-Free Flour Mix (page 322), plus more for kneading
- 1 tablespoon confectioners' sugar (optional)
- ½ teaspoon salt
- ½ cup (1 stick) cold unsalted butter, cut into small pieces
- 1 large egg, lightly beaten

Ding! Clever recipe alert for a reliable pie crust you'll make again and again! Double ding! Cute gift alert! Next time you're making your favorite pie, double the recipe and whip up some adorable individual-size pies using half-pint glass jars (see recipe on opposite page). For ease of use, purchase the widest-mouth jar you can find.

1. Preheat the oven to 375°F.

2. Put the flour mix, sugar (if using), and salt in a food processor and pulse a few times to combine. Add the butter and pulse until the mixture resembles coarse meal. Add the egg and pulse until completely combined.

3. Turn the dough out onto a wooden surface dusted with flour mix. Sprinkle more over the dough and knead gently, working in about 2 more tablespoons of gluten-free flour, until the dough holds together without being sticky but is still very pliable.

If not using right away, form a ball with the dough and wrap tightly with plastic wrap. Refrigerate for up to 5 days.

Mini Pies

Makes enough for 6 mini pies

1. Prepare the dough according to the recipe. On a floured surface, roll it out into a $\frac{1}{8}$-inch-thick circle. Use the ring of a half-pint mason jar to cut out perfectly sized pie tops. Cut at least one hole in each top to keep the pies from bursting when cooking. Use the rest of the dough to line the jars—no need to grease!—by taking little pieces and pressing them on the bottom and up the sides of the jars. Fill each with $\frac{1}{2}$ cup of your favorite pie filling and add a pie crust top, sealing the edges tightly. Place the lids on the jars and store the mini pies in your freezer.

2. If presenting the pies as a gift, remove the outer band of the lid, place a square of decorative fabric over the inner lid of the jar, then screw the outer band back on tightly. Add personalized labels with these instructions for cooking: No need to thaw. Simply remove lids and place jars on a sheet pan in a cold oven. Cook at 350°F for 50 to 60 minutes or until the pie crust is golden brown.

3. If you don't plan to use your dough immediately, you can freeze the dough with great results! Form a $\frac{1}{2}$-inch-thick dough disk, then wrap in plastic wrap and place in freezer until firm, about 2 hours. Once firm, place the dough disk in a freezer bag. Dough will last for up to 2 months in the freezer.

Homemade
Pizza Dough

Makes one 9 x 13-inch crust

- ½ teaspoon granulated sugar
- 1 cup warm water (110° to 115°F)
- 1 package active dry yeast (2½ teaspoons)
- 2½ cups all-purpose flour
- ½ cup yellow cornmeal
- ¾ teaspoon salt
- 2 tablespoons olive oil, plus more for the bowl

Nothing is better than pizza dough made from scratch. For the pizza connoisseur (and the pizza consumer), the crust can make or break the whole pie. It does take some extra time and patience, but we promise that it is well worth the effort.

1. In a large bowl, dissolve the sugar in the warm water. Sprinkle the yeast over the water and let stand until foamy, about 5 minutes. Stir in 2¼ cups of the flour, the cornmeal, salt, and 2 tablespoons of the oil, stirring until the mixture forms a dough. Put the dough on a floured surface and knead, incorporating as much of the remaining ¼ cup flour as necessary to prevent the dough from sticking, until smooth and elastic, about 5 minutes.

2. Put the dough in a deep, oiled bowl and turn to coat with the oil. Cover the bowl with plastic wrap and let the dough rise in a warm place for 1 hour or until doubled in bulk.

FREEZES WELL If you don't plan to use the pizza dough within 2 days of making it, form the dough into a disk and place in a zip-top freezer bag. The dough will last in the freezer for up to 2 months.

Pizza dough is not just for pizza anymore! It is a very flexible building block for tasty treats. Sandy likes to roll it out, brush it with melted butter, and sprinkle with cinnamon sugar for a quick and sweet dessert.

Mexican Cornbread

Makes 12 servings

- 1 cup (2 sticks) unsalted butter, melted, plus more for the pan
- 1 cup granulated sugar
- 4 large eggs
- 1 (15-ounce) can cream-style corn
- ½ (4-ounce) can chopped green chili peppers, drained
- ½ cup shredded Monterey Jack cheese (2 ounces)
- ½ cup shredded Cheddar cheese (2 ounces)
- 1 cup all-purpose flour
- 1 cup yellow cornmeal
- 4 teaspoons baking powder
- ¼ teaspoon salt

The Mexican flavors Sandy grew up with shine in this recipe. The sweetness of this cornbread blends so perfectly with the Southwestern spices. We love to serve it alongside most any grilled meat.

1. Preheat the oven to 300°F. Lightly butter a 9 x 13-inch casserole dish.

2. In a large bowl, whisk together butter and sugar until light yellow, about 3 minutes. Beat in the eggs one at a time and whisk until smooth. Stir in the corn, chilies, and cheeses.

3. In a separate bowl, combine the flour, cornmeal, baking powder, and salt. Add the flour mixture to the corn mixture and stir until smooth. Pour the batter into the prepared casserole dish.

4. Bake for 1 hour, until a toothpick inserted into center of the dish comes out clean. Let cool for 10 minutes before serving.

This dish can be made GLUTEN-FREE by replacing the flour with a gluten-free all-purpose mix, either store bought (see page 21 for recommendations of our favorite brands) or homemade (see page 322 for our recipe). Also, be sure to use a gluten-free baking powder.

Cook's
Cornbread

Makes 8 servings

Cooking spray

2 cups white cornmeal, plus more for the pan

1 teaspoon salt

2 cups boiling water

1 cup whole milk

2 large eggs

4 teaspoons baking powder

1 tablespoon unsalted butter, melted

Best made in a cast-iron skillet, this cornbread is a true Southern staple and can be served with almost any meal. It differs from our Mexican Cornbread (page 327) in that it is considerably less sweet. Crystal and her mom love to eat this with soup beans and a glass of buttermilk! How's that for a Southern delicacy?

1. Preheat the oven to 375°F. Spray an 8 x 8-inch pan with cooking spray and dust it with cornmeal.

2. In a large, heatproof bowl, sift together the cornmeal and salt. Slowly pour the boiling water over the cornmeal. Add the milk quickly, whisking constantly to avoid lumps. Add the eggs and beat well. Add the baking powder and melted butter, and beat well. Pour the batter into the prepared pan.

3. Bake for 30 to 35 minutes, or until golden brown.

This dish can be made GLUTEN-FREE by using a gluten-free baking powder.

Perfect Rice
Every Time

Makes 3 cups

1 cup long-grain rice

1 teaspoon salt

For even the most seasoned chefs, rice can prove to be a challenge. Yes, rice. One minute short and it's soggy; a minute extra, it can be sticky and clumped together. Unless you want to spend your hard-earned money on a rice steamer, we suggest you follow this tried-and-true method.

1. Put the rice and salt in a 2-quart saucepan, add 2 cups of water, and cover the pan with a tight-fitting lid. Bring to a boil, then reduce the heat to the lowest possible setting. Cook for 14 minutes.

2. Turn off heat and let the rice steam in the pan for 5 more minutes. Fluff the rice with a fork.

Seasoned Bread Crumbs

Makes 3 cups

- 1 loaf day-old bread
- 2 tablespoons dried thyme or oregano
- 2 tablespoons dried basil or parsley
- 1 teaspoon garlic powder
- 2 teaspoons salt
- ½ teaspoon freshly ground black pepper

Bread is too good of a thing to let go to waste. How many times does your uneaten bread go to the birds? If for some insane reason you didn't eat the entire baguette for dinner, use the leftovers to make some delicious bread crumbs, which are always handy for adding texture to casseroles. Bread crumbs can go stale quickly, so keep them fresh longer by storing in the freezer.

1. Preheat the oven to 300°F.

2. Cut the bread into 1-inch cubes and pulse in a food processor to make coarse crumbs. Spread the crumbs on a baking sheet and dry them out by baking for 10 to 15 minutes, stirring after 5 minutes. Allow the crumbs to cool completely.

3. Return the dried crumbs to the food processor. Add the thyme, basil, garlic powder, salt, and pepper, then pulse until the crumbs are finely processed and well mixed with the seasoning.

4. Store in an airtight container for up to 6 months in the freezer.

Creole
Seasoning

Makes 1 cup

- 3 tablespoons smoked paprika
- 2 tablespoons sweet paprika
- 2 tablespoons onion powder
- 2 tablespoons garlic powder
- 2 tablespoons dried oregano
- 2 tablespoons dried basil
- 1 tablespoon dried thyme
- 2 tablespoons freshly ground black pepper
- 1½ tablespoons cayenne
- 1 tablespoon celery seeds

Depending on what part of the country you live in, finding pre-mixed Creole spice blends can be a challenge. So why not make your own? This spice mix is easy enough to whip up and is great for seasoning rice, meats, stews, and veggies! In fact, it happens to be the star of our Cheesy Grits-Stuffed Eggplant Rolls with Tomato Sauce (page 180).

1. In a large bowl, combine the smoked and sweet paprikas, onion powder, garlic powder, oregano, basil, thyme, black pepper, cayenne, and celery seeds.

2. Store in an airtight container for up to 2 months.

Salsa Rio Grande

Makes 2 cups

- 1 large onion, finely chopped
- 3 garlic cloves, minced
- 1 jalapeño pepper, cored, seeds removed, and finely chopped
- 4 medium tomatoes, chopped
- ½ teaspoon ground cumin
- ¼ cup chopped fresh cilantro
- 1 tablespoon fresh lime juice
- Salt and freshly ground black pepper
- 2 or 3 dashes of hot sauce

Salsa is Sandy's condiment of choice. (Well, that and pickled jalapeños!) This recipe is one of her absolute favorites and provides her with a little taste of home. She typically adds this salsa to her morning eggs (she's spicy that way) or serves it as a flavorful dip to sit alongside a big pile of tortilla chips. If you like a really hot salsa, leave in some of the jalapeño seeds.

1. In a medium bowl, combine the onion, garlic, jalapeños, tomatoes, cumin, cilantro, lime juice, salt, pepper, and hot sauce.

2. The salsa can be stored in an airtight container in the refrigerator for up to 2 weeks.

Salsa Verde

Makes 2 cups

8 tomatillos, husked and washed (see Note)

1 medium onion, roughly chopped

1 jalapeño pepper, cored, seeds removed, and chopped

3 garlic cloves, roughly chopped

½ cup chopped fresh cilantro

1½ tablespoons fresh lime juice

Salt and freshly ground black pepper

This zesty salsa gets its flavor and green hue from tomatillos. Tomatillos have a tart, citrus-like flavor that works as a zingy accompaniment to fish (see Halibut Enchiladas with Salsa Verde, page 130). When choosing tomatillos, smaller is better. The smaller ones have a sweeter taste. Tomatillos should be green and about the size of a large cherry tomato. The inside is white and meatier than a tomato. They are covered by a papery husk that may range from pale green to a light brown. The husks are inedible and should be removed before use.

1. Into a pot of boiling water put the tomatillos, onion, jalapeño, and garlic, and cook for about 8 minutes. Strain the vegetables from the pot and reserve the cooking liquid.

2. Put the vegetables and cilantro in a blender or food processor and pulse. Add the reserved cooking liquid ½ cup at a time and process to the consistency of a pourable puree.

3. Transfer to a large bowl, add the lime juice, and season with salt and pepper to taste.

4. The sauce can be stored in an airtight container in the refrigerator for up to 2 weeks.

If you can't find fresh tomatillos in your local supermarket, you can use a 28-ounce can of tomatillos. The flavor of the canned isn't as bright as the fresh, but it's not too shabby in a pinch!

Marinara *Sauce*

Makes 3½ cups

- ¼ cup olive oil
- 4 garlic cloves, minced
- 2 shallots, chopped
- 1 (35-ounce) can crushed tomatoes
- 3 fresh basil leaves, chopped
- 1 teaspoon red pepper flakes
- ½ teaspoon dried oregano

  Salt and freshly ground black pepper

Fuggedaboutit! Marinara sauce is a great thing to have on hand at all times to make a fast and flavorful meal. Double or triple this recipe and freeze the sauce in pint-size containers. Just pull out of your freezer and make a quick and delicious dinner by tossing it with cooked pasta. Or for a quick snack, spoon on some toasted Italian bread and sprinkle with your favorite cheese (Parmesan and mozzarella work nicely).

1. Heat the olive oil in a medium saucepan set over medium heat. Add the garlic and shallots, and sauté until the garlic starts to brown, about 5 minutes. Do not burn the garlic or your sauce will be bitter. Add the tomatoes with their juice, basil, red pepper flakes, oregano, salt, and pepper, and stir well. Bring the mixture to a boil, stirring occasionally. Reduce the heat to low and simmer gently for 25 to 30 minutes or until the sauce has thickened.

2. Store in an airtight container in the refrigerator for up to 2 weeks or in the freezer for up to 2 months.

Chicken Broth

Makes 2 quarts

- 2 pounds chicken bones (from about 2 cooked chickens)
- 1 large onion (unpeeled), quartered
- 1 large carrot, roughly chopped
- 2 celery stalks, roughly chopped
- 1 leek, roughly chopped
- 2 bay leaves
- 2 fresh flat-leaf parsley sprigs
- 2 fresh thyme sprigs
- 5 whole black peppercorns
- Salt and freshly ground black pepper

So why make your own broth? The main reason is that you'll get a richness of flavor in your homemade broth that you just can't buy at the store. Homemade broth has an intense chicken flavor and an unbeatable smell. While the thought of making your own broth may seem intimidating, we promise that it's not! In fact, it requires little attention once all the ingredients hit the pot.

1. Place all of the ingredients except salt and pepper into a 5-quart stockpot and cover with cold water. Set the pot over high heat and bring to a boil. Reduce the heat to low and simmer for 3 to 4 hours. Check the seasoning after a couple of hours and season with salt and pepper to taste.

2. Remove the pot from the heat and let the broth sit for 10 to 15 minutes. Strain the broth through a fine sieve and place in the refrigerator overnight. The next day, skim the coagulated fat off the top of the broth.

FREEZES WELL If you don't plan to use your broth within 48 hours, pour the broth into ice cube trays and freeze, then put the broth cubes in zip-top freezer bags. The broth will keep in the freezer for up to 3 months.

Beef Broth

Makes 2 quarts

- 6 pounds beef soup bones (ask butcher for them)
- 2 medium onions, roughly chopped
- 3 medium carrots, roughly chopped
- 3 celery stalks, roughly chopped
- 1 large tomato, quartered
- 2 tablespoons tomato paste, thinned with 2 tablespoons water
- 1 garlic clove, crushed
- 3 to 4 parsley stems, roughly chopped
- ½ teaspoon chopped fresh thyme leaves
- 1 bay leaf
- 8 whole black peppercorns

Store-bought beef broth works just fine, but—just as with chicken broth—it simply doesn't compare in taste to the home-made version. The trick with beef broth is to roast the bones first in order to achieve a nice caramelized flavor.

1. Preheat the oven to 450°F.

2. Put the beef bones, onions, and carrots in the bottom of a 9 x 13-inch casserole dish. Bake, turning occasionally, for about 30 minutes or until the bones are very brown. Let cool for 30 minutes, then drain the fat out of the dish (keep the dish on hand).

3. Put the browned bones, onions, and carrots in a large stockpot. Pour about ½ cup water into the casserole dish, then scrape browned bits off bottom of the dish. Pour this liquid into the soup pot—this liquid holds a ton of flavor! Add the celery, tomato, tomato paste, garlic, parsley, thyme, bay leaf, and peppercorns. Add 12 cups of water and bring the mixture to a boil. Reduce the heat to low, cover, and simmer for 5 hours. Strain the broth, discarding the meat, vegetables, and seasonings.

4. Let the broth cool completely. Transfer to an airtight container and refrigerate overnight. The next day, skim off all the fat that's risen to the surface.

FREEZES WELL If you don't plan to use your beef broth within 48 hours, pour the broth into ice cube trays and freeze, then put the broth cubes in zip-top freezer bags. The broth will keep in the freezer for up to 3 months.

Veggie *Broth*

Makes 2 quarts

- 2 tablespoons vegetable oil
- 1 medium onion, peeled and chopped
- 1 medium celery stalk, chopped
- 1 medium carrot, peeled and chopped
- 1 tomato, chopped
- 3 garlic cloves, crushed
- 2 bay leaves
- 2 fresh thyme sprigs
- 3 to 4 fresh parsley sprigs
- 3 to 4 whole black peppercorns
- 2 teaspoons salt

Unlike the longer cooking times necessary for meat-based broths, vegetable broths come together fairly quickly and there is no fat to skim! Making this staple is one of those things that's really easy to do, and consists of ingredients that you are likely to always have on hand.

1. In a 5-quart stockpot set over medium heat, heat the oil. Add the onion, celery, carrot, tomato, and garlic and cook for about 5 minutes, or until the onions are soft and translucent.

2. Pour in enough cold water to cover the vegetables. Add the bay leaves, thyme, parsley, black peppercorns, and salt. Bring to a boil, reduce the heat to low, and simmer for 30 to 45 minutes.

3. Strain stock and let cool. Store the stock in an airtight container in the refrigerator for up to 1 week or in the freezer for up to 3 months.

Cream of Chicken Soup

Makes about 3 cups

2 tablespoons vegetable oil

1 medium onion, chopped

2½ tablespoons all-purpose flour

1½ cups whole milk

½ cup heavy cream

1 cup finely shredded roasted chicken (see page 340)

½ tablespoon granulated sugar

½ teaspoon dried thyme

½ teaspoon garlic powder

½ teaspoon salt

½ teaspoon freshly ground black pepper

Creamed soups are often used as a base ingredient in casseroles, and cream of chicken is among the most popular of choices. Trust us when we say that making this soup from scratch and using it in recipes will really make a huge flavor difference by highlighting the freshest ingredients and doing away with preservatives and artificial colorings. This soup is fantastic as an ingredient in recipes, but don't be afraid to make it as a stand-alone dish as well.

1. Heat the oil in a 3-quart saucepan set over medium-high heat. Add the onion and cook until translucent and soft, about 8 minutes. Gradually stir in the flour, then slowly add the milk and cream, stirring to break up any clumps of flour. Cook, stirring, until the mixture thickens, about 5 minutes. Add the chicken, sugar, thyme, garlic powder, salt, and pepper. Mix well and simmer for 10 minutes.

2. This soup can be stored in the refrigerator for up to 2 days. Cream-based soups do not freeze well, as they tend to separate when being reheated.

Cream of Mushroom Soup

Makes about 3 cups

- 1 quart Chicken Broth (page 335)
- ¼ cup (½ stick) unsalted butter
- ½ cup roughly chopped leek, white parts only
- 1 cup roughly chopped white button mushrooms
- ½ cup all-purpose flour
- ¾ teaspoon dried thyme
- 1 bay leaf
- ½ teaspoon salt, or more as needed
- ½ teaspoon freshly ground black pepper, or more as needed
- ½ cup heavy cream

There are some exceptions where homemade just makes good common flavor sense. This recipe boasts a lovely, woody mushroom flavor that doesn't compare to the canned variety. It's perfect for adding to your favorite recipes, such as our Oh Boy! Broccoli Casserole (page 197).

1. In a large pot set over high heat, bring the broth to a boil.

2. Meanwhile, in a large saucepan set over medium-high heat, melt the butter. Add the leek and mushrooms, and cook, without adding color, for 6 minutes. Sprinkle in the flour and thyme, and cook for 3 to 4 minutes. Let the mixture cool slightly.

3. Gradually whisk the hot broth into the leek and mushroom mixture, making sure to break up any lumps. Add the bay leaf and season with salt and pepper. Return the mixture to a boil. Reduce the heat to low, and simmer gently for 30 to 35 minutes, stirring occasionally.

4. Put the soup in batches into a blender and puree. Pass the blended soup through a fine strainer into a large saucepan. Put the soup over medium-high heat, add the cream, and return to a boil. Season to taste with more salt and pepper.

5. This soup can be stored in the refrigerator for up to 2 days. Cream-based soups do not freeze well, as they tend to separate when being reheated.

CQ Roasted Chicken

Makes 4 servings

1 (3-pound) whole chicken, giblets removed

1 tablespoon onion powder

Salt and freshly ground black pepper

½ cup (1 stick) unsalted butter, softened

1 celery stalk

If you are looking to save money, taking the time to roast your own chicken really can go a long way. Plus this foolproof method makes for a delicious chicken every time. After trying this traditional, scrumptious recipe, don't forget to make your own chicken broth from the chicken bones, which are rich in flavor. Talk about more cluck for your buck.

1. Preheat the oven to 350°F.

2. Place the chicken in a roasting pan and season it generously, inside and out, with the onion powder, salt, and pepper. Put 3 tablespoons of the butter in the cavity of the chicken. Rub 3 tablespoons of butter on the chicken's skin. Cut the celery into a few pieces and put them in the chicken cavity. Bake for 1 hour 15 minutes, until a meat thermometer inserted into the thickest part of the chicken breast registers 180°F.

3. Remove the roasting pan from the oven. Melt the remaining 2 tablespoons butter in a small saucepan. Baste the chicken with the melted butter and pan drippings. Cover with aluminum foil and allow to rest about 30 minutes before carving.

Caramel *Sauce*

Makes 3 cups

- 1 cup (2 sticks) unsalted butter
- 1 cup packed light brown sugar
- ¼ cup granulated sugar
- ¾ cup honey
- ¼ cup heavy cream

If you have never made caramel from scratch, once you make this recipe, you will ask yourself why you waited so long. In a few easy steps, you will have created a sinfully delicious sauce. Not only is it the perfect topper for our Brownies (page 306), but it is also a great topping for ice cream and dip for fruit and chocolate!

1. In a large saucepan set over medium-high heat, melt the butter. Add the brown sugar, granulated sugar, and honey. Bring to a boil, and cook for 4 to 5 minutes, stirring once or twice (watch carefully to avoid scorching), until the sauce begins to thicken.

2. Remove the pan from the heat and swirl in the cream until it is fully incorporated. Be very careful when adding the cream because the mixture will bubble up. Mix well and remove the pan from the heat. Use immediately, or let cool completely and store in the refrigerator for up to 3 weeks.

Index

Underscored page references indicate boxed text. An asterisk (*) indicates a photograph appears in the insert pages.